Metaphoricity and the Politics
of Mobility

QIGONG MOVES WEST

QIGONG +♡

ancient China's Gift to Our Well-Being

Thamyris
Intersecting: Place, Sex, and Race

Series Editor

Ernst van Alphen

Editorial Team

Isabel Hoving, Saskia Lourens, Yasco Horsman, Murat Aydemir

Metaphoricity and the Politics of Mobility

Editors

Maria Margaroni

Effie Yiannopoulou

Colophon

Design
Mart. Warmerdam, Halfweg

Printing
The paper on which this book is printed meets the requirements of "ISO 9706:1994,
Information and documentation – Paper for documents – Requirements for permanence".

ISSN: 1381-1312
ISBN-10: 90-420-2034-2
ISBN-13: 978-90-420-2034-4

Mission Statement

Thamyris **Intersecting: Place, Sex, and Race**

Thamyris/Intersecting is a new series of edited volumes with a critical, interdisciplinary focus.

Thamyris/Intersecting's mission is to rigorously bring into encounter the crucial
insights of black and ethnic studies, gender studies, and queer studies, and facilitate
dialogue and confrontations between them. *Intersecting* shares this focus with
Thamyris, the socially committed international journal which was established by Jan
Best and Nanny de Vries in 1994, out of which *Intersecting* has evolved. The sharp-
ness and urgency of these issues is our point of departure, and our title reflects our
decision to work on the cutting edge.

We envision these confrontations and dialogues through three recurring categories:
place, sex, and race. To us they are three of the most decisive categories that order society, locate power, and inflict pain and/or pleasure. Gender and class will necessarily figure prominently in our engagement with the above. *Race*, for we will keep analyzing this
ugly, much-debated concept, instead of turning to more civil concepts (ethnicity, culture)
that do not address the full disgrace of racism. *Sex*, for sexuality has to be addressed as
an always active social strategy of locating, controlling, and mobilizing people, and as an
all-important, not necessarily obvious, cultural practice. And *place*, for we agree with
other cultural analysts that this is a most productive framework for the analysis of situated identities and acts that allow us to move beyond narrow identitarian theories.

The title of the new book series points at what we, its editors, want to do: *think
together*. Our series will not satisfy itself with merely demonstrating the complexity of our
times, or with analyzing the shaping factors of that complexity. We know how to theorize
the intertwining of, for example, sexuality and race, but pushing these intersections one
step further is what we aim for: How can this complexity be understood in practice? That
is, in concrete forms of political agency, and the efforts of self-reflexive, contextualized
interpretation. How can different socially and theoretically relevant issues be *thought
together*? And: how can scholars (of different backgrounds) and activists think together,
and realize productive alliances in a radical, transnational community?

We invite proposals for edited volumes that take the issues that *Intersecting*
addresses seriously. These contributions should combine an activist-oriented perspective with intellectual rigor and theoretical insights, interdisciplinary and transnational perspectives. The editors seek cultural criticism that is daring, invigorating and self-reflexive;
that shares our commitment to thinking together. Contact us at intersecting@let.
leidenuniv.nl

Contents

Acknowledgements

We would like to thank our contributors for their hard work and unfailing commitment to the project during a span of over three years. We are also grateful to Professor Mieke Bal for her concrete assistance in difficult times and to Keith Piper and Doris Salcedo for their permission to reprint their work in this volume. Special thanks to the Thamyris/Intersections editors for their seriousness, invaluable feedback and patience.

Introduction

Theorizing Metaphoricity, Reconceptualizing Politics	Maria Margaroni and Effie Yiannopoulou

Metaphoricity: Definition and Theoretical Advantages

In his introduction to a recent book in the *Thamyris/Intersections* Rodopi series, Tim Cresswell assesses what has been seen as "the postmodern turn" in Western theorizations of mobility (see Cresswell 2002). As he argues, the humanistic "sedentarist metaphysics" that privileged place, roots and an identity firmly located in the particularity of its "Being-there" has given way to an equally problematic "nomadic metaphysics" that promotes a "fascination with all things mobile" ("Introduction: Theorizing Place" 11, "Mobilities – An Introduction" 9). Although, according to Cresswell, the contemporary re-evaluation of mobility has been necessary to counter the longstanding suspicion towards it, it has gone too far in the other direction, producing an a-historical conceptual framework that fails to do justice to our diverse, historical and geographically concrete experience of movement. In response to this nomadic metaphysics, Cresswell calls for the theorization of a "politics of mobility" ("Introduction: Theorizing Place" 11), in other words, for a critical and transformative *practice* that will restore the material, historical contexts of contemporary phenomena and that will remain attuned to their complexity and diversity.

Our contention in this volume is that at the heart of such a postmodern politics of mobility lies what we shall call "metaphoricity," a concept that we want to introduce into contemporary mobility studies. "Metaphoricity" draws on *metaphor* and its Ancient Greek root *metapherein*, the verb meaning to "transfer," to "move" from one context to another. The term refers, then, to the action of a (decontextualizing as much as recontextualizing) movement that blurs conventional boundaries and introduces difference in the self-same, opening up the "one" to receive the "other." Due to its connection with the rhetorical figure of metaphor, the term inscribes this action *within* the production of meaning, thus foregrounding the inextricable link between physical, social, conceptual and discursive movement.

Interestingly, this link, which is thrown into relief by the term "metaphoricity," has been recognized as one of the distinctive concerns of postmodern theory. As Cresswell notes, in the context of postmodern Western thought, "[n]ot only does the world appear to be more mobile but our ways of knowing the world have also become more fluid" ("Introduction: Theorizing Place" 17). For some commentators, the latter seems, in fact, to be the inevitable consequence of the former. "A starting point for many post-modernists is that conventional sociological and political categories have become too ossified to capture the fluidities of the contemporary world," Robin Cohen writes (129). Hence the favoring in the past three decades of a more "mobile" way of thinking over the philosophical and political foundationalism that characterized earlier decades. This mobile mode of thinking can be detected not only in the recent emergence within different fields of the Humanities of a cluster of concepts or metaphors drawn from the semantic field of movement, but also in the privileging of metaphor itself as the linguistic correlative of our contemporary experience, an experience marked by the instability of all types of (spatial, psychic, discursive or conceptual) borders.[1]

Though initially welcomed, postmodern theory's attempt to understand our contemporary mobile existence on the level of discourse is currently causing increasing dismay and is more often than not perceived as the reduction of complex historical phenomena to linguistic "play." In this light, it is no wonder that the critique of nomadic metaphysics has taken the form of a growing self-reflexivity with regard to prevalent metaphors of mobility and (in some cases) a suspicion of metaphor itself.[2] For those skeptical in the face of postmodern celebratory accounts of mobility, metaphor has functioned as a technology that obscures the politics of difference unfolding at the sites of tension between diverse historical experiences or theorizations of mobility. Caren Kaplan, for example, points to the reduction in Euro-American discourses of displacement of "immigrants, refugees, exiles, nomads, and the homeless" to "metaphors, tropes, symbols." Due to this reduction, and despite their radical intentions, she argues, such discourses "tend to absorb difference and create ahistorical amalgams" (2). In a similar vein, Smith and Katz warn against the universalizing gesture of postmodern spatial theories which allows metaphors "to take on something of a free floating existence that denies their referents and material results" (76).

What should not be missed in the critiques above is the striking convergence between the postmodern politics of mobility and a *politics of metaphor*, a politics, in other words, in the context of which the production and displacement of meaning(s) constitute the major stakes. For us, this convergence, rather than be deplored as the worrying symptom of an ailing "linguistic turn," needs to be taken seriously into account and foregrounded – which is what we wish to do by means of the term "metaphoricity." More specifically, in this volume we are interested in recording and analyzing instances of how discourse and material manifestations of movement interact. Is it the case that, as Rosi Braidotti has recently argued in *Metamorphoses*, the more people move, the more discourses (of difference) remain stagnant? Is this the basis of the continuing racism and xenophobia that the world is experiencing in spite of its rapid shrinking? Is this the cause of the fear that has swept the USA after September 11th? Or, alternatively, do discourses move and change along with social structures and people? In what contexts? To what effect? And to what extent do our "revolutions" in language have an impact on our ways of being *and* becoming?

What is at issue here is the relationship between materiality and discursivity, a relationship that, as more and more cultural theorists have begun to acknowledge, needs to be rethought.[3] One of our central aims in this volume is to engage in and actively promote such rethinking *outside* of what remain, in our view, the dominant paradigms of the relationship: on the one hand, the problematic assumption that the domains of materiality and discursivity are equivalent, which is what theorists such as Kaplan or Smith and Katz detect in postmodern accounts of mobility; and, on the other hand, the insistent reduction (traced in Kaplan more than in Smith and Katz) of the dialectic between materiality and discursivity to an idealizing gesture that erases the concreteness of contemporary formations as it carries them over into the domain of signification.[4] Thus, if in our attempt to reappraise the significance of movement in postmodern theory, politics and cultural practice, we have chosen to privilege the term "metaphoricity" over a number of possible substitutes which are currently being used in the Humanities (i.e., mobility, migrancy, nomadism, travel), this is because the term helps us situate our attempt to understand contemporary experience within what, for Minrose Gwin, is the distinctive function of metaphor: namely, the elucidation of the co-implication of the social and the discursive, language and power (11). All the contributors to this volume seek to throw light on the contexts, effects and stakes of this co-implication. For example, Paul Patton, Stuart Elden and Ginette Verstraete examine the politics of key contemporary mobile concepts (i.e., deterritorialization, nomad thought, diaspora) while Gareth Hoskins and Tim Cresswell trace the "making up" of Chinese Americans by laying bare the moral and material geographies produced by two different pieces of American legislation.

What is more, the term "metaphoricity" permits us to re-inscribe postmodern debates around mobility within a wider problematic, one that Mieke Bal in her contribution to this volume places at the heart of what she calls "metaphoring." This problematic relates to the necessity of re-conceptualizing the mediating act that opens the possibility of both theory and politics. As Bal argues in her analysis of the work of Colombian sculptor Doris Salcedo, this act should be perceived as involving not merely the transfer of the particular to the abstraction of theoretical reflection and to the "generality of the political domain" (224), but also a movement from one particular situation to another. Such a re-conceptualization is a corrective to views that reduce the act of metaphorization in postmodern theorizations of mobility to an act of idealization, for it invites us to rethink the employment of metaphor as the re-enactment/re-mobilization of a particular experience or situation within a new (and no-less-particular) signifying context. Bal's suggestion is, then, very significant for our purposes in this volume, given our aim to insist on the (difficult yet necessary) link between materiality and discursivity, theory and political practice, metaphor and mobility or, as Verstraete puts it in her essay in this volume, the link between generalities and "situated histories" (142).

Finally, the term "metaphoricity" has the additional advantage of spelling out what is at stake in postmodern experiences and theorizations of movement, namely the articulation of a postmodern ethics and the possibility of (political or subjective) innovation:

a) *Metaphoricity and ethics*: as more and more contemporary analysts point out, the challenge for the mobile citizen (and the culture receiving him/her) in the second millennium is how to create an effective bond from across the divide of difference. In this light, the postmodern politics of "metaphoricity" needs to be understood as inextricable from *ethics*, for what is at stake, as Nikos Papastergiadis demonstrates in his essay, is our relation to the (sometimes feared or hated) other.

b) *Metaphoricity and innovation*: it is true that a lot of the problems traced in postmodern accounts of mobility are the result of the uncritical association of the movement enacted in the process of metaphor with innovation (the renewal of thought and meaning). Hence, the essentialization and romanticization of movement that Cresswell describes, its association with "freedom, transgression and resistance in the face of state power" ("Mobilities – An Introduction" 21). As he insists, we should not forget that there are mobilities that "are produced to support the state, to support patriarchy or to support the power of multinational corporations in the globalized world of flexible capitalism" (21). This is why it is important to remain attuned to the diverse forms that movement takes in contemporary experience and its complex (sometimes ambiguous) effects.[5] This is also why the politics of reterritorialization that Elden proposes in his contribution to the volume is imperative, for we need to understand the new distributions of power formed in the constellation of postmodern mobility, the interests served by such distributions and the competing forms of attachments offered to us locally as well as globally.

Although, however, we need to remain suspicious of any theories of mobility that take innovation as a given, we should perhaps not abandon the concept as dangerous, an empty abstraction or a problematic return to modernist ideals. If our postmodern imaginary is dominated by metaphors of displacement and border-crossing, this is because it is the product of both a deep anxiety (indeed, a dissatisfaction) regarding the present facts of existence and of a futural, Utopian impulse; a desire, in other words, to push against the limits set for us by our particular circumstances or, as Fredric Jameson puts it, against "the mud of the present age in which the winged Utopian shoes stick" (75). In this volume we want to take this desire seriously and to reclaim it by means of the term "metaphoricity." For us, as well as for our contributors, the postmodern politics of mobility is inseparable from a commitment to social transformation. The link, of course, is far from "given" or innate but dependent on concrete historical contexts (and we need to examine which contexts are more conducive to its possible materializations). What is more, as we have tried to suggest in our definition of "metaphoricity," this link is always tested in discourse. It is precisely the trial and chance of the *speaking* subject. In *Tales of Love*, Julia Kristeva emphasizes that the question of mobility (traditionally raised in the context of physics and tied to the possibility of innovation) is now the concern of the speaking subject. "No longer physics but speaking subjectivity," she writes, "will henceforth ask the key epistemological question; what is mobility, what is innovation?" (274-75). As she explains, "what is" in this context means "how does one express them?" (275).

In effect, this is the "key epistemological question" that the volume raises, a question that forces us to think of the innovative or interventionist potential of present forms of mobility as inextricable from decisions taken at the level of representation. For, as Braidotti insists, "the project of finding adequate representations, which was raised to new heights by the poststructuralist generation, is neither a retreat into self-referential textuality, nor is it a form of apolitical resignation" (*Metamorphoses* 3). In its choice of the following three theoretical directions, the book reflects on the above conviction and makes its own contribution to what remains a valuable project: first, it seeks to rethink our concepts of mobility in order to open them up to the complexity and ambiguity of the phenomena that we, as global citizens in both the "centers" and the "peripheries," are witnessing today (phenomena as diverse as transnational migration; post-conflict refuge-seeking and psychic wandering; the trafficking in goods, information, sperm, sex workers or babies; the traveling of terms and theories across different intellectual communities and disciplinary borders). Second, it self-reflexively and critically examines the privileged position of concepts and metaphors of mobility in postmodern theory. In bringing together and juxtaposing theorists such as Patton and Bal, whose work has been conducive to such privileging, and theorists who are more critical of it (i.e., Elden, Cresswell, Landy), the book sets out to present the competing responses that fuel academic debates around this issue.

Finally, it aims at evaluating the influence of our increasingly mobile conceptual frameworks and everyday experience on the redefinition of politics currently under way, especially in the context of post-Marxist theory. This is a process that this volume is consciously promoting in the hope that it will ultimately lead to a reconfiguration of political practice, one that can accommodate the conflicting needs of establishing new forms of bonding and becoming more receptive to the destabilizing potential of difference.

Metaphoricity and Postmodern Theory

Following up on Kaplan's seminal work on travel, this book aims to de-essentialize our concepts of movement and to historicize our representations of and narratives about it. We are, therefore, far from claiming that movement *in itself* constitutes a distinctively postmodern phenomenon. There have already been enough studies that point to the significance of mobility in modernity and to the role it has played in the processes of industrialization and colonization.[6] The impetus behind our investigation in this volume lies, rather, in the following theoretical premises:

a) The premise that in postmodernity there have been changes in the patterns, scale, nature and the complexity of phenomena of mobility. As Papastergiadis, remarks, "[i]t is no longer possible to map movement with a series of arrows on a flat two-dimensional representation of the world" (*Turbulence of Migration* 24). In a similar vein, in their discussion of international population movements, Stephen Castles and Mark J. Miller emphasize that, though "migrations have been part of human history from the earliest times ... international migration has grown in volume and significance since 1945 and most particularly since the mid-1980s" (3-4). According to them, not only will migration continue to grow, but it "is likely to be one of the most important factors in global change" (3-4).

b) There are distinctively postmodern ways of understanding and relating to movement. If, for example, it is true that in modernity movement remains inscribed within the grand narratives of change, progress and a radical break with the past, is it legitimate to understand postmodernity as forcing such models of mobility into a crisis? How can we assess the contribution of anti-Western and post-colonial movements to the emergence of postmodernity as precisely this sort of crisis? Why have the dominant paradigms of mobility changed from modernity to postmodernity? And what can these changes tell us about the ways in which we relate not only to our experience of movement but also to our desire for locatedness and different forms of attachment?

c) Finally, movement has acquired a paradigmatic status in our very theorizations of postmodernity. The work of Paul Virilio, Gilles Deleuze and Felix Guattari, James Clifford, Iain Chambers and Edward Said (among others) is perhaps the best example here, though metaphors and terms connoting movement are increasingly being favored in different areas of the Humanities and the Social Sciences. Indeed, more and more theorists today have come to privilege "mobile concepts" (such as *différance*, dissemination, intertextuality, *sujet-en-procés*, becoming-woman/becoming-animal, diaspora, deterritorialization, nomadism, traveling theory, etc.) in their analyses of post-industrial societies and the philosophical traditions that value substance and permanence over chance and contingency. Our task in this book is to throw light on some of the contexts and reasons for this privileging. We also seek to determine the points of tension between such theorizations of postmodernity and rival conceptualizations of the present (in the Pentagon's New Map, for example, which Elden discusses here, or in Gianni Amelio's portrait of post-communist Albania, which constitutes the focus of Landy's contribution to the volume).

Based on the premises above, we hope to illuminate some of the distinctive stakes raised by movement in postmodernity. At the same time, we hope to understand the postmodern phenomenon of mobility not only as a complex of "actual" material processes but also as the product of particular conceptual transformations and discursive conjunctions. The advantage of such an understanding (which we have attempted to foreground through our use of the term "metaphoricity") is that it helps us appreciate the extent to which contemporary theories of mobility are caught up in specific power relations within academic circles. In doing so, it opens up a space from which we can begin to address productively the questions raised by the conflicting responses to the postmodern experience of mobility, responses ranging from unquestioning celebration to unmitigated condemnation.

Metaphoricity and Postmodern Politics

Two assumptions cut across all the essays in this volume: first, the belief that the character of the political is rapidly changing in postmodernity; and, second, the conviction that physical, affective and discursive forms of mobility are intrinsically connected with this transformation in a twofold manner. On the one hand, the meaning of politics and its material realities are being reconfigured following the increased global circulation of people, money, goods and information. On the other hand, radical political discourses are growing keener than ever to "mobilize" their oppositional strategies and interventionist tactics in order to negotiate the new hybrid geopolitical, economic and cultural formations at hand.

The fall of the Berlin Wall and the opening of the first McDonald's outlet in Beijing signaled not only the setting up of a new global trading network, but also the parallel weakening of the class-based ideological paradigm that regulated the bipolar, Cold-War politics of the twentieth century. They are symbolic moments in the dawning recognition that clear-cut economic and political systems, categories and institutions are in the process of being reconstructed, their past effectiveness posing today more as a question and less as a certainty. Jacques Derrida probably spoke for many when he warned us, in *Specters of Marx*, that "this form of organization called the party" and its correlative, the State, are becoming not only more suspect but "radically unadapted to the new – tele-techno-media – conditions of public space, of political life, of democracy, and of the *new* modes of representation" (102). Similarly, Papastergiadis's emphasis, in his analysis of the War on Terror in this volume, falls on the invisibility and unlocatability of the enemy in the post-September 11th climate of global warfare and dispersed fear. What is at stake here are both the conceptual limits of a modern political economy and its practical implementations at an everyday level. How is one to have politics without parties, blueprints for action, manifestos and well-defined enemies? Clearly, new types of political organization are emerging as new forms of domination and exploitation are rapidly settling in across the world's fast-paced societies, demanding kinds of analysis and action that are designed to address asymmetrical and constantly shifting power structures.

The present collection of essays responds to this demand by investigating, in its last part, how viable traditional political concepts, such as class, agency and resistance still are in the face of mobile enemies and fast-changing allies. Through her focus on the plight of Albanian immigrant workers, for example, Landy argues that, in order to preserve the category of "social class" in postmodernity, we need to reconceptualize it in terms of life and not merely of labor. It is important that we comprehend the "slipperiness," or rather, the "mobile character" of the term and to rethink it as operating in conjunction with other, often conflictual and internally contradictory, structures of difference. What Landy does in her essay is reconstruct the discursive boundaries of a seminal political concept and redefine it in terms of (carefully historicized) mobility to accord it political currency and usefulness as a tool of analysis. In her argument, concrete political effectiveness and analytical rigor are inextricably connected with the metaphoricity of politics, the mobilization, as it were, of the representational economies both of politics and mobility.

In line with Landy's position, this volume proposes that politics in a global context needs to refashion itself in response not only to physical movement but also to the concomitant traveling of meanings and ideas. Few would disagree that the processes of globalization are inscribed by a deep paradox as regards the new geography of movement: the more contemporary geopolitical and cultural formations celebrate the fast passage of populations, goods, trends and fashions across the globe, the more frequently we are confronted with the fixity underwriting religious and national fundamentalism. Rather than boundless and decentered, the emerging globe is, according to Elden, one of the new territorial configurations, hegemonies and power alliances, produced, not least, by the institution of new discursive divides and orientations. As Papastergiadis argues in a similar spirit, the meanings of war and terrorism have been radically revised since September 11th in the interest of situating a (disturbingly) mobile enemy within carefully policed geographical and discursive spaces. Far from being an abstract Deleuzean concept, re-territorialization, in both these instances, may be understood as producing a new kind of authoritarianism in the rhetoric, and above all, in the political practices of our times. If, as we maintain, fundamentalist resurgence and authoritarian political acts result from the freezing of discourse into positions of authenticity and naturalized fixity, then active resistance to proliferating injustices cannot but materialize on condition that the possibility of transformation come to bear on representation too. A radical postmodern politics cannot but be a politics of metaphoricity whose main task would be to end what Braidotti has graphically described as "displacement without movement" ("Metalflesh").

The argument that mobility can lend itself to anti-essentialist, anti-foundationalist political positions has been deployed effectively by many types of politically engaged critique in recent decades. Central among them are brands of poststructuralist, feminist and postcolonial theory which, through their interrogation of the Western binary logic, the universality of the subject, the authority of the real and the workings of power, have contributed substantially to the overall rethinking of the political and the conditions of its production. The emphasis in such theorizing falls on the critique of politics understood as a "representational discourse that presumes a fixed or ready-made subject" which operates within the public space of empiricism, rationality and universal values (Butler and Scott xiv). What these theories promote, instead, as alternative sites for political articulation are the domains of the private, the psychic, the local and the discursive. Implicit in this paradigm shift is an understanding of movement as that which can resist the fixity of hegemonic formulations and can structure the calculation of political strategies to suit the mutating context of multiple and interlocking differences. It is fitting here to remember Judith Butler arguing persuasively for the "contingent foundations" of feminist politics (Butler), Diane Elam for women's "groundless solidarity" (Elam), Chandra Talpade Mohanty for "strategic alliances" among diverse feminist groups (Mohanty) and Doreen Massey for the necessity of politicizing the concept of space by putting it in motion (Massey).

However, while alert to the oppositional potential of displacement, a politics of metaphoricity also insists that we need to pose the question of mobility in ways that make it historically viable in order to accord it political agency. Virilio is, after all, correct in reminding us that "revolution is movement but movement is not a revolution". In postmodernity's transnational spaces, where the *"freedom of movement"* has been replaced by the *"obligation to mobility"* (Virilio 30), a radical political practice needs to organize itself around historically grounded, carefully contextualized and concretely particularized discourses of mobility to be able to address the unequal power dynamic regulating border-crossings today.[7] In this vein, both the essays by Rinaldo Walcott and Hoskins and Cresswell caution against the postmodern politics of difference that inscribe the official multicultural policies of modern Western nation-states. Instead of impacting on how the nation imagines itself, Walcott suggests, Canadian multicultural practices continue to preserve the privileges of the dominant white hegemony and the notion of black peoples as perpetual outsiders to the Americas. In other words, Walcott's historicization of multiculturalism exposes this celebratory model of cultural exchange as one that, in fact, cancels out the very metaphoricity needed to develop more inclusive and positive ways of relating to others.

Finally, what is also important for the discussion at hand is that politics reconceived in light of metaphoricity produces new forms of oppositional agency and revised political agendas. Bal is to the point when she locates a dynamic form of political agency in the domain of affectivity. For her, "metaphoring" is a profoundly political gesture on condition that it transfers not only meanings but the specificity of affects from one context to another without losing it. Only then can discursive transferability activate viewers into political positions that allow them to deny the "generalities that belong to the self-evidences by which we live" (218). This is situated agency, enframed in the particularity of a historical location yet still mobile and non-foundational. It is also an enactment of "affirmative ethics," according to Braidotti who claims that "[t]his is a new form of activism, which takes seriously the active force of affects understood as affirmative ethical inputs. I call them positive processes of becoming which are neither abstract nor disengaged from concrete material and historical situations" ("Metalflesh").

In short, we hold that de-essentializing postmodern mobility requires that the political reconfigure itself into a space of *negotiation* between affect and discourse, the conceptual and the lived, diverse time-zones and places, or, as Jacques Derrida would have it, between the singularity of the here-now and "democracy to come" (*Negotiations* 179-80). For us, negotiation is the crucial word here, not insofar as it refers to a process that brings about consensus, a final harmony, but as long as it makes possible the constant revising of the terms of our engagement with the systems we inhabit, political or otherwise. Chantal Mouffe believes that the non-teleological movement inherent in this type of negotiation is the basis of a truly pluralist democracy (112). In a like manner, we also feel that negotiating the terms of its constitution is what can politicize the concept of mobility by setting it on the move on a journey that will have many stops, no end and many gifts to bear along the way.

Overview of Chapters

Having laid out the central principles that have guided us in the conception and realization of this volume, we move on to introduce the main concerns of each individual chapter. The task we have set ourselves in this section is to throw light on the different ways in which our contributors address the questions explored by the volume, focusing on the points of contact and tension between them.

In accordance with the main theoretical directions we have chosen to take, we have divided the essays in this volume into three parts. The first part, entitled *Metaphoricity and Postmodern Theory*, attempts to understand the workings and politics of "metaphoricity" in the context of the distinctively postmodern project of "putting metaphysics in motion," as Deleuze has defined it in *Difference and Repetition* (8). It is the work of Deleuze, in fact, and his collaborator Guattari that constitutes the focus of Part I as exemplifying a key direction in postmodern philosophy, one that privileges movement in its attempt to think beyond the foundational, oppositional categories of Western Metaphysics. In his essay "Mobile Concepts, Metaphor and the

Problem of Referentiality in Deleuze and Guattari" Paul Patton focuses on the philosophers' anti-metaphysics, arguing that their use of new mobile concepts originates in
their desire to "track" phenomena that are themselves in constant movement and
transformation. Situating himself at the point of convergence between the postmodern politics of mobility and the politics of metaphor, Patton engages with those interpretations of Deleuze and Guattari that insist on reducing their mobile concepts to
metaphors. His aim is to demonstrate that the philosophers' claim to write literally
needs to be taken seriously if the pragmatic character of their thinking is to be
appreciated. To this end, he traces the production in their work of particular mobile
concepts (i.e., "the order-word," "the war machine") and re-inscribes the philosophers'
thinking within a wider anti-representationalism in contemporary philosophy (as the-
orized most forcefully in the work of Derrida).

Though appreciative of Deleuze and Guattari's interventionist project, Stuart Elden
expresses his concern over current appropriations of this project in the contexts of
cultural and political theory. In "The State of Territory Under Globalization: Empire and
the Politics of Reterritorialization" he focuses on the concept of "deterritorialization"
and warns against any attempt to divorce "deterritorialization" from its conceptual
partner of "reterritorialization." He begins by tracing the ways in which the two concepts
are dialectically related in the philosophers' works and goes on to demonstrate how
this dialectical relation is obscured in Michael Hardt and Antonio Negri's Empire, one
of the most compelling contemporary deployments of Deleuze and Guattari's thought.
In his view, this is due to the fact that Hardt and Negri do not have a fully worked out
notion of "territory." As he emphasizes, it is only when this notion is re-thought within
the postmodern Imperial context that we will find ourselves in a position to understand both the deterritorializing effects of globalization and the new territorial configurations emerging alongside such effects.

The second part of the volume, entitled Mobilizing the Politics of Theory, restores
metaphoricity to its material co-ordinates, exploring the postmodern phenomenon of
mobility in terms of its social and cultural contexts as well as its political and ethical
stakes. The three essays included in this part seek to map out the effects of global
mobility on cultures and subjects and to investigate questions that arise from within
the lived experience of dislocation and movement. Firmly situated in the midst of current historical processes (i.e., European Unification, globalization, trans-national
migration, multiculturalism), they attempt to think through how we are to grasp the
significance of place and attachment in the current systems of transnational exchange
and mixture; how power is inflected through the dynamics of postmodern cross-border
mobility; how we express our resistance to the dominant forms of globalization and
whether hybridity can be a challenge to global homogenization. They also ponder over
the necessity of developing a new ethics attuned to the needs of a mobile world confronted with difference.

In their essay "Making up Chinese-Americans: Moral Geographies of Immigration in The Chinese Exclusion Act (1882) and the Peopling of America Theme Study Act (2001)" Gareth Hoskins and Tim Cresswell analyze how two pieces of American legislation (made at separate historical moments and serving disparate interests) produce distinctively different understandings of (Chinese) mobility. Drawing attention to the inseparability of the representational and the material in considerations of the politics of postmodern movement, Hoskins and Cresswell emphasize the necessity of remaining suspicious towards all uncritical celebrations of its "essentially transgressive" nature.

Rinaldo Walcott's "Land to Light On?: Making Reparation in a Time of Transnationality" addresses itself to the need of the black Canadian transnational to forge new ways of belonging. Walcott argues that (Canadian) multiculturalism as an official policy is a particular technique of nation building that might no longer be useful in a world riven by transnational and diasporic movements. With close reference to Dionne Brand's work (especially the novel *At the Full and Close of the Moon*), he proposes that we move beyond the old politics of national belonging. Drawing on Franz Fanon, he calls for the rethinking of the category of the "human" within a postcolonial context. It is this "new humanism," in his view, that constitutes the necessary condition for an ethical transnational citizenship.

Finally, in "Relocating the Idea of Europe: Keith Piper's Other Headings" Ginette Verstraete re-examines European identity in light of Europe's current transcultural situation and its recent re-evaluation of its imperial past. Engaging with Derrida's *The Other Heading*, she focuses on the aporetic movement between the universal and the particular that inscribes Europe's frequent idealization as the universal model of what is pure and authentic. She also proceeds to argue that it is this very metaphoricity at the heart of Europe's exemplary status that has the power to dislodge its Eurocentric basis and biases. Through patiently tracing the "digisporas" produced by the new technologies of communication, Verstraete seeks to throw light on the multiple communities gradually emerging beyond Derrida's philosophical idea of Europe. Her analysis of Keith Piper's digital online-project "Relocating the Remains" aims at recording precisely "the advent and event" of such alternative communities.

The third part of the volume seeks to open up a space for what we believe is the central task of cultural theorists today, namely, the task of re-thinking the theory of politics. In view of what feels like the increasing bankruptcy of the traditional categories of the political (such as class, the party, the State or the proletariat), this task becomes more and more urgent, especially in the context of contemporary attempts to develop new geopolitical institutions. Committed to this task, the three essays included in this part address the viability of the concept of "class" in an age of transnationalism, the necessity of reconceptualizing the relationship between political, socioeconomic and cultural practices and the contribution of the psychic dimension (the imaginary or the affective) in the formulation, but also the possible disruption, of political positions and strategies.

In "Ambient Fears," Nikos Papastergiadis explains why mobility is both a contradictory and a risky concept in the climate of perpetual anxiety prevalent in the West following the events of September 11th. Focusing his analysis on the "War on Terror," he examines the dispersed structure of terrorist warfare that has developed in response to the mobile technologies of globalization. He also identifies the conservative authoritarianism currently organizing world politics as the United States attempt to situate a mobile enemy on the map and, thus, justify its expansionist claims and rhetoric. By means of looking at the practice of contemporary artists, the essay also seeks to explore new models of cultural affiliation that would extend the aesthetic and ethical dimension of artistic experimentation to a broader political framework.

In her essay "On the Road with *Lamerica*: Immigrants, Refugees and the Poor," Marcia Landy explores the possibilities for re-inserting issues relating to class into discussions of postmodern politics. Focusing on Amelio's 1994 film *Lamerica* and drawing on Hardt and Negri's *Empire*, she puts forward a critique of the nature and effects of laissez-faire economics on a global scale, conventional conceptions of the nation state and unexamined celebrations of postmodern mobility.

Finally, in "Metaphoring: Making a Niche of Negative Space," Mieke Bal rethinks the relationship between materiality and discourse in ways that open up a vital "niche" for (the politics of) affectivity. Reinterpreting metaphor in the negative as what empties the viewer of her ordinary interpretive stock of meanings, she identifies "metaphoring," the act of transferring both meaning and affect from one specific context to another, as a crucial dimension of political art. In her argument, the translatability of affect and meaning re-imagines political agency as at once mobile and situated.

Notes

1. It is worth noting the frequent recourse to metaphor in contemporary theorizations of the experience of mobility. See, for example, de Certeau, Robertson et al, Chambers, Gwin.

2. See, for example, Ahmad, Smith and Katz, Kaplan, Cresswell 2001 and Cresswell 2002. Interestingly, in an attempt to respond to critics of postmodern theorizations of mobility, Rosi Braidotti reproduces these critics' suspicion of metaphor (a suspicion which is, in fact, strengthened by her Deleuzean background) and comes to draw a distinction between "figuration" and "metaphor": "A figuration is a living map, a transformative account of the self – it is no metaphor," she writes:

Being nomadic, homeless, an exile, a refugee, a Bosnian rape-in-war victim, an itinerant migrant, an illegal immigrant, is no metaphor. Having no passport or having too many of them is neither equivalent nor is it merely metaphorical, as some critics of nomadic subjectivity have suggested [...]. These are highly specific geo-political and historical locations – history tattooed on your body. One may be empowered or beautified by it, but most people are not; some just die of it. (Metamorphoses 3)

3. See Smith and Katz, Kaplan, and Gwin.

4. As Jacques Derrida demonstrates in his "White Mythology: Metaphor in the Text of Philosophy," this is precisely the gesture performed by metaphor in the context of Western philosophy. "Above all," he writes, "the movement of metaphorization ... is nothing other than a movement of idealization" (226). This is why, according to Heidegger, "the metaphorical exists only within the bounds of metaphysics" (quoted by Kristeva 268).

5. See, for example, Hoskins and Cresswell's discussion in this volume of the Peopling of America Theme Study Act (2001).

6. See Kaelbie, Canclini, Kaplan, Hochstadt, Morley, Papastergiadis 2000 and Rotberg.

7. See Mae Henderson, who highlights the conflictual power matrices within which postmodern mobility is embedded when she writes that "Border crossings move in different directions and from different locations, some from positions of centrality and dominance, others from positions of marginality and powerlessness" (26).

Works Cited

Ahmad, Aijaz. In Theory: Classes, Nations, Literatures. London: Verso, 1992.

Braidotti, Rosi. Metamorphoses: Towards a Materialist Theory of Becoming. Cambridge: Polity Press, 2002.

—. "Metalflesh." Essay emailed to the authors. 5 July 2004.

Butler, Judith. "Contingent Foundations: Feminism and the Question of 'Postmodernism'." Feminists Theorize the Political. Ed. Judith Butler and Joan W. Scott. New York: Routledge, 1992. 3-21.

Canclini, Nestor Garcia, et al. Hybrid Cultures: Strategies for Entering and Leaving Modernity. Minneapolis: U of Minnesota P, 1995.

Castles, Stephen and Mark J. Miller. The Age of Migration: International Population Movements in the Modern World. London: Macmillan, 1993.

Chambers, Iain. Migrancy, Culture, Identity. 1994. London and New York: Routledge, 1995.

Cohen, Robin. Global Diasporas: An Introduction. London: UCL Press, 1997.

Cresswell, Tim. "Introduction: Theorizing Place." Mobilizing Place, Placing Mobility: The Politics of Representation in a Globalized World. Ed. Verstraete, Ginette and Tim Cresswell. Amsterdam and New York: Rodopi Press, 2002. 11-32.

—. "Mobilities – An Introduction." Mobilities. Ed. Tim Cresswell, spec.issue of New Formations: A

Journal of Culture/Theory/Politics 43 (2001):
11-25.

De Certeau, Michel. *The Practice of Everyday
Life.* Berkeley, Los Angeles and London: U of
California P, 1988.

Deleuze, Gilles. *Difference and Repetition.* Trans.
Paul Patton. New York: Columbia UP, 1994.

Derrida, Jacques. "White Mythology: Metaphor in
the Text of Philosophy." *Margins of Philosophy.*
Trans. Alan Bass. New York and London:
Harvester Wheatsheaf, 1982.

—. *Specters of Marx: The State of the Debt, the
Work of Mourning, and the New International.*
Trans. Peggy Kamuf. New York: Routledge, 1994.

—. *Negotiations: Interventions and Interviews,
1971-2001.* Ed., Trans. and Intro by Elizabeth
Rottenberg. Stanford: Stanford UP, 2002.

Elam, Diane. *Feminism and Deconstruction: Ms.
En Abyme.* London: Routledge, 1994.

Gwin, Monrose C. *The Woman in the Red Dress:
Gender, Space, and Reading.* Urbana and
Chicago: U of Illinois P, 2002.

Henderson, Mae. "Introduction." *Borders,
Boundaries, and Frames: Cultural Criticism and
Cultural Studies.* Ed. Mae Henderson. New York:
Routledge, 1995. 1–30.

Hochstadt, Steve. *Mobility and Modernity.* Ann
Arbor, MI: U of Michigan P, 1999.

Jameson, Fredric. *The Seeds of Time.* New York:
Columbia UP, 1994.

Kaelbie, Hartmut. *Social Mobility in the 19th and
20th Centuries.* Oxford: Berg Publishers, 1985.

Kaplan, Caren. *Questions of Travel: Postmodern
Discourses of Displacement.* 1996. Durham and
London: Duke UP, 2000.

Kristeva, Julia. *Tales of Love.* Trans. Leon
S. Roudiez. New York: Columbia UP, 1987.

Morley, David. *Home Territories: Media, Mobility
and Identity.* London and New York: Routledge,
2000.

Mohanty, Chandra Talpade. "Under Western
Eyes: Feminist Scholarship and Colonial
Discourses." *Colonial Discourse and Post-colonial
Theory: A Reader.* Ed. Patrick Williams and Laura
Chrisman. New York: Harvester Wheatsheaf,
1993. 196-220.

Massey, Doreen. *Space, Place and Gender.*
Cambridge: Polity Press, 1994.

Mouffe, Chantal. "For a Politics of Nomadic
Identity." *Travellers' Tales: Narratives of Home and
Displacement.* Ed. Robertson, George, Melinda
Mash, Lisa Tickner, Jon Bird, Barry Curtis and
Tim Putnam. 1994. London and New York:
Routledge, 1998. 105-13.

Papastergiadis, Nikos. *The Turbulence
of Migration: Globalization, Deterritorialization
and Hybridity.* Cambridge: Polity Press,
2000.

Robertson, George, Melinda Mash, Lisa Tickner,
Jon Bird, Barry Curtis and Tim Putnam, eds.
*Travellers' Tales: Narratives of Home and
Displacement.* 1994. London and New York:
Routledge, 1998.

Rotberg, Robert I., ed. *Social Mobility and
Modernization.* Cambridge, MA: MIT Press,
2000.

Smith, Neil and Cindi Katz. "Grounding
Metaphor: Towards a Spatialized Politics." *Place
and the Politics of Identity.* Ed. Michael Keith and
Steve Pile. London and New York: Routledge,
1993.

Virilio, Paul. *Speed and Politics.* Trans. Mark
Polozzotti. New York: Semiotext(e), 1986.

I. Metaphoricity and Postmodern Theory

Mobile Concepts, Metaphor, and the Problem of Referentiality in Deleuze and Guattari

Paul Patton

Deleuze and Guattari's distinctive version of poststructuralist theory relies upon a metaphysics of process as opposed to product, becoming as opposed to being, and lines of flight or deterritorialization as opposed to the capture of primary flows. This metaphysics affects their conception of thought as well as its objects. They undertake a rhizomatic or nomadic practice of thought in which concepts are not built in orderly fashion upon secure foundations but constructed, as it were, on the run, in the course of an open-ended series of encounters with diverse empirical contents. This philosophical practice is not well understood by critics, who often understand them to be employing metaphors rather than constructing concepts. Thus, they are often read as proposing figures of multiplicity by analogy with botanical rhizomes, or figures of movement or deterritorialization by analogy with real nomads, and so on. In turn, this reading leaves them open to criticism directed at both the accuracy and the ethics of the referential claim imputed to them. On the one hand, for example, Christopher L. Miller argues that their reliance on anthropological sources in the discussion of nomadism commits them to an "anthropological referentiality" which is open to question both with regard to its accuracy and its complicity with colonial discourse (Miller, "Beyond Identity" 179; see also 181, 196). While he recognizes that Deleuze and Guattari's project is not straightforwardly representational, Miller's criticism supposes that it must rely either upon direct representation or metaphor (indirect representation). On the other hand, Caren Kaplan argues that their privileging of the "nomadic" and related processes of becoming-minor and deterritorialization amounts to a "metaphorical mapping of space" which reproduces the modern Eurocentric valorization of distance and displacement (88). She argues that:

Deleuze and Guattari appropriate a number of metaphors to produce sites of displacement in their theory. The botanical metaphor of the rootlike "rhizome," for example,

enacts the subjectivities of deterritorialization: burrowing through substance, fragment-
ing into simultaneous sprouts, moving with a certain stealth, powerful in its dispersion.
Rejecting the classic Western humanist metaphors *of family trees and genealogies, the*
rhizome destabilizes the conventions of origins and endings … As a metaphor *for pol-*
itics, then, the rhizome constitutes an anarchic relation to space and subjectivity, resist-
ant to and undermining the nation-state apparatus. (87; emphasis added)[1]

Kaplan's criticism is not directed at the supposed referential aspect of their claims so much as at their participation in a modernist European imaginary construction of col- onized peoples. More generally, she argues that the "metaphors of explanation" uti- lized by poststructuralist critics such as Deleuze and Guattari "reinforce and depend upon specifically modernist versions of colonial discourse" (85-86).

Such a reading flies in the face of the authors' repeated denials that their novel use of words involves the use of metaphor. They insist that societies may be regarded as machines "in the strict sense, without metaphor" (Deleuze and Guattari, *Anti-Oedipus* 251) and that, when they characterize capital as an "axiomatic" they are using the word in a literal rather than a metaphoric sense (Deleuze and Guattari, *A Thousand Plateaus* 454, 455).[2] In conversation with Claire Parnet, Deleuze is unequivocal in his rejection of metaphor: "There are no proper words (*mots propres*), neither are there metaphors (all metaphors are sullied words [*mots salés*], or else make them so). There are only inexact words to designate something exactly" (Deleuze and Parnet 3; trans. modified).[3]

What are we to make of this persistent refusal of the status of metaphor for such an apparently idiosyncratic vocabulary? Moreover, supposing we do take at face value Deleuze and Guattari's claim to write literally rather than metaphorically, what does this imply with regard to the referential status of their philosophical concepts? What does it imply for those critical readings that do not take seriously their refusal of metaphor? My goal in this essay is, firstly, to examine what is at stake in this hostil- ity towards metaphor; and, secondly, to ask what relationship this has to their con- ception of philosophy as the creation of "mobile" concepts. Finally, I will suggest that the critics who see no alternatives aside from interpreting Deleuze and Guattari as con- cerned with empirical social science or with metaphor miss an important dimension of their novel practice of philosophy. To this extent, their criticisms fall short of their intended target.

Anti-Representationalism and Mobile Concepts

Deleuze's renunciation of metaphor flows from some of the most fundamental commit- ments upheld throughout his philosophy. First among these is his rejection of the rep- resentational image of thought. In *Difference and Repetition*, this takes the form of a characterization and criticism of the dogmatic image of thought modeled on the act of recognition, where this supposes a fundamentally passive relation to the world. Against the dominant philosophical tradition that supposes that the world is already named and that the task of thinking is to discover the names of things, he advocates an image of thought as engagement with problems. He abandons the idea that human thought has a natural affinity with the truth in favor of an image modeled on the involuntary response of an apprentice struggling to come to terms with a new craft, recalcitrant material and unfamiliar tools (Deleuze, *Difference and Repetition* 164-65). This image reappears at the beginning of *What is Philosophy?*, where it introduces the definition of philosophy as the creation of concepts. Since an apprentice is someone who learns how to identify particular problems and how to characterize them in a way that points toward their solution, this conceptual persona suggests a pragmatic conception of thought.

Second, *A Thousand Plateaus* outlines an explicitly pragmatic conception of thought and language as means of intervention in, rather than representation of, the world.[4] The concept of the order-word or slogan (*mot d'ordre*) best exemplifies this conception: a slogan is not something that is evaluated for its accuracy or truth-value but for its effectiveness. (I discuss this concept in more detail below). *What is Philosophy?* proposes a no less pragmatic conception of philosophy in suggesting that it "does not consist in knowing and is not inspired by truth" (Deleuze and Guattari, *What is Philosophy?* 82). The point is not to reduce philosophical concepts to mere slogans, but to suggest that, like slogans, philosophical descriptions should be evaluated in terms of their usefulness rather than their truthfulness. Of course, in order to be effective, philosophical concepts must in some way "map" the world. However, "mapping" should not be understood as a matter of naming, copying or tracing the pre-existing articulations of the world. Mapping has to do with performance rather than representation and what distinguishes mapping from "imitation" or tracing is that "it is entirely oriented toward an experimentation in contact with the real" (Deleuze and Guattari, *A Thousand Plateaus* 12). *What is Philosophy?* is unequivocal with regard to the pragmatic ambitions of this kind of philosophy. As Deleuze and Guattari see it, the task is to help summon "a new earth and people that do not yet exist" (*What is Philosophy?* 108). In common with Marx, Foucault, Derrida, Rorty and many others, they see the philosophical creation of concepts as serving the larger goal of making the future different from and in some sense better than the past. Philosophy serves this goal by virtue of the manner in which the concepts it creates enable us to see things differently. New concepts provide new ways of describing the events and states of affairs that form the circumstances of our actions. They provide new ways of describing the problems to which philosophical thought is a response.

A third distinctive feature of Deleuze's anti-representational image of thought relates to his long-standing interest in the mobility of philosophical concepts. On more than one occasion he expresses his admiration for those philosophers, such as Nietzsche, Kierkegaard and Bergson, who aspired to put concepts in motion.[5] On other occasions, he expresses antipathy towards ways of thinking that serve to block movement, such as the appeal to "eternal values": "These days it's the rights of man that provide our eternal values. It's the constitutional state and other notions everyone recognizes as very abstract. And it's in the name of all this that thinking's fettered, that any analysis in terms of movements is blocked" (Deleuze, *Negotiations* 122). This remark does not imply opposition to rights in general but only to a way of understanding these, which refers back to an already determined and static set of human rights. His comments on jurisprudence in the interview with Negri make it clear that he prefers a conception of rights as in perpetual transformation in accordance with the requirements of a particular situation (Deleuze, *Negotiations* 169-70).

Deleuze and Guattari's anti-representational conception of thought appeals to another kind of adequation between concepts and material states of affairs, in which the open-endedness and mobility of concepts parallels the movement in things themselves. This emerges in remarks such as the suggestion in *Dialogues* that inexact words are needed to designate things exactly (Deleuze and Parnet 3), or the suggestion in *A Thousand Plateaus* that the "anexactitude" of mobile concepts is necessary in order to think a world that is in constant movement. For this reason, the authors suggest that "anexactitude is in no way an approximation; on the contrary, it is the precise movement of that which is under way" (Deleuze and Guattari, *A Thousand Plateaus* 20; trans. modified). As these remarks imply, their interest in mobile concepts is related to their ontological commitment to a world of events. Unlike things or states of affairs, events are mobile rather than static phenomena, constantly changing and becoming-other than they were. Deleuze and Guattari understand events in the manner of the Stoics, as incorporeal entities which are attributed to things and states of affairs but expressed in propositions or in the infinitive form of the verb: to go, to encounter, to capture, to deterritorialize etc. In *What is Philosophy?* they insist that philosophical concepts do not represent states of affairs but rather express pure events.

The Impossibility of Metaphor

There is considerable agreement or, as Deleuze and Guattari would say, a "zone of proximity" between Derrida's reasons for relocating the distinction between concept and metaphor within a field of generalized metaphoricity and their own reasons for rejecting the concept of metaphor in favor of a generalized process of concept creation. Even though Derrida takes issue with the suggestion that philosophy creates concepts, it is not clear on what grounds he is entitled to do so (Derrida, "I'm Going to Have to Wander All Alone" 193). Deleuze and Guattari do not suppose that concepts are created ex nihilo and, in any case, Derrida's own deconstructive practice of philosophy involves the creation of a whole series of "a-conceptual" concepts such as writing in general, *différance*, trace, *supplément*, generalized metaphoricity and so on. These a-conceptual or non-concepts in many respects conform to Deleuze and Guattari's description of specifically philosophical concepts.[6] More significantly, the apparent differences between Deleuze and Derrida over the "creation" of concepts only serve to obscure the underlying affinity between their non-representational views of the nature of language and thought.

In "White Mythology," Derrida shows how the concept of metaphor in its canonical Aristotelian sense presupposes a primitive representational view of the relation between words and independently existing things. It is because he supposes that there is a metaphysically literal language in which the proper concepts or names of things may be formulated that Aristotle can define metaphor as the act of calling something by the name of something else. It is because language allows for the imitation of things that both metaphor and literal speech are able to convey truth about what is. However, Derrida argues, since the concept of metaphor relies upon the idea of transposing or carrying over the content of a given name onto something else, it is already irreducibly metaphoric. Moreover, to the extent that literal language is understood as a means of conveying that which might be conveyed by other means, this representational con-ception of meaning involves the very same spatial metaphors of movement and transport. For these reasons, Derrida concludes that Aristotle's conception of lan-guage and meaning is thoroughly "implicated in metaphor" (241) and that the quasi-concept of a generalized metaphoricity forms a more appropriate backdrop for the everyday contrast between literal and metaphoric uses of language.

The common ground between Deleuze and Guattari and Derrida emerges when we consider the consequences of abandoning the representational image of thought along with the idea that there is a "proper" relationship between particular words and things: the ground of the distinction between literal and metaphorical uses of words col-lapses. When a word is transposed from its usual sphere of application and employed in another sphere, there is no more justification for calling this metaphorical than for calling it the creation of a concept. Thus, when Deleuze employs mathematical terms in order to define his own concept of problematic Ideas in *Difference and Repetition*, he denies that his procedure is metaphorical in any sense other than that which coin-cides with the creation of new concepts: there is no metaphor here, he writes, "except the metaphor consubstantial with the notion of Ideas, that of the dialectical transport or '*diaphora*'" (Deleuze, *Difference and Repetition* 181). In the terminology of *A Thousand Plateaus*, there is no metaphor but only the deterritorialization of signs from one location and their reterritorialization in another (see the passage from *Dialogues*, 117; cited in note 3).

For his part, Derrida proposes the rhetorical term "catachresis" to describe the "imposition of a sign upon a meaning which did not yet have its own proper sign in language" ("White Mythology" 255). In the terms in which Fontanier defined it, cat-achresis still relies upon the logocentric assumption that meanings exist prior to being named or expressed in language. Derrida therefore uses it "by analogy" to refer to the "discovery" of new objects of thought. He engages in precisely this kind of forced extension of the meaning of words in creating his own series of a-conceptual or quasi concepts. For Deleuze and Guattari, there are no metaphors only concepts and occasions of their use which can involve either the unexpected extension, transformation or variation of an existing concept or, in extreme cases, the coinage of new words to express novel concepts.

Just as Derrida presents philosophical thought as advancing by catachresis, Deleuze and Guattari present philosophical concepts as inherently subject to variation in the course of being applied to different problems: concepts developed in relation to one set of problems may be applied in relation to another set of problems, thereby transforming the original concept. However, this propensity for historical movement within and between concepts over time is not the most important sense in which concepts are mobile. Their ambition, as we saw above, is to create concepts that are in themselves mobile.[7] The means by which this task is achieved constitutes the philosophical style of a given work, since "style in philosophy is the movement of concepts" (Deleuze, *Negotiations* 140). What needs to be explained, however, is just what this style amounts to and what it means to put concepts in motion.

Mobile Concepts 1: The Order-Word

For Deleuze and Guattari, style always involves a procedure of continuous variation, whether in thought, in music, or in the writing of those literary figures who succeed in creating their own minor language within a language. Two things militate against style in philosophy, namely "homogeneous language" and "a heterogeneity so great that it becomes indifferent, gratuitous, and nothing definite passes between its poles" (Deleuze, *Negotiations* 141). *A Thousand Plateaus* embodies a definite philosophical style that seeks to avoid both of these dangers. The book is written in the form of a series of plateaus where "plateau" is not a metaphor but a name for the "zones of continuous variation" in which intellectually mobile concepts are produced (Deleuze, *Negotiations* 142). The heterogeneity of the writing within each plateau produces the openness and instability of the concepts, while the organization of the book into distinct segments of writing allows for movement between the concepts developed in each plateau: "we watched lines leave one plateau and proceed to another like columns of tiny ants. … Each plateau can be read starting anywhere and can be related to any other plateau" (22). The best way to appreciate the practice of creating mobile concepts in this book is to retrace the paths followed in the construction of particular concepts.

Take as an example the plateau devoted to "Postulates of Linguistics." This is laid out in the form of a series of extended commentaries upon postulates shared by a range of approaches within linguistics and philosophy of language: language is informational and communicational; there is an abstract machine of language that does not appeal to any "extrinsic" factor; there are constants or universals of language that enable us to define it as a homogeneous system; language can be scientifically studied only under the conditions of a standard or major language.[8] Deleuze and Guattari's rejection of the latter postulate implies abandonment of the view that language may be defined as a system independent from the social and political circumstances of its use. In turn, this implies reversing the traditional relationship between pragmatics and syntactico-semantical theories of language. They appeal to William Labov's socio-linguistic studies of African-American English to argue against the idea that the syntactic or semantic structure of language might be defined independently of the pragmatic dimensions of use in particular circumstances. In this manner, through detailed rebuttals of each of these postulates, Deleuze and Guattari develop their own account of the pragmatic conditions and consequences of linguistic utterance. The postulates of linguistic theory ensure that the heterogeneity of the text remains within limits, but this heterogeneity is ensured by the manner in which they weave together elements of Austin's speech act theory, Stoic logic and its metaphysics of the incorporeal, Hjelmslev's distinction between content and expression, assorted historical and socio-linguistic studies of the politics of language, along with their own theory of assemblages, the abstract machines which govern their operation, and the movements of deterritorialization and reterritorialization to which these are subject.

The aspect of language use that interests them most is the relationship between the acts performed in speaking and the social, institutional and political conditions of such acts. In the course of the plateau, they outline a pragmatic conception of language use. The mobile concept at the heart of this pragmatics is that of the "order-word." Initially presented in terms of the function served by explicit or implicit commands, this concept is extended in the course of the plateau so that, by the end, it does not refer to a particular class of utterances but to an entire dimension of language use. It is from this perspective, they argue, that language must be understood as "the set of all order-words, implicit presuppositions or speech acts current in a language at a given moment" (A Thousand Plateaus 79). Deleuze and Guattari's procedure in outlining this concept parallels Austin's movement in the course of How to Do Things With Words, from performatives as a class of utterances to illocutionary force as a universal dimension of language use. In similar fashion, they pass from explicit commands to a concept of the order-word as "a function co-extensive with language" (A Thousand Plateaus 76), from there on to the acts or incorporeal transformations expressed in utterances and, finally, to the assemblages of enunciation of which these are the variables.

Deleuze and Guattari further develop the Austinian concept of illocutionary force embedded in their concept of the order-word by recourse to a concept of incorporeal transformation derived from the Stoics. The explicit performatives that Austin used as the basis for his theory of speech acts provide the clearest cases of such transformative events: a judge's sentence transforms an accused person into a convicted felon. What took place before (the murder, the trial) and what takes place after (the punishment) are corporeal changes affecting the passions and interrelations of particular bodies, but "the transformation of the accused into a convict is a pure instantaneous act or incorporeal attribute ... The order-words or assemblages of enunciation in a given society (in short, the illocutionary) designate this instantaneous relation between statements and the incorporeal transformations or noncorporeal attributes they express" (*A Thousand Plateaus* 80-81). All such incorporeal transformations are identifiable by reference to the date and time of utterance, hence the title of this plateau: "November 20, 1923," which refers to the day on which, in response to runaway inflation in Germany, the old *reichsmark* was declared invalid and was replaced by a new currency. History is replete with such events but so is everyday life. Whether they are world historical events such as declarations of independence, of war, the assertion of sovereignty over vast areas of land previously unclaimed by European powers, or familiar interpersonal events such as a declaration of love, such incorporeal and "pure" events have lasting consequences for the actions and passions of the material bodies to which they are addressed or attributed.

Two consequences of Deleuze and Guattari's conception of language as the set of order-words current at a given time are significant for their view on the pragmatic character of the relationship between utterances and non-linguistic components of the world. First, they draw attention to the historical and social character of what is said and suggest that "language always seems to presuppose itself," in the sense that a given utterance always carries the trace of previous utterances of the same form within it. Utterance, therefore, "does not operate between something seen (or felt) and something said, but always goes from saying to saying" (*A Thousand Plateaus* 76). For this reason, they suggest that free indirect discourse rather than declarative judgment is the essential linguistic operation.[9] In other words, it is not the representation of a non-linguistic reality that is the primary function of language but the capacity to repeat and therefore transmit something already said. On this basis, they question the importance that some theorists have attributed to metaphor and metonymy and propose instead that "the translative movement proper to language is that of indirect discourse" (77). While this remark does not contradict the appeal to generalized metaphoricity as a means of opposing the representational conception of language, it does highlight the importance of another kind of translative movement that has nothing to do with the structure of metaphor. In this sense, despite the common ground between the appeal to generalized metaphoricity and their own theory of concept creation, Deleuze and Guattari's pragmatism leads them even further away from the structure of representation which informed both traditional theories of language and the dominant image of thought in philosophy.[10]

Second, the manner in which the order-word function of language accounts for the expression of the incorporeal transformations present in a given society at a given time, allows Deleuze and Guattari to redescribe the relationship between the world and language use in terms of intervention rather than representation. This is where the everyday sense of *mot d'ordre* as "slogan" is especially significant for this concept. The order-word or slogan-function of language is a matter of effectivity: it refers to the manner in which bodies and states of affairs are transformed by a particular utterance which describes them in a particular way, thereby effecting an instantaneous incorporeal transformation or simply enabling the participants to perceive things differently. Deleuze and Guattari go on to describe the forms of interaction between language (forms of expression) and the world (forms of content) in terms of the double movement of deterritorialization and reterritorialization, thereby renewing the connection between their pragmatic theory of language and the theory of assemblages developed across the other plateaus which make up this book-rhizome.

To return to the question of the mobility of the order-word concept: the conceptual consistency of the concept can be understood in terms of the complex function that maps linguistic elements such as words and well-formed strings of words onto the circumstances or context of utterance. It is this function linking language to its outside that transforms the utterance of such linguistic elements into a linguistic act or statement. It is in this sense that Deleuze and Guattari suggest that the order-word "effectuates the conditions of possibility of language" (*A Thousand Plateaus* 85). At the same time, the heterogeneity of the order-word concept lies in the fact that its meaning cannot be determined apart from its connection to a series of further concepts such as free indirect discourse, collective assemblages of enunciation, regimes of sign, majority and minority treatments of language and the concept of events as incorporeal transformations. The inherent mobility of the concept lies in the manner in which it preserves its own unity of composition across the range of differential relations to the other concepts in terms of which it is defined, where the series of these other concepts remains open-ended. In this sense, the mobility of the concept is built into its exposition in the text. The series of connections with additional concepts through which it is expounded opens up the order-word concept to a range of potential paths of theorization with regard to the social and political character of language use, the manner in which enunciation or utterance is bound up with discursive as well as non-discursive conditions of the possibility of saying certain things, and to the manner in which these conditions and, therefore, the form as well as the content of utterances, are subject to constant variation.

Mobile Concepts 2: The War-Machine

The concept of the "war-machine" outlined in Plateau 12, "1227: Treatise on Nomadology – the War Machine" provides a particularly striking example of a concept in motion. Deleuze and Guattari provide no definitive list of characteristics of the war-machine. Instead, they outline a number of defining characteristics by means of a series of axioms and propositions, where there is no reason to suppose that this series is either definitive or closed. They then proceed to demonstrate these axioms using empirical material drawn from the study of mythology, literature, anthropology, historical epistemology and the history of philosophical images of thought. The first axiom asserts the exteriority of the war-machine in relation to the State. By the "exteriority" of the war machine, they mean that it is in all respects "of another species, another nature, another origin" than the State apparatus (Deleuze and Guattari, *A Thousand Plateaus* 352). In other words, these are assemblages of such a completely different kind that no direct comparison between them is possible. Deleuze and Guattari state at the outset the problem that their mode of exposition is designed to address:

The exteriority of the war machine in relation to the State apparatus is everywhere apparent but remains difficult to conceptualize. It is not enough to affirm that the war-machine is external to the apparatus. It is necessary to reach the point of conceiving the war-machine itself as a pure form of exteriority, whereas the State apparatus constitutes the form of interiority we habitually take as model, or according to which we are in the habit of thinking. (A Thousand Plateaus *354)*

This problem may be stated either from the point of view of the object or from the point of view of the style of thought in which conceptualization is attempted.

From the point of view of the object, the State is an apparatus of capture, which always involves the constitution of a field of interiority. As such, it is a well-defined entity in the sense that these are the constant features of all forms of State. Despite the differences between ancient empires, early modern monarchies or contemporary democratic States, they all share a "unity of composition" (*A Thousand Plateaus* 427). By contrast, there is no such unity of composition among war machine assemblages. These are the expression of a peculiar kind of abstract machine which "exists only in its own metamorphoses" (360). As such, war-machine assemblages are a fundamentally different kind of thing to forms of State. The war-machine is more like a function, process or recurrent event than a well-defined object (a characteristic shared with the order-word concept discussed above). The essentially differential and diverse character of the war-machine makes it a paradoxical "object" from the standpoint of the traditional understanding of concepts and concept formation. It is incapable of being captured in a stable concept, where this implies the specification of necessary and sufficient conditions for something to fall under a given concept. The war-machine is not the kind of thing of which there can be a concept in the traditional sense of a series of features or marks that will determine necessary and sufficient conditions for something to be an assemblage of this kind. The problem, then, is to arrive at a way of thinking the war-machine that is adequate to its nature as a "pure form of exteriority."

From the point of view of the concept, the problem of adequately conceptualizing the war-machine is the same as that of arriving at a non-representational style of thought capable of putting concepts in motion. Moreover, this is a problem precisely because the traditional understanding of concepts as the constitution of a form of interiority in thought is modeled on the State form that understands it as an apparatus of capture. Deleuze and Guattari point to the manner in which the traditional representational image of thought expresses the essence of the State form in general (*A Thousand Plateaus* 374ff).[11] The problem of how to give conceptual expression to a pure form of exteriority, therefore, calls for another, non-State style of thought which Deleuze and Guattari call "nomad" thought. This is a mode of thinking which delineates its object not by conceptual capture but by following a variable path of conceptual oppositions such as those between the two poles of sovereignty identified in Dumézil's studies of Indo-European mythology, between the games of chess and go, or between the different styles of epic drama found in Shakespeare and Kleist. This is how the war-machine concept is defined: by retracing a line of continuous conceptual variation through the various kinds of content addressed under the successive axioms and propositions in this plateau. In this sense, the mobility of the war machine concept implies an indeterminacy or an exactitude that parallels the differential and dispersed nature of the object.

The Problem of Referentiality

As noted at the outset above, the non-representational character of Deleuze and Guattari's mobile concepts creates an interpretative problem for commentators on their work. Critics tend to assume that they are engaged either in a form of empirical social science or in a form of philosophy that relies upon metaphor. Either way, they are supposed to be vulnerable to criticism directed at the empirical basis of their concepts. Caren Kaplan provides an example of the latter reading to the extent that she treats Deleuze and Guattari's nomads as mere metaphors of a deterritorialized mode of existence. To say that the figure of nomadism as it functions in Deleuze and Guattari's text is a metaphor is to imply that it relies upon a comparison with real nomadic peoples. Understood in this manner, Deleuze and Guattari's use of the terms "nomad" and "nomadic" in spelling out their concept of the war-machine implies a comparison between the characteristics of the war-machine and the relations to territory, weapons and signs found among supposedly nomadic peoples. As a result, their text is open to criticism on the basis of its misrepresentation of one of the parties to this comparison, or, more generally, on the basis of its participation in misrepresentations maintained by European colonial discourse. Thus, Kaplan argues that:

> the nomad as metaphor may be susceptible to intensive theoretical appropriation because of a close fit between the mythologized elements of migration (independence, alternative organization to nation-states, lack of opportunity to accumulate much surplus, etc.) and Euro-American modernist privileging of solitude and the celebration of the specific locations associated with nomads: deserts and open spaces far from industrialization and metropolitan cultural influences. (90)

The term "mythologized" here makes it clear that, beneath the charge of perpetuating Eurocentric discourse about its colonial others, lies the accusation of misrepresentation of the realities of life among those who came to be called "nomads."

At this point, Kaplan's criticism coincides with Christopher Miller's suggestion that the referential authority of their discourse is threatened by its reliance upon colonial anthropological sources (Miller, "Beyond Identity"). The question of the referential status of their characterization of nomadism also lies at the heart of a recent exchange between Miller (Miller, "We Shouldn't Judge Deleuze and Guattari") and Eugene Holland (Holland, "Representation and Misrepresentation," "To The Editor"). In response to Holland's reminder that Deleuze and Guattari's "nomad" is a conceptual persona rather than a social scientific concept, Miller insists that their philosophical concept of nomadism is nevertheless in some sense reliant upon anthropological sources and to that extent "derived from" real nomads. To this extent, the "taint of mortal representation remains in *A Thousand Plateaus*" (Miller, "We Shouldn't Judge Deleuze and Guattari" 136). He reiterates his earlier criticism that their characterization of nomadism is compromised by the primitivism and colonialism of the anthropological sources on which they rely: Deleuze and Guattari's concept of nomadism is corrupt because it is epistemologically supported by suspect anthropological material sources. The only alternative to this empirical reading of the concept of nomadism is to treat it as a metaphor. Thus, when he does take into account the concluding remarks of the Nomadology plateau which deny that nomads "hold the secret" of the war-machine, Miller resorts to the metaphorical reading in commenting that "nomads and their war-machine seem to have disappeared into horizonless space, become historical metaphors, inventions serving some other purpose" ("Beyond Identity" 204). Similarly, in his response to Holland, he accuses Deleuzians of turning real nomads into metaphors in a manner which is "philosophically dubious – producing as it does a 'world without others' – and historically reprehensible – being, as it is, indissociable from colonialism" ("We Shouldn't Judge Deleuze and Guattari" 137).

Miller and Kaplan's criticisms dovetail in supposing that Deleuze and Guattari present either straightforwardly empirical concepts or metaphors. Either way, the argument goes, they are guilty of complicity with colonialism. However, what follows if we take at face value their claim to produce philosophical concepts rather than metaphors? To persist in treating nomadism, the war machine, the various types of minority becoming and so on as metaphors is simply to fail to recognize their non-representational practice of thought. For Deleuze and Guattari, the choice is not between concepts and metaphors understood in terms of the representational image of thought, but between this representational image and a new image of thought that allows for the creation of mobile concepts. On these terms, the real issue here is that of the relationship of their concepts to their apparently empirical claims. It is undoubtedly true that they make statements about nomadic peoples and cultural practices in the course of outlining concepts of nomadism, the war-machine and minority-becoming. It may well be true that some of these statements are open to question on empirical grounds. However, the important question is what the function of such statements is in the text.

The fact that Deleuze and Guattari make it an axiom that the war-machine is invented by nomads, and their assertion that nomads are defined by the constellation of characteristics which define assemblages of the war-machine type, suggests that their "nomadism" is only contingently related to the empirical claims made about actual nomadic peoples. They draw upon accounts of the life of desert peoples to make a connection between nomadism and smooth space, suggesting that nomadic existence follows paths that distribute individuals and groups across an open and smooth space, in contrast to the roads and highways that connect the regions of sedentary social space. Sedentary space is striated by enclosures and paths between enclosures, whereas nomadic space is a pure surface for mobile existence, without enclosures or fixed patterns of distribution. However, in the end, these quasi-empirical claims are no more than discursive means to express the characteristics of smooth space. Ultimately, it is the active relation to smooth space that defines the fundamental nature of the nomad as well as that of the war-machine: "the nomads make the desert no less than they are made by it. They are vectors of deterritorialization" (A Thousand Plateaus 382). The concept of nomadism is not derived from empirical facts about nomads. The statements about nomadic existence in the text only serve to express a concept of nomadism of which the real sources lie elsewhere. The definition of nomadic existence in terms of its relation to smooth space follows conceptual paths already traced by Deleuze's characterization of a nomadic distribution of being in Difference and Repetition.[12] The hostility to figures of unity, totality and closure expressed in the Deleuzian world of "free differences" is a direct antecedent of the concept of nomadism. This philosophical and moral inspiration, rather than any derivation from anthropological sources, is the real origin of the concept in Deleuze and Guattari's thought.

In the terms of their definition of war-machine type assemblages, a political, scientific or artistic assemblage can be a potential war-machine to the extent that "it draws, in relation to a phylum, a plane of consistency, a creative line of flight, a smooth space of displacement. It is not the nomad who defines this constellation of characteristics; it is this constellation that defines the nomad, and at the same time the essence of the war-machine" (422-23). It follows that their account of the conditions of nomadic existence is really no more than a means to demonstrate key characteristics of assemblages of the war-machine kind: the relation to smooth as opposed to striated space, the affinity with lines of flight or deterritorialization, and a capacity for absolute, intensive speed.[13] In turn, the war-machine is really Deleuze and Guattari's term for machines of metamorphosis, outside of, and fundamentally opposed to, the State-forms that express the forces of unity, totality and closure in thought or in society

(Patton, *Deleuze and the Political* 109-10). As such, the war-machine is an abstract assemblage, an abstract machine of pure exteriority, not to be confused with any concrete social, much less military, apparatus. Its essence is not war but creative displacement, deterritorialization and the propagation of smooth spaces in which new connections between different forces are possible. The function of this concept is to give expression to the forces and processes of metamorphosis and deterritorialization. Along with the concept of nomadic existence, it is intended to counter-actualize those forces in contemporary society that resist processes of capture. Since the concept of nomadism is definitionally bound to that of the war-machine, the characterization of nomadic existence serves to give expression to this paradoxical object. At the same time, however, neither this concept nor its "object" can be considered bound to any given form of expression. Deleuze and Guattari's nomadism is abstract to the same degree that the war-machine is an abstract assemblage irreducible to its particular artistic, technological or political incarnations. The quasi-empirical claims made about nomadic existence only serve to demonstrate these characteristics of this abstract machine.

It follows that the unreliability of these claims is no threat to the task of conceptual specification. Miller may well be correct to suggest that many of the sources for these claims are corrupt. However, the appropriate response to such criticism from the point of view of the task of outlining a non-representational concept of nomadism is to abandon such material and look for other ways of specifying the concept. As Miller notes, this amounts to salvaging nomadology from *A Thousand Plateaus* ("We Shouldn't Judge Deleuze and Guattari" 137). However, this response is justified in terms of what I described above as Deleuze and Guattari's pragmatic conception of philosophy. To say that the accounts of nomadism and the war-machine serve the philosophical purpose of constructing concepts of a certain kind does not mean that these are good concepts in the sense that they achieve the goal of counter-actualizing certain kinds of transformative agency. The conditions of nomadic social life do not necessarily offer the most effective means to grasp the nature of machines of metamorphosis and deterritorialization in contemporary societies. The strongest reason for rethinking the concept of nomadism comes not from the supposed referential deficiencies of the concept but from the argument, advanced by both Miller and Kaplan, that the choice of nomads to specify the characteristics of war-machines and smooth space perpetuates a long tradition of Eurocentric primitivism and a fascination for the Other. To this extent, Kaplan argues, they perpetuate the rhetorical structures of a modernist European imaginary.

As a comment on Deleuze and Guattari's text, there is undoubtedly some truth to this diagnosis, although it engages only with the relatively superficial question of their choice of means of expression. As a comment on their concept of nomadism, these charges are much less compelling, since Deleuze and Guattari's association of

nomadism with qualitative multiplicity, smooth space and the conditions of transformation can be seen to controvert the Eurocentric priority attached to sedentary forms
of agriculture and social life at the expense of more fluid and mobile relations to the
earth. In this sense, their concept of nomadism runs counter to a deep stratum of
the modern European social imaginary, which we find in Locke's *Second Treatise on
Government* as well as in Rousseau's *Essay on the Origins of Inequality*. This Eurocentric
prejudice in favor of sedentary forms of life worked its own magic in the justifications
it provided for the appropriation of land and the subjugation of so-called "primitive"
peoples. The absence of sedentary institutions and agricultural practices was considered sufficient reason to relegate indigenous peoples to a condition of primitive
savagery and to a cultural time before the advent of "civilization." Deleuze and Guattari's
concept of nomadism and its association with processes of deterritorialization and
transformation directly challenges this normative structure.

Kaplan further argues that Deleuze and Guattari perpetuate colonial discourse by
relying on Eurocentric images of the other rather than allowing the other to speak for
itself: "The Third World functions simply as a metaphorical margin for European oppositional strategies, an imaginary space, rather than a location of theoretical production itself" (88). This argument also assumes that Deleuze and Guattari's oppositional
strategies rely on metaphor: becoming-minor is said to require "emulating the ways
and modes of modernity's 'others'," in much the same way that some feminist critics
initially assumed that becoming-woman required men to imitate women.[14] The inappro-
priateness of the strategy is largely an effect of supposing that it relies on "emulating"
the ways of minority groups. If we do not take the concepts of minority or nomadism
for metaphors, then no such emulation is implied. In addition, the argument assumes
that the authors are responsible for the inappropriate generalization of this oppositional strategy, so that when they recommend minority-becoming for "us all" they
speak on behalf not just of Europeans and North Americans but all peoples everywhere. In this manner, Kaplan argues, a strategy of becoming-minor that only makes
sense for those majoritarian figures at the center of power "is presented as an imperative for 'us all'" (88). However, it is not the authors who are at fault here, but rather
the reader who assumes that a book written from within and against one particular
cultural tradition can be simply transposed onto another context without undergoing
significant transformation. By claiming that the "utility of their methodology … is
always generalized" (88), Kaplan herself transforms the limitation implicit in Deleuze
and Guattari's critical gesture into a defect.

By contrast, if we take their text to be an intervention in a specific cultural context,
along the lines suggested by their account of language as the current set of order-words,
then it is inappropriate to generalize their critical gesture in this way. As Kaplan herself notes, we need to be aware of the sense in which Deleuze and Guattari's use of the
figures of marginality and displacement involves an "attempt to displace the sedimented

bulk of European humanist traditions" (88). There is no guarantee that the means adopted to do so will be effective in all contexts. It is a consequence of the manner of presentation of Deleuze and Guattari's concepts that their critical force remains largely internal to the European cultural imaginary.[15] The interpretation of their practice of philosophy as non-representational and pragmatic as outlined above teaches us that the effective counter-actualization of processes of metamorphosis, transformation and deterritorialization requires contextually appropriate means of expression. It shows that the question of metaphor is irrelevant. Finally, it enables us to appreciate the essential mobility of these concepts and to dissociate these from their means of expression. Effective criticism must start from the presumption that we do not have the same relation to such concepts.[16]

Notes

1. See also N. Katherine Hayles: "Deleuze and Guattari use metaphors indispensable to their argument and treat them as if they were literally true" (Hayles 156).

2. Elsewhere in *A Thousand Plateaus*, in the course of describing the physical, organic and semiotic stratification of an unstratified, deterritorialized plane of consistency on which the most disparate kinds of things and signs freely circulate and collide, they insist that this metaphysics does not rely on a metaphorical use of words: "There is no 'like' here, we are not saying 'like an electron,' 'like an interaction,' etc. The plane of consistency is the abolition of all metaphor" (69).

3. Deleuze here plays on the ambiguity of "propre" which can mean both "proper" and "clean." Later in *Dialogues*, he comments with reference to the concept of faciality which he and Guattari put forward on the basis of an extension and combination of the concepts of white wall, black hole and a particular social machine of overcoding the human body:

Here is a multiplicity with at least three dimensions, astronomical, aesthetic, political. In none of the cases are we making a metaphorical use of it: *we don't say that it is "like" black holes in astronomy, that it is "like" a white canvas in painting. We are using deterritorialized terms, that is, terms which are torn from their area, in order to reterritorialize another notion, the "face,"* "faceity" is social function. (Deleuze and Parnet 18; emphasis added)

Finally, he and/or Parnet write with reference to their conception of language as a combination of fluxes of expression and content in immanent variation:

When a word assumes a different meaning, or even enters into a different syntax, we can be sure that it has crossed another flux or that it has been introduced to a different regime of signs. ... It is never a matter of metaphor; there are no metaphors only combinations. (117)

4. Deleuze and Guattari reject the representational idea of the book as image of

the world in favor of a conception of the book as forming a rhizome with the world: "the book assures the deterritorialization of the world, but the world effects a reterritorialization of the book, which in turn deterritorializes itself in the world (if it is capable. ...)" (*A Thousand Plateaus* 11).

5. In *Difference and Repetition*, Deleuze explains the interest in theatre shared by Nietzsche and Kierkegaard by reference to their common desire "to put metaphysics in motion" (8). In an interview in *Negotiations*, he suggests that just as the invention of cinema brought motion into images so Bergson provides us with "one of the first cases of self-moving thought" (122).

6. For comments on some of these similarities, see Patton "Strange Proximity" and *Deleuze and the Political* 15–17.

7. As Deleuze comments in an interview, "it's not enough simply to say that concepts possess movement; you have to also construct intellectually mobile concepts" (*Negotiations* 122).

8. These postulates are discontinuously numbered from I to III and then VI.

9. "Indirect discourse is the presence of a reported statement within the reporting statement, the presence of an order-word within the word. Language in its entirety is indirect discourse" (*A Thousand Plateaus* 84).

10. Commenting on the fundamental points of his and Guattari's approach to language, Deleuze singles out for mention "the importance of indirect discourse (and the recognition of metaphor as something that just confuses matters and has no real importance)" (*Negotiations* 29).

11. Applying their concept of the State form as involving two poles or types of capture to the image of thought, they point out that "it is not simply a metaphor when we are told of an imperium of truth and a republic of spirits.

It is the necessary condition for the constitution of thought as principle, or as a form of interiority, as a stratum" (*A Thousand Plateaus* 375).

12. Deleuze refers to a "completely other distribution which must be called nomadic, a nomad nomos, without property, enclosure or measure. Here, there is no longer a division of that which is distributed space which is unlimited, or at least without precise limits" (*Difference and Repetition* 36).

13. "The nomad distributes himself in a smooth space; he occupies, inhabits, holds that space; that is his territorial principle ... we will say by convention that only nomads have absolute movement, in other words, speed ... [the

nomads] are vectors of deterritorialization" (*A Thousand Plateaus* 381-82).

14. For a summary of these criticisms, see Grosz 163-64 and 173-79. For more recent feminist responses to Deleuze's political and conceptual nomadism, see Buchanan and Colebrook and Braidotti 65-116.

15. Curiously, she notes as a consequence of this implied limitation that it is a critical gesture of use primarily to "Europeans and some North Americans," as though, apart from Europeans, the colonial imaginary was operative only in North America.

16. I am grateful to Maria Margaroni, Effie Yiannopoulou and to Charles J. Stivale for their helpful comments on earlier drafts.

Works Cited

Austin, J. L. *How To Do Things With Words*. Ed. J.O. Urmson and Marina Sbisà. Oxford: Oxford UP, 1975.

Braidotti, Rosi. *Metamorphoses: Towards a Materialist Theory of Becoming*. Cambridge: Polity, 2002.

Buchanan, Ian and Claire Colebrook, eds. *Deleuze and Feminist Theory*. Edinburgh: Edinburgh UP, 2000.

Deleuze, Gilles. *The Logic of Sense*. Trans. Mark Lester with Charles Stivale. Ed. Constantin Boundas. New York: Columbia UP and London: Athlone, 1990.

—. *Difference and Repetition*. Trans. Paul Patton. London: Athlone Press and New York: Columbia UP, 1994.

—. *Negotiations 1972–1990*. Trans. Martin Joughin. Columbia: Columbia UP, 1995.

Deleuze, Gilles and Felix Guattari. *Anti-Oedipus: Capitalism and Schizophrenia*. Trans. Robert Hurley, Mark Seem and Helen R. Lane. New York: Viking P, 1977.

—. *A Thousand Plateaus: Capitalism and Schizophrenia*. Trans. Brian Massumi. Minneapolis: U of Minnesota P, 1987.

—. *What is Philosophy?*. Trans. Hugh Tomlinson and Graham Burchell. New York: Columbia UP, 1994.

Deleuze, Gilles and Claire Parnet. *Dialogues*. Trans. Hugh Tomlinson and Barbara Habberjam. London: Athlone Press, 1987.

Derrida, Jacques. "White Mythology: Metaphor in the Text of Philosophy." *Margins of Philosophy*. Trans. Alan Bass. Chicago: The U of Chicago P, 1982. 207-71.

—. "I'm Going to Have to Wander All Alone." *The Work of Mourning*. Trans. and ed. Pascale-Ann Brault and Michel Naas. Chicago: U of Chicago P, 2001. 192-95.

Grosz, Elizabeth. *Volatile Bodies: Towards a Corporeal Feminism*. Bloomington, Indiana: Indiana UP/Sydney: Allen and Unwin, 1994.

Hayles, N. Katherine. "Desiring Agency: Limiting Metaphors and Enabling Constraints in Dawkins and Deleuze/Guattari." *SubStance* 94/95 (2001): 144-59.

Holland, Eugene W. "Representation and Misrepresentation in Postcolonial Literature and Theory." *Research in African Literatures* 34. 1 (Spring 2003): 159-72.

—. "To The Editor." *Research in African Literatures* 34. 4 (Winter 2003): 187-90.

Kaplan, Caren. *Questions of Travel: Postmodern Discourses of Displacement*. Durham and London: Duke UP, 1996.

Miller, Christopher. "Beyond Identity: The Postidentitarian Predicament in *A Thousand Plateaus*." *Nationalists and Nomads: Essays on Francophone African Literature and Culture*. Chicago and London: The U of Chicago P, 1998. 171-244. [Revised version of "The Postidentitarian Predicament in the Footnotes of *A Thousand Plateaus*: Nomadology, Anthropology, and Authority." *Diacritics* 23.3 (1993): 6-35.]

—. "'We shouldn't Judge Deleuze and Guattari': A Response to Eugene Holland." *Research in African Literatures* 34. 3 (Fall 2003): 129-41.

Patton, Paul. "Strange Proximity: *Deleuze et Derrida dans les parages du concept*." *The Oxford Literary Review* 18 (1997): 117-33.

—. *Deleuze and the Political*. London and New York: Routledge, 2000.

Thamyris/Intersecting No. 12 (2006) 47-66

The State of Territory under Globalization

Empire and the Politics of Reterritorialization	Stuart Elden

Mais un jour, peut-être, le siècle sera Deleuzien

(Foucault 1994: 76)

Michel Foucault's suggestion is often misconstrued. The usual translation, found in the *Language, Counter-Memory, Practice* collection, is: "perhaps one day, this century will be known as Deleuzian" (165). Unsurprisingly, it is regularly referenced in books on Gilles Deleuze (see, for example, Marks 79 and Dumoncel 67), and indeed there was a special issue of the journal *SAQ* entitled "A Deleuzian Century?" (Buchanan).[1] But, as James Faubion, following Paul Rabinow, notes: the *double entendre* is neglected – *le siècle* can also mean "the circle of courtiers," and the phrase can therefore also be translated as "some day, the in-crowd will be Deleuzian" (xix, xxxix n. 30). We might be content with this, laughing gently at Foucault's prophetic irony. Deleuze himself certainly saw the suggestion as a joke, or at least as provocative (*Negotiations* 88-89).[2] But there is yet more to this polysemantic phrase. *Le siècle*, especially in religious contexts, can mean the worldly life or the world as a whole, an exchange of a temporal marker for a spatial signifier.

Attempts to understand the world as Deleuzian have been widespread in recent years, with a range of studies taking up his concepts with alacrity. Of course, the "his" obscures the way in which many of his most used concepts are the ones he developed in conjunction with Félix Guattari, published in four important works. Indeed, in *What is Philosophy?* he and Guattari describe the task of the philosopher as that of formulating concepts (5) and, in his well-known interview with Foucault, Deleuze suggests that "a theory is exactly like a box of tools ... it must be useful. It must function" (*Language, Counter-Memory, Practice* 208). Does this mean that we should simply sit back and watch while terms such as schizoanalysis, hybridity, smooth and striated space, the molar and the molecular, the rhizome, the refrain and others are paraded for the entertainment and edification of the multitude? Conceptual policing may seem to go against the very nature of the Deleuzian enterprise.

In spite of this, it seems instructive to me to slow down, to hesitate, to read and to think, before embarking on such an appropriation. That was certainly the way in which Deleuze approached his thinkers in studies of, among others, Nietzsche, Spinoza and Leibniz. Here, I am particularly concerned with thinking about the notion of deterritorialization that Deleuze developed in some of the works written in collaboration with Guattari. This term has been widely used in recent literature on globalization (for a critique see Elden, "Missing the Point"), but is usually divorced from its conceptual partner of reterritorialization. What is interesting about these terms in Deleuze and Guattari is the way in which they function both as a linguistic medium and in terms of organisms and their movement. Metaphoricity and mobility are, therefore, intertwined in important and complicated ways. Perhaps the most important recent study utilizing these terms has been Michael Hardt and Antonio Negri's *Empire*, where sometimes they are used together and at times separately. The separation raises a number of problems, but in utilizing and developing these terms in a much more explicitly political way, they make space for further potential utilizations. Taking this forward, the conclusion of the essay stresses not the politics of deterritorialization but the politics of reterritorialization. It suggests that we can see this at play in recent events, but that, before we speak too freely of either deterritorialization or reterritorialization, we need to think far more carefully about territory itself, conceptually, historically and politically.

Deterritorialization/Reterritorialization

There are a number of ways in which these terms are used in the work of Deleuze and Guattari. As Ronald Bogue has usefully cautioned, the concept of *territory* is discussed "in its narrow ethological sense in *A Thousand Plateaus*," but "is inseparable from the general notions of territorialization, reterritorialization and deterritorialization, which play through their thought in a wide range of contexts" ("Minority, Territory, Music" 114). These contexts have been helpfully discussed in some of Bogue's own works, but in the wider field of literature they are often conflated. Bogue notes that the first recorded use of these terms is in 1966, in Guattari's work on group psychology ("Art and Territory" 466). As Holland has also noted, the uses of deterritorialization/reterritorialization "derive from Lacanian usage" ("Schizoanalysis and Baudelaire" 241).[3] Territorialization, in Lacan, refers to the way in which parental care structures and organizes the child's body, how feeding and cleaning focuses behavior on specific zones or sites of the body (the mouth, the genitals, the anus, etc.). As Holland notes, in Deleuze and Guattari, deterritorialization shows how this centering on particular sites can be applied elsewhere. Holland gives the examples of movement from the mother's breast and the Oedipal complex ("Schizoanalysis and Baudelaire" 241-42; see also "Deterritorializing Deterritorialization").

The point, though, for both Bogue and Holland, is that this is not just a move toward the psychological register, but also toward the social, where the terms can allude to capitalism, "the disconnection and reconnection of working bodies and environments – for example, the disconnection of peasants from grazing land by the Enclosures Acts in England, and their reterritorialization onto textile looms as wage-labor in the nascent garment industry" (Holland, "Schizoanalysis and Baudelaire" 242). For Bogue, the aim of Guattari's early work "is to extend to the domain of the social Lacan's essentially psychological use of 'territorialization'," a process which is continued in Anti-Oedipus, where "deterritorialization" and "reterritorialization" "figure prominently in tandem with the concepts of 'decoding' and 'recoding' " ("Art and Territory" 466). In Anti-Oedipus, Deleuze and Guattari discuss different ways in which the world has been configured, as primitive-territorial, barbarian-despotic, or civilized-capitalist (also see Marks 95). What is significant about the capitalist machine is that it "seeks to mul-tiply deterritorialised schizophrenic flows, never reaching a limit" (Marks 96). For Marks, following Lyotard (1972), "Marx was the first to locate the fluidity and deterritorialisation which is axiomatic of capitalism," but it is Deleuze and Guattari who are capable of revealing this (Marks 97). As Marx and Engels famously proclaimed, "all that is solid melts into air" (70).

But although the term deterritorialization is found within Anti-Oedipus, it is in Deleuze's work on Kafka that it takes a central role. Here, Kafka's writings in German are seen as disruptive because of his position as a Czech Jew outside of Germany. Kafka himself, in a diary entry from Christmas Day 1911, discusses these issues: the springboard for the reflections of Deleuze and Guattari (see Kafka 148-53 and Bogue, "Minority, Territory, Music" 114-15). Other studies that Deleuze, in particular, undertook, emphasized these disruptive tendencies in writers such as Marcel Proust, Jack Kerouac, Samuel Beckett, Herman Melville and Henry Miller (Critique et clinique and Deleuze and Parnet. Also see Goodchild 55 and Bryden, Buchanan and Marks). Some of Deleuze's work on Nietzsche functions in a similar way. Indeed, in a piece written a couple of years before the book on Kafka, he explicitly relates the two: "The only parallel I can find here is with Kafka, in what he does to German, working with the language of Prague Jewry: he constructs a battering ram out of German and turns it against itself" ("Nomad Thought" 143 and see Marks 58-59).

This forms a distinct understanding of the concept of deterritorialization, based on the notion of a minor literature (Kafka: Toward a Minor Literature 16-17 and see also A Thousand Plateaus: Capitalism and Schizophrenia 97-98, 104-05). The notion of minor literature, which, rather than coming from a minor language, is that which "a minority constructs within a major language" (Kafka: Toward a Minor Literature 17), has been developed in recent work from the field of sociology, literary and cultural studies (see, among others, Appadurai and Papastergiadis). For Papastergiadis, for example, "the concept of deterritorialization has been a useful mode of understand-ing the fissures within language and cultural identity" (118). As he notes, "the cultural dynamic of deterritorialization has decoupled previous links between space, stability and reproduction; it has situated the notion of community in multiple locations; it has split loyalties and fractured the practices that secure understanding and knowledge within the family and social unit" (117).

It is essential to note that these are quite narrow understandings, interesting in their own right, but limited to specific issues. Bogue notes that it is only in "1837: Of the Refrain" in *A Thousand Plateaus* that Deleuze and Guattari discuss "territory *per se*, engaging the subject via an analysis of music's relation to animal ethology" ("Minority, Territory, Music" 125, also see "Art and Territory" 466). Bogue then leads us through a range of discussions of animal territoriality, touching on the work of Henry Eliot Howard, Bernard Altum, J. S. Huxley, Konrad Lorenz, Jacob von Uexküll and Raymond Ruyer, among others, spending most time on the last two, because of their importance to Deleuze and Guattari ("Art and Territory" 466-75). It is worth citing Bogue at length here:

In essence, what Ruyer is describing at such length are biological instances of de/reterritorialization, of the detachment or unfixing of elements and their reorganisa-tion within new assemblages. Ruyer's work, then, supports Deleuze and Guattari's con-tention that a territory, *in the biologic sense of the term, is created through the general process of* deterritorialization, *whereby milieu components are detached and given greater autonomy, and* reterritorialization, *through which those components acquire new functions within the newly created territory. (475)*

From this we can stress one key thing: the continual process of de- and reterritorial-ization. In other words, the reconfiguration of spatial relations rather than their end. This is often missed: deterritorialization is part of a process. We find this insisted upon in several places in *A Thousand Plateaus*. They are "always connected, caught up in one another;" deterritorialization "always occurs in relation to a complementary reterritorialization" (10, 54; also see 181, 508 and *What is Philosophy?* 67-68). Indeed, they make this point more strongly when they stress the territoriality that is the condition for change: "we must therefore take a number of factors into consideration: relative territorialities, their respective deterritorializations, and their correlative reterritorial-izations" (*A Thousand Plateaus* 303, also see 203). In this, we see that deterritorial-ization, in spite of its name, does not mean the end of the importance of territory. Indeed, far from it, because territory is both its condition of possibility and, in some newly configured form, its necessary outcome.

In this light, it is worth turning our attention to Deleuze and Guattari's discussion of the nomad in *A Thousand Plateaus*. Contrary to visions of the nomad as without territory, they emphasize how nomads, too, follow "customary paths ... from one point to another," noting water, dwelling and assembly points. But these points are reached only in order to be left behind, they are stages on a life's way, "strictly subordinated to the paths they determine, the reverse of what happens with the sedentary." This is in con-trast to the migrant, "for the migrant goes principally from one point to another, even if the second point is uncertain, unforeseen or not well localized" (*A Thousand Plateaus*

380). Deleuze and Guattari make a distinction here between a closed space and an open one. In the first, land is parceled out and divided between people, in the second, people are distributed in space. This leads them to suggest the difference between these understandings of space, a distinction between striated and smooth space (380-81, 474ff).

The migrant moves in striated space, space that is divided and limited – "walls, enclosures, and roads between enclosures." Every deterritorialization is partnered by a reterritorialization (381). Agriculture, therefore, is a form of both, with land distributed between people (rather than the other way round), and, for Deleuze and Guattari, "earth, unlike other elements, forms the basis of a striation, proceeding by geometry, symmetry, and comparison" (441). For the nomad, "there is no reterritorialization *afterward* as with the migrant, or upon *something else* as with the sedentary;" instead, "it is deterritorialization that constitutes the relation to the earth, to such a degree that the nomad reterritorializes on deterritorialization itself. It is the earth that deterritorializes itself, in a way that provides the nomad with a territory" (381). Even here, with the stress on deterritorialization, there is an insistence on the importance of reterritorialization. The nomad has a territory, but it is a territory in the process of making and remaking, one in which they are always changing, without a final resting point. The distinction between smooth and striated space is an important one, and relatively well-known. What is sometimes neglected is the emphasis they place on the fact that "the two spaces in fact exist only in mixture. Despite the important qualification that "the de facto mixes do not preclude a de jure, or abstract, distinction between the two spaces" (475), they note that "smooth space is continually being translated, transversed into a striated space; striated space is constantly being reversed, returned to a smooth space" (474). This point seems to be crucial to an actual comprehension of the ways in which contemporary events are played out in space, and the way in which the spaces of Empire operate. It is a point to which I will return.

In terms of this project, the other issue of interest is the wide historical scope of the book. It is no surprise that the various plateaus all carry dates, given the range of examples. From Kleisthenes' reforms in ancient Athens, through to the Roman Empire and the Crusades, and onwards to the discovery of the New World, we see that deterritorialization and reterritorialization (in Deleuze and Guattari's terms) are not a new phenomenon. Rather, the continual remaking and reshaping of spatial relations may take on, indeed must take on, different forms in different times and places, but this is not a vision of a static world of fixed territories suddenly thrown into flux, as it is in much of the literature on deterritorialization. Here, I would sound a note of caution, suggesting that, although without a doubt spatial relations and territorial configurations have been continually under process of review, this does not mean that earlier periods had anything like a sense of "space" or "territory." There is a weak version of this argument – which suggests that earlier periods had different perceptions of these and other terms, and a strong version – which argues that they did not have a sense of them at all (on Kleisthenes in this context, see Elden "Another Sense of *Demos*").

There are other uses of these terms in Deleuze and Guattari. Indeed, in *What is Philosophy?* thinking itself is a form of deterritorialization (Patton, *Deleuze: A Critical Reader* 9), but this is hopefully a useful enough survey to reflect on (see also Colebrook). The terms emerge from an engagement with Lacan, and function as a way of moving from the psychological to the social sphere. They are used to analyze minor literatures and the potential for disruption and they re-emerge through engagement with ethology and ideas of nomads and migrants. For Paul Patton, the political implications are great: "Minority provides an element capable of deterritorialising the dominant social codes. Conversely, it is the process of deterritorialisation which constitutes the essence of revolutionary politics for Deleuze and Guattari" (*Deleuze and the Political* 7). For Philip Goodchild, who defines deterritorialization as "leaving home and travelling in other parts," and reterritorialization as "making a new dwelling place" (218-19), they are, despite the title of his book, largely apolitical. In his view, issues surrounding desire are more important. Indeed, following the suggestions in *What is Philosophy?* he suggests that "Deleuze and Guattari's concepts are entirely deterritorialized: they have no meaning, and only express a kind of nonsense – 'deterritorialized' means 'outlandish' " (56, citing Deleuze, *Critique et clinique* 93).

Empire, Sovereignty and Territory

One of the most interesting adaptations of these ideas is found in Michael Hardt and Antonio Negri's *Empire*. As they state in a note, "two interdisciplinary texts served as models for us throughout the writing of this book: Marx's *Capital* and Deleuze and Guattari's *A Thousand Plateaus*" (415 n. 4). But this is not an idle claim, Hardt having written one of the best introductions to Deleuze's thoughts (see also Negri, "On Gilles Deleuze and Félix Guattari") and Negri having corresponded and written with both Deleuze and Guattari (Deleuze *Negotiations*, Negri, *The Politics of Subversion* and Guattari and Negri). Equally, a few years before, Negri argued that he had found in *A Thousand Plateaus* "the fundamental elements of the renewal of historical materialism, in function of the new dimensions of capitalist development" ("On Gilles Deleuze and Félix Guattari" 104, cited in Patton, *Deleuze and the Political* 6, also see Negri, *The Politics of Subversion* 95 note). He also admitted that his own work on Spinoza would have been impossible without Deleuze's work (*The Savage Anomaly* 267, cited in Patton, *Deleuze and the Political* 143 n. 1).

In philosophical terms, *Empire* is perhaps the most sophisticated attempt to come to terms with the new world order that has partnered "an irresistible and irreversible globalization of economic and cultural exchanges" (xi). At its root, it is a reformulation of perceptions of sovereignty, with a recognition that models of sovereignty developed in the early modern period – by Hobbes, for example – are no longer valid. There is a "new form of sovereignty," and it is Empire that is the political subject that "effectively regulates these global exchanges." Instead of the sovereignty of nation-states, we now have sovereignty of the world. This is important, because it underlines the way in which Hardt and Negri dismiss claims that sovereignty itself has declined (xi). It is a new *logic* of rule that is under investigation here. That rule might be exercised in different ways, in different places, and by a range of bodies, but the underlying "single logic of rule" is consistent (xii).

Hardt and Negri claim that the concept of sovereignty, in its modern sense, evolved in tandem with that of modernity. It was tied both to conflict within Europe and the colonial project, where it was formulated through Europe's relation to its outside. It was also tied to developments in modern science (70). Elsewhere, I have discussed how sovereignty, political theory and scientific practices come together principally in the seventeenth century, with the Thirty Years War and the English Civil War showing the problems of divided rule and overlapping territoriality, with theoretical solutions offered by Hobbes and Leibniz, respectively. While Hobbes' solution to the question of sovereignty is to concentrate it in one place, unlimited and undivided, Leibniz proposes a distinction between sovereignty and majesty, with the Emperor having the latter, meaning the power to command obedience and loyalty, and the princes of the Empire the former, tied explicitly to territory (Leibniz 347, for a discussion, see Elden, *Missing the Point*).

Hardt and Negri draw upon Weber and Foucault to theorize the emergence of modern sovereignty, but, in contrast to Foucault, suggest that, instead of a development from sovereignty to governmentality, there is "a passage *within* the notion of sovereignty" (88). Citing the famous principle from the 1555 Diet of Augsburg, they argue that "cuius regio, eius religio" means that "religion had to be subordinated to the territorial control of the sovereign" (94). The real issue here, though, is in danger of being missed due to the speed of their progress.[4] Augsburg laid down a principle that the territorial princes in the Holy Roman Empire had religious freedom and that they could determine the religion of their subjects. This was only partly upheld at Westphalia a hundred years later, which proclaimed the "free exercise of territorial right" of the princes. In other words, rather than sovereignty being exercised over territory and then over religion, it is territory that makes the sovereign. Sovereignty, in this weak sense that is the first modern version of the term, is "territorial superiority," in distinction to the majesty proposed by Bodin and claimed by the Emperor. Hobbes' absolute version, proposed just a few years after Westphalia, should not blind us to the way in which it was Leibniz's formulation that was a more accurate reflection of the situation at the time.

Nevertheless, Hardt and Negri recognize that the model of sovereignty in the imperial period was tied to boundaries, strictly defined and demarcated territories, with the partitioning of the world into discrete portions. "Wherever modern sovereignty took root, it constructed a Leviathan that overarched its social domain and imposed hierarchical territorial boundaries, both to police the purity of its own identity and to exclude all that was other" (xii). Modern sovereignty is framed in terms of its territory and its relation to an outside (187), where "the spiritual identity of the nation rather than the divine body of the king now posed the territory and population as an ideal abstraction" (95). In contrast, Hardt and Negri argue that:

Empire establishes no territorial center of power and does not rely on fixed boundaries or barriers. It is a decentered and deterritorializing apparatus of rule that progressively incorporates the entire global realm within its open, expanding frontiers. Empire manages hybrid identities, flexible hierarchies, and plural exchanges through modulating networks of command ... Capital seems to be faced with a smooth world – or really, a world defined by new and complex regimes of differentiation and homogenization, deterritorialization and reterritorialization. (xii-xiii)

There is obviously much here that derives from and parallels the ideas of Deleuze and Guattari. Perhaps particularly when they suggest that Empire is a concept, not a metaphor (xiii), and that the book's aim is to be "a general theoretical framework and a toolbox of concepts" (xvi).

However, in places, they can seem to be proposing an understanding of the world as merely deterritorialized, without considering the concomitant process of remaking – of reterritorialization.[5] In part, this is because, like many other theorists of globalization, Hardt and Negri do not seem to have a fully developed notion of what territory itself might be. The best I can find, by Negri alone, in an earlier work, is that "in advanced capitalism *territory* becomes the framework of productive potential; that is, it becomes the spatial ontology of the productive society" (*The Politics of Subversion* 90). But in *Empire*, for example, we find a discussion of the "deterritorializing capacities of communication," bringing about both the "dissolution of territorial and/or national sovereignty" as well as "the very possibility of linking an order to a space" (346-47). They recognize that analysis meets an obstacle here: "At this point we cannot conceive of this relationship except in *another space*, an elsewhere that cannot in principle be contained in the articulation of sovereign acts," but they do claim that "the space of communication is completely deterritorialized" (347). They attempt to justify this by suggesting that it does not fit the pattern of space analyzed in "terms of the monopoly of physical force and the definition of monetary measure" (347), which perhaps reveals the problem of that very definition.

Elsewhere, we find the suggestion that the "deployments of the imperial machine are defined by a whole series of new characteristics, such as the unbounded terrain of its activities" (35). Hardt and Negri also argue that "perhaps the fundamental characteristic of imperial sovereignty is that *its space is always open*" (167). While they are right in noting that political sovereignty in the modern period "conceived space as bounded, and its boundaries were always policed by the sovereign administration" (167), this seems to me to confuse things somewhat. Space was understood in such a way in the modern period so as to allow it to be restricted, which would then enable it to be policed. Space was conceived of as something extending into three dimensions, qualitatively measurable and thereby amenable to partitioning, regulation and order. The sense of "space," of *spatium*, that emerges in the late medieval period, which finds its most clearly worked through argument in Descartes, is not *necessarily* something that is circumscribed and divided politically into separate sovereign entities. But this sense of space is a necessary *condition* for such a political system: it makes it possible.

In contrast, rather than the strict differentiation of an earlier time, "the world market both homogenizes and differentiates territories, rewriting the geography of the globe" (310). It is clear that this phrase rests on the inclusive logic of the "both ... and...." Change both homogenizes *and* differentiates. If the homogenization is a process of deterritorialization, the differentiation and, indeed, the homogenization itself evokes a passage of reterritorialization. This may not be based on what we commonly understand by territory, but the spatial context is clear. We find this most strikingly illustrated in a central passage:

The striated space of modernity constructed places that were continually engaged in and founded on a dialectical play with their outsides. The space of imperial sovereignty, in contrast, is smooth. It might appear to be free of the binary divisions or striation of modern boundaries, but really it is crisscrossed by so many fault lines that it only appears as a continuous, uniform space. In this sense, the clearly defined crisis of modernity gives way to an omni-crisis in the imperial world. In this smooth space of Empire, there is no place of power – it is both everywhere and nowhere. Empire is an ou-topia, or really a non-place. (190, also see Hardt and Negri, Multitude 101-02)

There is much going on here, and its conceptual prevarication can easily lead us to misconstrue its purpose. There is a danger that striated and smooth space are perceived as polar opposites, and we are, supposedly, seeing the passage from one to the other. For here, even if smooth space only *appears* to be free of striation, it is still being conceived of in such a way that it is different from, and seen in opposition to, striated space in the strict sense. While striated space is scored, chamfered, grooved, channeled and divided into shapes of various sizes, the smooth space of Empire is crisscrossed with lines, overlapping and creating jumbled points in a web of connections. Politically, we have the nation-state map of ordered Europe that progressively eradicates the overlapping sovereignties of medievalism, redistributing land in order to remove almost all the enclaves and exclaves, in contrast to the globalized world of the third millennium, a world of far-flung points connected in a network society like nodes in a system. But as Sparke puts it, "Hardt and Negri fail to distinguish between the globalist enframing of smooth space and the much more messy, uneven and asymmetrical political-economic geography of globalization that the vision of a decentred and deterritorialized globe serves simultaneously to obscure and enable" (385). In other words, there may be a conceptual division within globalization, rather than a passage from a prior mode of spatial ordering. Indeed, it seems to me to make more sense to think of the two spaces as overlapping, the smooth space of Empire imposed over the striated spaces of modernity, the nation-states still attempting to cling to their sovereignty and territorial integrity in an age of globalizing markets and culture and emergent global modes of governance. The unevenness and asymmetry show the messiness, the incompleteness, the striation of the smooth. In other words, it reveals deterritorialization partnered with reterritorialization.

A Politics of Reterritorialization

I am not convinced that Deleuze and Guattari's understandings of de- and reterritorialization, important and interesting though they are, are the most useful ways of understanding what is happening at the moment. In particular, I think that there is a danger in using ethological understandings of territoriality as a basis for understanding territory. In *A Thousand Plateaus*, Deleuze and Guattari analyze how bird-song is used to mark a territory, broadening this into a discussion of how the refrain functions as a "territorial assemblage [*agencement*]." What this means is that, whatever other functions it has, "it always carries earth with it; it has a land (sometimes a spiritual land) as its concomitant" (312. Also see 326-27). Earth [*terre*] and territory [*territoire*] are not the same, but as they describe it, earth "is the intense point at the deepest level of the territory or is projected outside it like a focal point, where all the forces draw together in close embrace" (338-39). Territory "is the product of a territorialization of milieus and rhythms" (314), and they give examples of birds and fishes, rabbits and monkeys, drawing upon a wide range of ethological literature in the process (also see *What is Philosophy?* 67). My concern is that there is not only a latent vitalism evoked here, in spite of the critique of some of this literature, notably in Konrad Lorenz's work on aggression (*On Aggression*), but that, by this logic, all periods of human behavior have exhibited some sense of territoriality.[6] It seems to me that territory is something rather more historical and limited. In other works, I have tried to develop an understanding of space (as opposed to place) as both a historical development and one centrally tied to understandings of calculation, in particular to a new mode of geometry that emerges from late scholasticism and finds its central exponent in Descartes (also see Casey and Malpas). Territory is, I believe, the political corollary of the notion of space – much more about calculation than boundedness, boundaries being a consequence of, and made possible by, "space" and the emergence of new techniques in cartography and surveying.

But even if we are to use Deleuze and Guattari as a tool, it seems important to see the push-pull, almost dialectical, balance of de- and reterritorialization. As Deleuze and Guattari insistently argue, every deterritorialization is partnered by a reterritorialization;

striated and smooth space can be theoretically disassociated, but are perpetually entwined in practice. In terms of contemporary insights, such a dialectical under-standing of Deleuze and Guattari's territorial politics remains underdeveloped. In one of the most interesting discussions of the politics of Deleuze's work, Patton suggests that "Deleuze and Guattari's mature political philosophy might be regarded as a pol-itics of deterritorialisation" (*Deleuze and the Political* 136).

The concept of deterritorialisation implies a contrast between "earth" and "territory" (terre and territoire) understood as the two fundamental dimensions of nature. Territory is in the first instance territorialised earth, but it produces its own movements of deter-ritorialisation, while conversely the earth gives rise to processes of reterritorialisation and the constitution of new territories. Stable identities or territories are therefore sec-ondary formulations upon the mobile earth. Deleuze and Guattari describe a world in which the overriding tendency is deterritorialisation. (9)

By contrast, I want to argue that perhaps in the current climate, as we try to come to terms with both *Empire* and Empire, it is rather a politics of reterritorialization that we need to think about and articulate. How is the globe being reconfigured, remade, re-divided?

David Harvey's recent book *The New Imperialism*, a book that explicitly perceives itself as operating in the wake of *Empire*, makes a persuasive distinction between two contrasting elements within capitalist imperialism: its fundamental basis in state politics and the flow of capital between and beyond such strict territorial boundaries. Harvey calls this the logic of territory and the logic of capital (26, 33). Trading upon his earlier writings (for example *The Limits to Capital* and *Spaces of Capital*), Harvey discusses the strains between these two forms of logic. For example, the endless accumulation of capital creates tension with the territorial logic because of a need to "create a parallel accumulation of political/military power" (183). The boundaries of the state are necessarily exceeded by the capitalist demand for bigger and better markets, a tendency Marx perceptively noted in the *Grundrisse*: "capitalism by its nature drives beyond every spatial barrier ... to conquer the whole world for its mar-ket" (524, 539). Political demands may require military solutions, especially when the state takes on the role of protecting and promoting the internal economy on the world stage, what Lefebvre has called the state mode of production (*De l'État,* also see Elden, *Understanding Henri Lefebvre* 222-26, 231-35).

Harvey is certainly on the right track when he suggests that "imperialism cannot be understood, therefore, without first grappling with the theory of the capitalist state in all its diversity" (183), but this must be understood to include the state's territorial foundation. By this I mean more than a simple cataloguing of its material base, but a deeper understanding of territory itself. Indeed, the recent events in Afghanistan and Iraq have shown how it became easier for the US to fight a territorially identifi-able foe rather than the Al-Qaeda "network of networks."[7] A deterritorialized challenge was reterritorialized, situated by the US government and forced onto a geographically located base. Baghdad could be found and targeted and Saddam located more easily than could a dispersed and splintered organization. Harvey identifies this clearly when he suggests that "with most of the American public uncaring and uninformed about almost anything geographical, it proved fairly easy to parlay the hunt for terrorists into a campaign to hunt down and remove Saddam" (15, see Leaman). In a quote variously attributed to Ambrose Bierce or Paul Rodriguez, war is supposedly "God's way of teaching Americans geography." Reversing Marx, this is comedy replayed as tragedy (Marx, "The Eighteenth Brumaire of Louis Bonaparte" 146).

But the territorial aspects of the war on terror go beyond these straightforward, if important, geographies.[8] One of the key issues is the way in which the term "territorial integrity" is being used. Territorial integrity is a term with two interlinked and usually compatible meanings. The first is that states should not seek to promote border changes or secessionist movements within other states. This also applies to attempts to seize territory by force. The second meaning is the standard idea that within its own borders, within its own territory, a state is sovereign. Territorial integrity, in this sense, can be found enshrined within the UN Founding Charter:

All Members shall refrain in their international relations from the threat or use of force against the territorial integrity or political independence of any state, or in any other manner inconsistent with the Purposes of the United Nations. (Charter of the United Nations, Chapter 1: Purposes and Principles, Article 2 Paragraph 4)

It is also found in numerous Security Council Resolutions, and in the constitutions of several countries. States are supposed to recognize the equal legal standing of other states, and, therefore, respect their sovereignty within the limits of their boundaries.

In recent years, though, this notion of non-intervention in the internal affairs of other states has come under scrutiny. Tony Blair was one of the first to make this assumption problematic, notably in a speech in Chicago in April 1999, where he called for a "new doctrine of international community." Under this doctrine, intervention could be justified, not on the basis of "any territorial ambitions but on values" (1999). At the time, this was a justification of the actions in Kosovo, but it was used soon after to legitimize British involvement in Sierra Leone. Since the war on terror commenced, however, several other examples have been given. One of the most striking is that given by Richard Haass, Director of Policy at the US State Department, in April 2002:

Sovereignty entails obligations. One is not to massacre your own people. Another is not to support terrorism in any way. If a government fails to meet these obligations, then it forfeits some of the normal advantages of sovereignty, including the right to be left alone inside your own territory. Other governments, including the United States, gain the right to intervene. In the case of terrorism, this can even lead to a right of preventive, or peremptory, self-defense. You essentially can act in anticipation if you have grounds to think it's a question of when, and not if, you're going to be attacked. (quoted in Lemann)

Blair too, has warmed to this theme:

So, for me, before September 11th, I was already reaching for a different philosophy in international relations from a traditional one that has held sway since the treaty of Westphalia in 1648; namely that a country's internal affairs are for it and you don't interfere unless it threatens you, or breaches a treaty, or triggers an obligation of alliance ... The best defence of our security lies in the spread of our values ... But we cannot advance these values except within a framework that recognises their universality. If it is a global threat, it needs a global response, based on global rules. (Speech, Sedgefield, 5 March 2004)

Blair has similarly called for revisions to the UN charter that allow this changed position (Mansion House Speech on Foreign Policy, 16 November 2004).

While there are clearly numerous problems with such positions, not least the Eurocentric projection of universal values, it is notable that the notion of "territorial integrity" in the other sense is continually stressed by Blair and others. In fact, Blair generally goes out of his way to underline the importance of the territorial integrity of most regions he subsequently orders to be bombed. Security Council resolutions stressed the territorial integrity of Yugoslavia, even as its government complained to the UN that it was being violated. It has similarly been articulated for Sierra Leone and Afghanistan, and even, recently, for Sudan. Challenges to territorial integrity have been identified as terrorism: China has used the notion to protest against Muslim separatists in Xinjiang province calling for a separate East Turkestan; Russia has stressed its importance in relation to Chechnya; and India has long insisted on it in relation to Kashmir. The US has generally subscribed to these recodings. As I write these lines, the outcome of the Ukraine election is still in doubt and concerns regarding the viability of that country's unity are being voiced. Most notably, the term has been insisted upon in relation to Iraq. Despite the artificial construction of a country from three provinces of the Ottoman Empire – Mosul, Baghdad, Basra – under British mandate following World War One, this most important territorial issue in Iraq can not even be mentioned now. Bush, Blair and Aznar stressed that they envisaged "a unified Iraq with its territorial integrity respected" as an outcome of the war (Azores Summit Statement, 16 March 2003), and subsequent UN resolutions and the express wishes of several of Iraq's neighbors have supported this. Only dissident voices, such as Naqishbendi in *The Kurdistan Observer*, have suggested that the maintenance of the arbitrary unity is the root of the problem, proposing three states – from north to south: Kurdish, Sunni, Shiite – with the Kurds and Shiite's providing some kind of financial recompense to make up for the uneven distribution of oil reserves.

While dominant powers are, therefore, able to suggest that the precepts of international law should be revised in accordance to their values, it seems that the other side of the coin is that secessionist movements, that is, those who want to challenge any notions of territorial integrity, are increasingly being recoded as terrorists. This can be profitably related to Weber's famous definition of the state: "The state is that human community, which within a certain area or territory [*Gebietes*] – this 'area' belongs to the feature – has a (successful) monopoly of legitimate physical violence" (510-11). The point here is not just that standard discussions of the state neglect the territorial aspect of its character; nor that this definition renders any use of violence by non-state actors necessarily illegitimate; but that any potential redrawing of the borders of a state limits the extent of the state's ability to use violence and is, therefore, in itself, necessarily violent and illegitimate. As Blair noted in 2002, "today boundaries are virtually fixed. Governments and people know that any territorial ambition threatens stability, and instability threatens prosperity."

This explicit linking of territorial issues, stability and prosperity is revealing. It is a concern that is important in the various strategies that the US, notably, has adopted in recent years in order to safeguard its interests. Of the many strategies, one is particularly worth noting, because it makes explicit the territorial issues that are implicit within globalization. This is the "Pentagon's New Map," a map of a world where, as Thomas Barnett puts it, "disconnection defines danger" ("The Pentagon's New Map" and *The Pentagon's New Map: War and Peace in the Twenty-First Century*).

Barnett's map shows a world with a "functioning core" and a "non-integrating gap," formed by those countries that share American values and can be seen as part of a globalized world, and those which do not. The map is represented in two ways. One is a picture of the globe in two halves, showing its physical geography, but with a dark "stain" spreading over the center, across the equator and running north and south to various degrees. On the other map, "major U.S. military operations 1990-2003," these "excluding humanitarian operations," are plotted. These operations are subdivided into combat, show of force, contingent positioning, reconnaissance, evacuation, security, and peacekeeping ("The Pentagon's New Map" 144-45). A line snakes around these plotted areas, demarcating the "non-integrating gap," like a lasso thrown around the problem places, a hole in the global ozone layer. This gap is a contiguous area, including Central and South America, with the exception of Brazil, Argentina, Uruguay and Chile; Africa (except for South Africa); the Middle East and the Balkans; the Central Asian Republics of the former USSR; South-East Asia, Indonesia and the Philippines. There are but a few exceptions to the inclusion of all the places that the US military has been involved since the end of the Cold War, notably North Korea (149). For Susan Roberts, Anna Secor and Matthew Sparke, "the map is both that which is to be explained and the explanation itself, descriptive of the recent past and predictive of future action" (890, also see Barnett, "The Pentagon's New Map" 153). These authors usefully discuss how the "common neoliberal imagined geography of the globe as a smooth, de-centred, borderless, level playing field" is seemingly in tension with this model of the world as divided and orientated around a new US hegemony, which we might perceive as striated and scarred. For them, following Thomas

Friedmann (373), this tension is implicit in the neoliberal project, with the US as the hidden fist that abets the economy (894). Barnett talks of decreasing the gap, effectively tightening the noose around the non-globalized world. What is significant is that the map operates with no outside: the gap is within its core.

Conclusion

What these and other examples show is the concomitant reterritorialization that coincides with deterritorialization. New geographies, maps and territorial configurations are emerging. If John Locke founded his seventeenth-century argument for property accumulation on the basis that "in the beginning all the World was *America*" (II §49), perhaps today we are seeing an attempt to turn back the clock. Indeed, Barnett's solution to the global malaise is "more Locke" ("The Pentagon's New Map" 166). Although Hardt and Negri are careful to argue against seeing Empire as an American venture, the organization *Project for the New American Century* (set up during the Clinton years by a number of prominent conservatives, including Jeb Bush, Dick Cheney, Francis Fukuyama, Donald Rumsfeld, Dan Quayle, and Paul Wolfowitz) seems determined to mould it in its own image. In its founding Statement of Principles, it calls for "a Reaganite policy of military strength and moral clarity," which, although it "may not be fashionable today ... is necessary if the United States is to build on the successes of this past century and to ensure our security and our greatness in the next" ("Statement of Principles"). It subsequently lays out the military program required for this new century in a major report (*Rebuilding America's Defenses*), which has clearly influenced "The National Security Strategy of the United States of America" (United States, The White House, *The National Security Strategy*).

If the century is, indeed, defined in this way, the world will be reshaped. This shift is worth stressing: a persuasive point made by Neil Smith is that Henry Luce's 1941 editorial for *Life* magazine, "The American Century," masks its territorial, imperial ambitions by means of a temporal aspiration (18-20). As Harvey notes, PNAC "deliberately repeats, therefore, all the evasions that Smith exposes in Luce's presentation" (*The New Imperialism* 191).

Perhaps, then, in the current global climate (and however loosely we define ourselves as a crowd of followers of such thoughts as Deleuze and Guattari's), we need both to articulate a response to such geographical obfuscation and understand what is actually taking place. Although some important steps have been taken in this direction by geographers and other spatially minded social theorists, it seems to me that discussions of deterritorialization and reterritorialization require more than a straightforward deployment. In attempting to demonstrate how these terms are utilized in the work of Deleuze and Guattari and to show how they are deployed in a more explicitly political sense in *Empire*, and to highlight some contemporary territorial issues, I have essentially opened up a much deeper and more difficult problematic in this article. That is, that before we attempt to understand deterritorialization, and to articulate a politics of reterritorialization, we need to undertake a more detailed – that is conceptual, historical, and political – analysis of territory itself. In other words, what precisely is it that we have supposedly gone beyond?

This is a long-term project investigating the interrelation of mathematical, philosophical and political conceptions of space. The guiding theme is that there is a relation, but that this is not a strict, causal relation, but rather a complicated set of shifts and developments that needs to be investigated carefully. What is at stake in this project is an understanding of the ways in which advances in geometry and calculus allow more exact mapping of the territories of states in Europe and increasingly abstract geometries of division in the New World. For if territory can be re-thought not as bounded space, but as the political form of the type of conceptualization of space that makes boundaries possible, we may well find that contemporary events are a variant within an existing spatial-political configuration, rather than the ontological shift they are often presumed to be.[9]

Notes

1. The fact that Dumoncel writes in French shows that this is not merely an issue of translation.

2. See also the comment made at the very beginning of *A Thousand Plateaus*: "The two of us wrote Anti-Oedipus together. Since each of us was already several, there was already quite a crowd" (Deleuze and Guattari, *A Thousand Plateaus* 3).

3. We should remember that Guattari was trained by Lacan.

4. Tellingly, when they discuss this in *Multitude* they entirely neglect the spatial content (16).

5. On this criticism of *Empire*, see Painter, more generally Minca and Balakrishnan.

6. This would not have concerned Deleuze. See his suggestion that "everything I've written is vitalistic, at least I hope it is" ("Lettre-préface" 5, Negotiations 143, cited in Daniel Smith, "A Life of Pure Immanence" xiii).

7. I owe this phrase to Burke 14.

8. There is a key question, raised by Meiksins Wood, as to whether the thesis of *Empire* can "accommodate the military actions of an imperial nation-state, and least of all the 'democratic' U.S.A.?" (71). Hardt and Negri's answer can be found in *Multitude*, the first part of which is entitled "War," although it seems to require quite a lot of conceptual back-pedaling to do so.

9. I am grateful to Paul Harrison for some very useful conversations in the early development of this essay and Antonis Balasopoulos and Effie Yiannopoulou for their useful comments. A version of this paper was given as a lecture at the Globalization and Comparative Cultural Studies symposium, University of Cyprus, 19-20 November 2004. I owe a particular debt to Maria Margaroni for this invitation, and for continually encouraging me to develop the claims of this paper by means of successive versions.

Works Cited

Appadurai, Arjun. *Modernity at Large: Cultural Dimensions of Globalisation*. Minneapolis: U of Minnesota P, 1996.

Balakrishnan, Gopal, ed. *Debating Empire*. London: Verso, 2003.

Barnett, Thomas P. M. "The Pentagon's New Map." *Esquire* March 2003. 29 Nov. 2004 <http://www.thomaspmbarnett.com/published/pentagonsnewmap.htm>

—. *The Pentagon's New Map: War and Peace in the Twenty-First Century*. New York: G. P. Putnam's Sons, 2004.

Blair, Tony. Speech. The Chicago Economic Club. 22 April, 1999. 29 Nov. 2004 <http://www.pbs.org/newshour/bb/international/jan-june99/blair_doctrine4-23.html>

—. Speech. The George Bush Senior Presidential Library, Texas. 8 Apr. 2002. 29 Nov. 2004 <http://politics.guardian.co.uk/speeches/story/0,11126,680866,00.html>

—. Speech. Sedgefield. 5 Mar. 2004. 29 Nov. 2004 <http://politics.guardian.co.uk/iraq/story/0,12956,1162991,00.html>

—. Mansion House Speech on Foreign Policy. 16 Nov. 2004. 29 Nov. 2004 <http://politics.guardian.co.uk/foreignaffairs/story/0,11538,1352442,00.html>

Bogue, Ronald. "Art and Territory." *A Deleuzian Century?* Ed. Ian Buchanan. Spec. issue of *The South Atlantic Quarterly* 96. 3 (1997): 465-82.

—. "Minority, Territory, Music." *An Introduction to the Philosophy of Gilles Deleuze.* Ed. Jean Khalfa. London: Continuum, 2002. 114-32.

Bryden, Mary. "Deleuze and Anglo-American Literature: Water, Whales and Melville." *An Introduction to the Philosophy of Gilles Deleuze.* Ed. Jean Khalfa. London: Continuum, 2002. 105-13.

Buchanan, Ian, ed. *A Deleuzian Century?* Spec. issue of *The South Atlantic Quarterly* 96. 3 (1997). 465-82.

Buchanan, Ian and John Marks. *Deleuze and Literature.* Edinburgh: Edinburgh UP, 2000.

Burke, Jason. *Al-Qaeda: The True Story of Radical Islam.* Harmondsworth: Penguin, 2004.

Bush, George W., Tony Blair and Jose Maria Aznar. Azores Summit Statement. 16 Mar. 2003. 29 Nov. 2004 <http://news.bbc.co.uk/2/hi/middle_east/2855567.stm>

Casey, Edward S. *The Fate of Place: A Philosophical History.* Berkeley: U of California P, 1997.

Colebrook, Claire. "The Sense of Space: On the Specificity of Affect in Deleuze and Guattari." *Postmodern Culture* 15: 1 (2004). 29 Nov. 2004 <http://www.iath.virginia.edu/pmc/current.issue/15.1colebrook.html>

Deleuze, Gilles. "Nomad Thought." *The New Nietzsche.* Ed. David B. Allison. Cambridge: MIT Press, 1985. 142-49.

—. "Lettre-préface." *Sahara: L'esthétique de Gilles Deleuze.* Mireille Buydens. Paris: Vrin, 1990. 5.

—. *Critique et clinique.* Paris: Éditions de Minuit, 1993.

—. *Negotiations, 1972-1990.* Trans. Martin Joughlin. New York: Columbia UP, 1995.

Deleuze, Gilles and Félix Guattari. *Anti-Oedipus: Capitalism and Schizophrenia.* Trans. Robert Hurley, Mark Seem and Helen R. Lane. London: Athlone, 1984.

—. *Kafka: Toward a Minor Literature.* 1975. Trans. Dana Polan. Minneapolis: U of Minnesota P, 1986.

—. *A Thousand Plateaus: Capitalism and Schizophrenia.* Trans. Brian Massumi. London: Athlone, 1988.

—. *What is Philosophy?* Trans. Hugh Tomlinson and Graham Burchill. London: Verso, 1994.

Deleuze, Gilles and Clare Parnet. *Dialogues.* Trans. Hugh Tomlinson and Barbara Habberjam. London: Athlone, 1987.

Dumoncel, Jean-Claude. *Le Pendule du Docteur Deleuze: Une introduction à l'Anti- Œdipe.* Paris: Cahiers de l'Unebévue, 1999.

Elden, Stuart. "The Place of Geometry: Heidegger's Mathematical Excursus on Aristotle." *The Heythrop Journal* 42. 3 (2001): 311-28.

—. *Mapping the Present: Heidegger, Foucault and the Project of a Spatial History.* London: Continuum, 2001.

—. "Another Sense of *Demos*: Kleisthenes and the Greek Division of the *Polis*." *Democratization* 10. 1 (2003): 135-56.

—. "The Importance of History: A Reply to Malpas." *Philosophy and Geography* 6. 2 (2003): 219-24.

—. *Understanding Henri Lefebvre: Theory and the Possible.* London: Continuum, 2004.

—. "Missing the Point: Globalisation, Deterritorialisation and the Space of the World." *Transactions of the Institute of British Geographers* 30. 1. (2005).

Faubion, James D. "Introduction." *Aesthetics, Method, and Epistemology.* Michel Foucault. Ed. James D. Faubion. Harmondsworth: Penguin, 1998. xi-xli.

Foucault, Michel. *Language, Counter-Memory, Practice*. Ed. Donald F. Bouchard. Oxford: Basil Blackwell, 1977.

—. *Dits et écrits 1954-1988*. Ed. Daniel Defert and François Ewald. Vol. II. Paris: Gallimard, 1994.

Friedmann, Thomas L. *The Lexus and the Olive Tree: Understanding Globalization*. New York: Farrar Straus Giroux, 1999.

Goodchild, Philip. *Deleuze & Guattari: An Introduction to the Politics of Desire*. London: Sage, 1996.

Guattari, Félix. *Psychanalyse et transversalité*. Paris: François Maspero, 1972.

Guattari, Félix and Toni Negri. *Communists Like Us: New Spaces of Liberty, New Lines of Alliance*. Trans. Michael Ryan. New York: Semiotext(e), 1990.

Hardt, Michael. *Gilles Deleuze: An Apprenticeship in Philosophy*. Minneapolis: U of Minnesota P, 1993.

Hardt, Michael and Antonio Negri. *Empire*. Cambridge: Harvard UP, 2000.

—. *Multitude: War and Democracy in the Age of Empire*. New York: The Penguin Press, 2004.

Harvey, David. *The Limits to Capital*. 1982. London: Verso, 1999.

—. *Spaces of Capital: Towards a Critical Geography*. Edinburgh: Edinburgh UP, 2001.

—. *The New Imperialism*. Oxford: Oxford UP, 2003.

Holland, Eugene W. "Deterritorializing Deterritorialization: from the *Anti-Oedipus* to *A Thousand Plateaus*." *Substance* 66 (1991): 55–65. Department of French and Italian, Ohio State University. 29 Nov. 2004 <http://people.cohums.ohio-state.edu/holland1/deterritorializing.htm>

—. "Schizoanalysis and Baudelaire: Some Illustrations of Decoding at Work." *Deleuze: A Critical Reader*. Ed. Paul Patton. Oxford: Blackwell, 1996. 240-56.

Kafka, Franz. *The Diaries of Franz Kafka*. Ed. Max Brod. Harmondsworth: Penguin, 1964.

Lefebvre, Henri. *De l'État*. 4 vols. Paris: UGE, 1976-78.

Leibniz, Gottfried. *Œuvres de Leibniz*. Vol. 6. Ed. Louis Alexandre Foucher de Careil. Hildesheim: Olms Verlag, 1969.

Leaman, George. "Iraq, American Empire, and the War on Terrorism." *Metaphilosophy* 35. 3 (2004): 234-48.

Lemann, Nicholas. "The Next World Order." *The New Yorker*. 1 Apr. 2002. 29. Nov. 2004 <http://www.newyorker.com/fact/content/?020401fa_FACT1>

Locke, John. *Two Treatises of Government*. Ed. Peter Laslett. Cambridge: Cambridge UP, 1988.

Lorenz, Konrad. *On Aggression*. London: Methuen, 1966.

Lyotard, Jean-François. "Capitalisme énergumène." *Critique* 306 (1972): 923-56.

Malpas, Jeff. "On the Map: Comments on Stuart Elden's *Mapping the Present: Heidegger, Foucault and the Project of a Spatial History*." *Philosophy and Geography* 6. 2 (2003): 213-18.

Marks, John. *Gilles Deleuze: Vitalism and Multiplicity*. London: Pluto, 1998.

Marx, Karl and Friedrich Engels. "Manifesto of the Communist Party." *The Revolutions of 1848: Political Writings, Volume I*. Karl Marx. Ed. David Fernbach. Harmondsworth: Penguin, 1973. 62-98.

Marx, Karl. *Grundrisse: Foundations of the Critique of Political Economy (Rough Draft)*. Trans. Martin Nicolaus. Harmondsworth: Penguin, 1973.

—. "The Eighteenth Brumaire of Louis Bonaparte." *Surveys from Exile: Political Writings, Volume II*. Trans. David Fernbach. Harmondsworth: Penguin, 1973. 143-249.

Meiksins Wood, Ellen. "A Manifesto for Global Capitalism." *Debating Empire*. Ed. Gopal Balakrishnan. London: Verso, 2003. 61-82.

Minca, Claudio. "Empire goes to War, or, The Ontological Shift in the Transatlantic Divide." *ACME: An International E-Journal for Critical Geographies* 2. 2 (2003): 227-35. 29 Nov. 2004 <www.acme-journal.org/vol2/minca.pdf>

United States. The White House. *The National Security Strategy of the United States of America*. Washington D.C, 2002. 29 Nov. 2004 <http://www.whitehouse.gov/nsc/nss.pdf>

Naqishbendi, Rauf. "Maintaining Iraq's Territorial Integrity Is Causing United States' Failure and Continuing Hardship For The Iraqi People." *The Kurdistan Observer* 8 Sept 2004. 29 Nov. 2004 <http://home.cogeco.ca/~kurdistan/8-9-04-opinion-naqishbendi-us-failure-irq-integrity.html>

Negri, Antonio. *The Politics of Subversion: A Manifesto for the Twenty-First Century*. Trans. James Newell. Cambridge: Polity Press, 1989.

—. *The Savage Anomaly: The Power of Spinoza's Metaphysics and Politics*. Trans. Michael Hardt. Minneapolis: U of Minnesota P, 1991.

—. "On Gilles Deleuze and Félix Guattari, *A Thousand Plateaus*." Trans. Charles T. Wolfe. *Graduate Faculty Philosophy Journal* 18. 1 (1995): 93-109.

Painter, Joe. "*Empire* and Citizenship." *ACME: An International E-Journal for Critical Geographies* 2. 2 (2003): 248-53. 29 Nov. 2004 <www.acme-journal.org/vol2/painter.pdf>

Papastergiadis, Nikos. *The Turbulence of Migration: Globalization, Deterritorialization and Hybridity*. Cambridge: Polity Press, 2000.

Patton, Paul. "Introduction." *Deleuze: A Critical Reader*. Ed. Paul Patton. Oxford: Blackwell, 1996. 1-17.

—. *Deleuze and the Political*. London: Routledge, 2000.

Project for the New American Century. "Statement of Principles." 1997. 29 Nov. 2004 <http://www.newamericancentury.org/statementofprinciples.htm>

Project for the New American Century. *Rebuilding America's Defenses: Strategy, Forces and Resources for a New Century*. Washington D.C.: Project for the New American Century. 2000. 29 Nov. 2004 <http://www.newamericancentury. org/RebuildingAmericasDefenses.pdf>

Roberts, Susan, Anna Secor and Matthew Sparke. "Neoliberal Geopolitics." *Antipode* 35. 5 (2003): 886-97.

Smith, Daniel W. " 'A Life of Pure Immanence': Deleuze's 'Critique et Clinique' Project." *Essays Critical and Clinical*. By Gilles Deleuze. Trans. Daniel W. Smith and Michael A. Greco. London: Verso, 1998. xi-liii.

Smith, Neil. *American Empire: Roosevelt's Geographer and the Prelude to Globalization*. Berkeley: U of California P, 2003.

Sparke, Matthew. "American Empire and Globalisation: Postcolonial Speculations on Neocolonial Enframing." *Singapore Journal of Tropical Geography* 24. 3 (2003): 373-89.

United Nations. *Charter of the United Nations*. 1945. 29 Nov. 2004 <http://www.un.org/aboutun/charter/index.html>

Weber, Max. "Politik als Beruf." *Gesammelte Politische Schriften*. Ed. Johannes Winckelmann. Tübingen: Mohr, 1971: 505-60.

II. Mobilizing the Politics of Theory

Making up Chinese-Americans

Moral Geographies of Immigration in the Chinese Exclusion Act (1882) and The Peopling of America Theme Study Act (2001)	Gareth Hoskins and Tim Cresswell

Introduction

In 1970 a park ranger, Alexander Weiss, was busy checking some old buildings on Angel Island in the San Francisco Bay. The California Department of Parks and Recreation was in the process of demolishing these buildings as they were considered unsafe and unsightly by the increasing number of the city's residents who visited for the purposes of picnicking and, fog permitting, enjoying views of the city skyline. Several buildings had already been bulldozed and an old wooden pier had been removed. As he inspected the two-storied detention barracks, Weiss noticed some writing on the wall and believed them to be carvings left by Chinese immigrants once detained there for questioning. He informed his superiors at the department, but apparently they shared neither his enthusiasm nor belief in the significance of the writings. The ranger eventually contacted Dr George Araki of the San Francisco State University, who, along with a local photographer, recorded the hundreds of poems scrawled all over the inside of the building.

The poems are written in classical Chinese verse in the Tang Dynasty style and are part of a legacy of literature left by different authors recording their feelings of frustration, confusion and sadness at having been detained in the building under the 1882 Chinese Exclusion Act. These two examples appear with others in the book *Island: Poetry and History of Chinese Immigrants on Angel Island 1910-1940* collected and translated by Him Mark Lai, Genny Lim and Judy Yung.

> *I hastened here for the sake of my stomach*
> *And landed promptly in jail.*
> *Imprisoned I am melancholy; even when I*
> *eat, my heart is troubled.*
> *They treat us Chinese badly, and feed us*
> *yellowed greens.*

My weak physique cannot take it; I am truly
miserable. (Lai, Lim, Yung 102)

The low building with three beams merely
shelters the body.
It is unbearable to relate the stories
accumulated on the Island slopes.
Wait till the day I become successful and
fulfil my wish!
I will not speak of love when I level the
immigration station. (Lai, Lim, Yung 94)

The discovery of these poems and recognition of their cultural importance sparked widespread interest from the local Asian-American community, enough to success-fully lobby $250, 000 dollars for the preservation of the site. Today, accounts of the immigration experience have become part of the heritage landscape and are consid-ered to be significant national treasures.

From 1910 to 1940 Angel Island functioned as an immigration station and deten-tion/quarantine headquarters for an estimated 175,000 Chinese seeking to find work and residence in America. As we write, it is in the process of becoming some-thing else – a museum and heritage center memorializing Asian immigration into the United States. The writing on the wall, following careful preservation, has become the central focus of this new heritage space.

These inscriptions are a material expression of the socio-geographical construc-tion of Chinese immigrants. In this essay we examine two pieces of American legis-lation concerning the mobility of Chinese citizens to the United States that have formed key moments in this process and that have, in significant ways, played impor-tant roles in the history of these poignant poems. The first is the Chinese Exclusion Act of 1882 and the second is the Peopling of America Theme Study Act of 2001. We show how the first act constructed the Chinese as radically different and a threat to the ongoing process of American identity construction. The second act, on the other hand, seeks to incorporate the experience of the Chinese into a unifying story of the "Peopling of America," which cannot help but negate the difference that it attempts to recognize. The latter statute envisages a reworking of American history and roots in a manner befitting a society of paradox, that is, one ever more fixated on its plural identity while simultaneously living out and selling its image of a coherently bounded and concrete nation. So, this essay will explain how, in two instances divided by 118 years, the movement of Chinese groups into the United States has been made mean-ingful in different ways by the United States within its legislature. In effect, we chart how knowledge concerning the mobility of the Chinese changed from the late nineteenth century, that constructed them as a threat to the economic, social, physical and moral order of a Eurocentric civilization, to the situation today where that mobility is given another meaning – as flagship for tolerance, acceptance of difference and accomplishment over adversity that all peoples in the nation can share.

The attribution of meaning to the Chinese is neither apolitical nor outside of human construction but always cultivated, articulated, reinforced or contested within uneven relations of power. In some sense, then, this is an exercise in social constructionism – the social construction of Chinese immigrants. We have a number of reservations about this label. First, social constructionism is too often understood as "merely" discursive where the term "discursive" is taken to refer to the world of meaning and representation. We insist that discourse refer to the sum of representation, practice and material contexts that construct or produce social facts. This is not in order to oppose the discursive and the material but to insist on the materiality of discourse. This leads to our second objection, which is that we are interested in the way in which Chinese immigrants are "geographically constructed." Since the social is always already geographical this might not seem like much of a distinction. We simply want to high-light the role of geography in the process of constructing people. Geography is par-ticularly important in our story because the legislation we discuss is thoroughly embedded in moral geographies of mobility and of place, and because a particular network of material spaces – detainment centers, offices, places to check identities – arose to support and enact the legislation.[1] Geography is part of the discourse at all levels. In this sense, our project supports the contentions of the editors of this vol-ume concerning *metaphoricity* – that is, the insistence on the materiality of discourse and meaning. It is one thing to say that meanings are constructed around Chinese immigrants to America; it is quite another, and, in our view, more productive thing to say that the materiality of being a Chinese immigrant is fabricated. Our third caveat about social construction is connected to this. Following Ian Hacking, we insist that it is necessary to be more literal about the process of construction. The concept of "Chinese immigrants," after all, could never be anything other than a social con-struct. To make the story interesting, it is necessary to show how this construction is assembled both in terms of the meanings ascribed to the immigrants and the mate-rial facts of their lives.

A further central strand in our argument is rooted in the entanglement of the politics of mobility (Massey, Hyndman, Cresswell, "The Production of Mobilities") with the politics of difference (Lyotard and Thébaud, Young, *Justice and the Politics of Difference*). The ways in which mobility is given meaning and then enacted is intimately tied to notions of sameness and difference. We show how the Chinese Exclusion Act was based on notions of essential difference between forms of mobility, while the Peopling of America Theme Study Act, although often ambivalent, is ultimately based on the notion of unity, totality, sameness – the idea that American national identity is based on a common experience of mobility. The next section of the paper examines notions of unity and difference through the work of Jean-François Lyotard and Iris Young and relates their formulation of a politics of difference to the theme of mobility.

Politics, Difference and Mobility

In *The Postmodern Condition*, Jean François Lyotard describes the "incredulity toward meta-narratives" (xxiv) and the heterogeneity of language games that mark the post-modern condition. This leads him to ask us, somewhat cryptically, to "wage a war on totality" (82), as "[t]he nineteenth and twentieth centuries have given us as much ter-ror as we can take. We have paid a high enough price for the nostalgia of the whole and the one" (81). In discussion with Jean-Loup Thébaud, he develops this ethical and political commitment to difference in *Just Gaming*:

> if one has the viewpoint of a multiplicity of language games. If one has the hypoth-esis that the social bond is not made up of a singular type of statement, or, if you will, of discourse, but that it is made up of several kinds of these games ..., then it follows that, to put it quickly, social partners are caught up in pragmatics that are different from each other. (93)

Once, he argues, we have abandoned the Parsonian idea of a singular and coherent "society" and we recognize the variety of "language games" that exist side by side and in conflict with each other, we necessarily have to jettison the political idea of "unity" and accept multiplicity and difference.

> The picture that one can draw from this observation is precisely that of an absence of unity, an absence of totality. All of this does not make up a body. On the contrary. And the idea that I think we need today in order to make decisions in political matters can-not be the idea of the totality, or of the unity, of a body. It can only be the idea of a mul-tiplicity or of a diversity. (94)

Lyotard admits the lack of an answer to what this new form of postmodern politics and justice might look like.

This line of questioning has been inherited by Iris Marion Young, who has consis-tently called for a new "politics of difference" to challenge the hegemony of modernist liberal doctrines of rights and equality (Young, *Justice and the Politics of Difference* and *Intersecting Voices*). Her starting point is the recognition that there has always been a politics of difference based on essentialist notions of absolute difference – "a time of caste and class, when tradition decreed that each group had its place" (*Justice and the Politics of Difference* 156). Here, social inequality was based on the hierarchical difference of people's natures. This politics of essential difference was overturned (not completely and not everywhere) by an Enlightenment project in which the use of impartial reason was central to a multitude of struggles of liberty and equality – struggles against the tyranny of irrational prejudice. Recent manifestations of this project include the fights for women's rights and the civil rights movements.

Today in our society a few vestiges of prejudice and discrimination remain, but we are working on them, and have nearly realized the dream these Enlightenment fathers dared to propound. The state and law should express rights only in universal terms applied equally to all, and differences among persons and groups should be a purely accidental and private matter. We seek a society in which differences of race, sex, religion, and ethnicity no longer make a difference to people's rights and opportunities. (Young, Justice and the Politics of Difference *157).*

Young refers to this enlightenment dream of sameness as an "assimilationist ideal" – an ideal that places "equal treatment" at the heart of the idea of justice. A new anti-essentialist politics of difference, on the other hand, rejects both this view and the older politics of essential difference. Instead, it argues for a liberatory self-definition of group difference. Here, however, difference is not rooted in nature but within social processes. It is not absolute but relational. Rather than thinking of difference as distance from a norm in which some groups simply function as an "other" to a pre-established neutral group, Young asks us to conceptualize difference as simply a variation defined by means of social processes in a way that undermines the previously universalized position of privileged groups that "others" have been constituted as different from. So while the liberal assimilationist ideal calls for all people to be subject to the same rules and standards, the politics of difference argues that "equality as the participation and inclusion of all groups sometimes requires different treatment for oppressed and disadvantaged groups" (*Justice and the Politics of Difference* 158). In this way, Young takes the discussion of totality and difference out of the realm of philosophy and into the domain of policy and legislation, showing how such abstractions impact on the material lives of people. In this sense, Young is less reticent than Lyotard and is able to give an answer to the question of how a politics based on multiplicity might work.

Returning to our theme of the role of mobility in the geographical imagination that informs legislation on and about Chinese-Americans, we can utilize some of the lessons learned from Lyotard and Young concerning the challenge to "totality." In particular, we focus on specifically geographical ideas of sameness and difference as expressed through legislation concerning Chinese immigration. Thinking about the different ways in which mobility is given meaning and experienced (in legislation and elsewhere) leads to a focus on the politics of mobility (Hyndman, Cresswell, "The Production of Mobilities").

Analysis of the politics of mobility involves delineating the ways in which human movement is given meaning in particular contexts. As such, it resists totalizing accounts of mobility and instead looks at how differences in both the meaning and experience of mobility are socially and culturally produced and how these differences are then mobilized to reproduce or contest the social arrangements that produced them in the first place. Such an approach stands in opposition to accounts of mobility that describe it in essentialist terms – as being at the core of "American identity," on the one hand, or as essentially transgressive and resistant, on the other. Mobility is not simply a geographical fact of getting from A to B but an activity that has social relations embedded within it and which, in turn, produces social relations. While many forms of mobility have been historically seen as threatening, unruly and transgressive due to the crossing of boundaries which are supposed to inscribe order on the chaos of life (Cresswell, *The Tramp in America*, Sibley), other forms of mobility have been seen as essential to the well-ordered machinery of global capitalism (Castells) or at the heart of American national identity (Baudrillard, Pierson, Boorstin). Rather than read mobility as either transgressive or a key part of "normal" life, in the analysis below we show how these different readings swirl around each other in the ongoing politics of sameness and difference. In this spirit, we turn our attention to the mobilization of discourses of difference and sameness around Chinese mobility into the United States.

Constructing Chinese Mobility: Act One

The mobility of migrants to the United States and the mobility of people within the nation has been portrayed in a positive light as a general fact of American cultural identity (Zelinsky, Jasper, Boorstin, Turner). While this movement has been cast as a universal experience at the heart of collective identity, it has, however, most often selectively referred to the mobility of white European migrants. The problem with totalities is that they often obscure the situatedness of the knowledge that is produced and claim it to be universal. This mobility – represented as general – has been placed at the heart of America's creation myth, a story created by means of a selective use of history combined with strategic forgetting that helps to cement ideas of a single and common national identity. Even this selected aspect of migrancy cannot be so simply coded. The movements of the Irish, Italians, East European Jews and Germans were all, at one time or another, seen as a threat to the body politic as well as to the literal human body. As they passed through Ellis Island and were squashed into the maze of tenements on New York's lower east side, these immigrants were variously coded as lazy, excitable and diseased (Ward, Kraut). Over time, however, the migration of white Europeans into the United States has been celebrated and given a home at the Immigration Museum on Ellis Island. Conversely, the mobility of the Chinese to America has more often been regarded and represented as a threat and a danger to the moral and physical well-being of established American citizens.

We recognize that both groups had similar experiences of poverty and deprivation, whether in Europe or China, enough to compel them to settle elsewhere. However, the meaning given to European migrants has been largely affirmative – as actors in a narrative of nation building (Turner). Chinese migration, on the other hand, was popularly understood and represented as a threat that required defense in the form of racially determined exclusion acts. In 1882, the forty-seventh Congress passed the Chinese Exclusion Act.

Preamble.

Whereas, in the opinion of the Government of the United States the coming of Chinese laborers to this country endangers the good order of certain localities within the territory thereof: Therefore, Be it enacted by the Senate and House of Representatives of the United States of America in Congress assembled, *That from and after the expiration of ninety days next after the passage of this act, and until the expiration of ten years next after the passage of this act, the coming of Chinese laborers to the United States be, and the same is hereby, suspended; and during such suspension it shall not be lawful for any Chinese laborer to come, or, having so come after the expiration of said ninety days, to remain within the United States.*

Section 14. *That hereafter no State court or court of the United Sates shall admit Chinese to Citizenship; and all laws in conflict with this act are hereby repealed. (The Chinese Exclusion Act 1882)*

The Chinese Exclusion Act of 1882 incorporated understandings of race, class and mobility to define the individual as an illegitimate job seeker and denied at one stroke a wider appreciation of economic and structural relations. Furthermore, sections of the Chinese Exclusion Act differentiate mobilities along class and occupation lines. The coding of people as raced is seldom free of class connotations. Section 6 reads:

That in order to the faithful execution of articles one and two of the treaty in this act before mentioned, every Chinese person other than a laborer who may be entitled by said treaty and this act to come within the United States, and who shall be about to come to the United States, shall be identified as so entitled by the Chinese Government in each case, such identity to be evidenced by a certificate issued under the authority of said government, which certificate shall be in English ... Such certificate shall be prima-facie evidence of the fact set forth therein, and shall be produced to the collector of customs, or his deputy, of the port in the district in the United States at which the person named therein shall arrive. (The Chinese Exclusion Act 1882, Section 6)

Section 13 makes it clear that diplomats and other officers of the Chinese Government must be able to present credentials that will be taken in lieu of a certificate. Section 15 reads: "That the words 'Chinese laborers' whenever used in this act, shall be construed to mean both skilled and unskilled laborers and Chinese employed in mining." The Chinese Exclusion Act, then, mobilized a set of suppositions about race and class in order to enact strict controls on some forms of mobility for some sorts of people. The mobility was to be policed by a bureaucratic handling of certificates which provided the necessary details including "name, title, or official rank, if any, the age, height, and all physical peculiarities, former and present occupation or profession" (Section 6). People without such certificates were prohibited from entering the United States. The Act was thereby enacting a politics of mobility at a number of levels. At one level, it ascribed a particular set of meanings to certain kinds of Chinese mobility based on the danger posed to "the good order of certain localities" (Section 1). On another, connected, level it was producing a new set of material institutional arrangements to police and enforce exclusion ranging from the certificates themselves to the offices and material spaces needed to enact that exclusion. One of these material spaces was the detention center on Angel Island. All of this was based on the fine-tuned definitions of mobility implicit in the Act. These did not come from nowhere, however. Instead, they were merely one part of a wider set of representations and practices directed against the Chinese.

The Chinese were the first numerically significant non-white group to enter the United States as free immigrants. The first wave of Chinese immigration began around 1849 after the discovery of gold in California, where their subordination was at once obvious due to their reworking of gold claims abandoned by white miners and because they earned only 12 cents per hour laying tracks as section hands for the Central Pacific Railroad.

Roger Daniels tells of the most dangerous part in the railway's completion: the crossing of the Sierra Nevada in California. Here, Chinese laborers worked with large quantities of dynamite to blast a passage through the rock and open up the west to the rest of the world. The eventual conclusion of this task had implications that helped to inform an understanding of Chinese mobility over the next decades:

When that road was completed at Promontory Point, Utah, perhaps ten thousand Chinese workers were discharged; most of them found their way back to San Francisco where their presence in a depressed labor market helped an existing and virulent anti-Chinese movement gain strength in the late 1860's. (Daniels 7)

The formulation, policing and challenge of numerous laws during the late nineteenth century allows a wealth of insight into the construction of knowledges about the Chinese expressed variously as alien, inassimilable, uncivil, immoral and unhealthy (Anderson, Craddock). Indeed, preceding the Exclusion Act of 1882, there are many attempts not only to prevent entry but also to withdraw rights for existing legitimate Chinese residents. A highly symbolic decision defining the Chinese individual as outside of society occurred in 1854, for instance, when the California Supreme Court ruled in the case of *People vs Hall* that the testimony of a Chinese witness against any white person could not be accepted in court. Additionally, the Page Act of 1875 focused on preventing the importation of Chinese women due to fear of prostitution and subsequent health risk to white men (Daniels).

It was not only by Congress and the courts that the Chinese endured persecution owing to essentialist conceptions applied to them as a group. Local resistance hindered Chinese inclusion in many professions from mining to laundry by means of race-specific taxation. Moreover, anti-Chinese sentiment was put into operation with The State of California's 1879 Constitution forbidding corporations from employing any Chinese people, barring them from all public works and calling upon legislature to protect the State from the evils and burdens arising from their presence. There are countless sources that tell of violent treatment given to Chinese communities all over the West during the cycle of late nineteenth-century depressions, when resentment was at its peak. In 1885, the white citizens of Humboldt County evicted many Chinese from the area after the shooting of councilman David Kendall, allegedly by a Chinese American. A year later, further north, Del Norte County expelled all Chinese Americans to San Francisco. In May 1887, a fire destroyed San Jose's Chinese-American community under suspicious circumstances. Newspapers noted the following day that the fire had started in three places at once and that the water tanks were empty at the time.

What these actions reveal is the enactment of a particular kind of essentialist politics of difference in which the Chinese are categorized as a threatening "other" to white Americans – and particularly white American laborers. The Act's careful delineation of difference is clearly part of a process of differentiation that is at the same time part of the process of social construction. We share Ian Hacking's suspicion of the term "social construction," as it is too often used in banal and self-evident ways. Following Hacking, we take the process of "making up" the Chinese threat more literally. The processes through which discourse is made to act on its objects is more than by means of "mere words." Rather, discourses have their own geographies, their own brute materialities, that act on the bodies of those being constructed. The Chinese Exclusion Act necessitates certificates to be carried by Chinese people entering the United States. As John Torpey has noted, the Chinese Exclusion Act was the "[f]irst serious attempt in American history specifically to exclude members of a particular group whose relevant characteristics were knowable only on the basis of documents" (Torpey 97). As the 1882 Act only prohibited Chinese laborers from entering the United States, these people had to be distinguished from Chinese people who were already present when the Act was passed and from Chinese people entering who were not laborers. The right to remain in or enter the United States could only be policed by means of passport-like documents and a system of registration of identification. "Inspectors" at ports needed to be appointed in order to check over the certificates and inspect the Chinese people for "physical peculiarities." Offices were created for these inspectors with desks where the process of differentiation could be enacted. Spaces needed to be constructed where the Chinese could stand in line awaiting decisions. Courtrooms became spaces in which attorneys specializing in immigration law could make carefully crafted arguments over whether a Chinese person was really a "laborer" or belonged to some more exalted category. In these material spaces categories came to life. Perhaps the most obvious material geographic component of this discourse of difference was the detention center at Angel Island where tens of thousands of Chinese people would be incarcerated while they awaited decisions over whether they were leaving or arriving.

(Re)Constructing Chinese Mobility: Act Two

With such a regrettable past it is no wonder that totalizing historical narratives have written the Chinese out of American space and not surprising that heritage sites have typically directed our gaze away from the experience of minorities (Loewen, Solnit). Today a postmodern culture is combining with a renewed fascination for history and roots to begin to readdress this imbalance with the legitimacy it affords to marginalized groups and their alternative voices.

Just as earlier essentialized views of difference were inscribed in the legislation of the Chinese Exclusion Act, so more recent cultural currents have been expressed in legislature. On July 27, 2000, the 106th Congress of Senate sat for a second reading of, and subsequently approved, a Bill that set out a strategy to reassess and then rework the entire social history of North America. The Peopling of America Theme Study Act, Bill S.2478, strives to:

Direct the secretary of the Interior to conduct a theme study on the peopling of America to provide a basis for identifying, interpreting and preserving sites related to the migration, immigration and settling of America. (Peopling of America Theme Study Act 2000) The statute seeks to rework knowledge about the roots of America by directing investigation on mobility to show how the continent was populated. The broad term "The Peopling of America" is defined in section two of this Act as characterized by:

i. The movement of groups of people across external and internal boundaries of the United States and territories of the United States, and
ii. The interactions of those groups with each other and with other populations.
(Peopling of America Theme Study Act 2000, Section Two)

This bill is co-written, sponsored and brought before the house by Senator Daniel Akaka, representative of Hawaii and the first native Hawaian voted to Congress. Throughout his political career, Akaka has sought to communicate the role played by Asian-Americans in the growth of the nation. With this new statute, the United States' success and the spiritual, intellectual, cultural, political and economic strength of its national fabric is attributed to pluralism, its embrace and accommodation of diversity. This is how Senator Akaka promoted his bill in a press release before it was presented to the house:

Americans are all travelers from other regions, continents and islands. We need a better understanding of this coherent and unifying theme in America. This is the source of our nation's greatest strength.

Looking back, we understand that our history, and our very national character, is defined by the grand entangled process of people to and across the American landscape – through exploration, colonization, the slave trade, traditional immigration, or internal migration – that gave rise to the rich interactions that make the American experience unique. (Official Press Release, February 14, 2001, our emphasis)
The Bill's purpose, therefore, is to develop a system of knowledge about mobility, use it to rewrite the history of the nation, and foster a new inclusive identity for the American nation that all can share. It intends to highlight the power of the nation through

a wider understanding of the positive contributions made by diverse and marginal groups; it is a success story using minorities as its tool. Those minorities who were once excluded from the story of America are now at the forefront of demonstrating its strength.

Interpretation of the Bill is not straightforward. Perhaps as a reflection of Akaka's ambiguous position – a representative of the Asian-American community and agent of the State – the text of the Bill and supporting statements constantly shift from a recognition of difference and diversity to unified statements of American mobile identity. In the above quotation, for instance, we hear of the clearly differentiated mobilities of "exploration, colonization, the slave trade, traditional immigration, or internal migration." This is preceded, however, by statements about "*our* national character" and followed by the unifying tag of "*the* American experience." According to the bill, the very exceptional and distinctive nature of Americans is that they have all experienced mobility within and across national boundaries and have been shaped by all the "positive" attributes of diversity – social, cultural, ethnic and racial – that the experience of mobility brings. However, despite its willingness to promote inclusion and celebrate diversity, the Bill constantly slips from acknowledging difference to the valorization of universal mobility. Textually, the mobilities of Americans are stripped of their peculiarities and reduced to the simple act of movement, which is the essential core of a unified "American experience."

Here, as Steven Hoelscher has indicated, the State's need to recognize diversity is at odds with the necessity to uphold the notion of a coherent national identity. Hoelscher questions the appropriateness of a strategy that acknowledges cultural pluralism while containing it within a universal theme or unifying narrative. Applying Barbara Kirshenblatt-Gimblett's idea of the "banality of difference" to historical accounts of Wisconsin and the United States, he recognizes the risks of stripping difference of its politics by painting it as ubiquitous. With such problems, then, is it possible to achieve unity in diversity? And what kind of poly-ethnic culture can we appreciate while pursuing integration within a secular nation state? Can any such intention take difference seriously (Hoelscher 394)?

The framework of the Peopling of America Theme Study Act provides advance funding for preservation and education and effectively claims all stories of movement as a universal national trait of success that is to be emphasized and celebrated. It valorizes travel and renders the vast differences in experience between Chinese and other immigrant groups as secondary to the prime importance of the unified experience of movement. When looking at the particular context that groups entering Ellis Island and groups entering Angel Island encountered because of their mobility, we see how different the types of mobility and the meanings construed from them actually are. To carefully observe the experiences of those entering America via Ellis Island (even if only in retrospect and despite much that was degrading about the process of entry) is to witness one set of meanings defining mobility as positive, a civilizing force over nature where the homesteader migrates to the west and eventually defines "America." The difficulties encountered by the incoming Chinese, on the other hand, can only be equated with the experiences of earlier European immigrants fallaciously, because of the very different character of their mobility and how it was perceived, and because they were, after all, only retrospectively written into the metanarratives of American history.

Conclusion

Groups experiencing cultural imperialism have found themselves objectified and marked with a devalued essence from the outside, by a dominant culture they are excluded from making. The assertion of a positive sense of group difference by these groups is emancipatory because it reclaims the definition of the group by the group, as a creation and construction, rather than a given essence. (Young, Justice and the Politics of Difference *172)*

On the basis of the theme study authorized by the Peopling of America Act, the Secretary of the Interior will identify and recommend for designation new historic land-marks and encourage the nomination of other properties to the National Register of Historic Places. Section 4B reads:

The purpose of the theme study shall be to identify regions, areas, trails, districts, communities, sites, buildings, structures, objects, organizations, societies and cultures that best illustrate and commemorate key events or decisions affecting the peopling of America and can provide a basis for the interpretation of the peopling of America that has shaped the culture and society of the United States. (Peopling of America Theme Study Act 2000, Section 4B)

It is thus mandated that sites that help to tell the story of migration should be inter-preted as such and preserved in line with that interpretation. The barracks building used to detain Chinese immigrants, Japanese, German and Italian Prisoners of War as well as Federal Prisoners, for instance, is now used as a museum communicating a story in the context of the peopling of America. Indeed, Federal funds for the Angel Island museum have a specific aim – to build on a migrational account of nation build-ing and American roots rather than on the specific history of Chinese exclusion and its associated racist legislation. Importantly, monies released as part of the Peopling of America Act require the reworking of the Angel Island story from one that is in part a specific history of specific Chinese exclusion to one that gets repackaged as com-patible with a larger picture of American history that is positive and coherent.

Whether this happens in practice remains to be seen. Many of the groups involved in the restoration project are seeking to assert the particularity of the Chinese expe-rience in ways that interrogate the construction of social categories informing inclusion and exclusion. What we can also see, however, is that the project was orig-inally the product of a very particular discourse about mobility and difference which finely differentiated mobilities along race and class lines. The place as a functioning immigration station was an embodiment of the Chinese Exclusion Act – a necessary material part of the socio-geographical construction of Chinese mobility. What the Peopling of America Theme Study act encourages today is the embodiment of a very different conception of mobility – the idea that mobility is a central and unifying experience for Americans. Crucially, the mobility propagated by Akaka as a unifying experience acknowledges diversity within a prioritized national experience. The discourses, therefore, neglect any thorough engagement with the construction and representation of race and class-based differences that did and still does cause tension between the Chinese and other experiences of immigration to America. At Angel Island the politics of difference, mobility and heritage intersect.

Similar themes of difference and sameness have emerged in recent work on holocaust memorialization. Steven Cooke and Andrew Charlesworth point to the ill feelings caused by the current vogue of historical representation: statues, memorials, and museums that reproduce a generalized universal message rather than the particularities of Jewish experience. Questions should be and are being raised about the purpose of restoring sites as spaces of memory either for purposes of perpetrator catharsis, or for a kind of collective therapy of the persecuted, or both (Paris, Grunebaum-Ralph). Such studies have examined the value of presentations of modified histories staged in the very place in which the original experience occurred. In this narrow sense, Angel Island Immigration Station and the Holocaust Museum at Auschwitz risk being robbed of their particular histories to become heritage receptacles that use the past to articulate "appropriate" universal messages.

The framework of remembrance being applied to the Theme Study Act is constructed by means of a well-established and oft-repeated story of mobility as generalized, abstracted, unifying and valuable. Angel Island is in the process of becoming a site that tells a story that all Americans can share. Through a delicate balancing act between unity and difference that, in the end, prioritizes unity over difference, a generalized mobility is given value and the places that are taken to symbolize it can be preserved with a message that is intentionally abstract and emptied of politics. This message is based on a set of perceptions about the American people being travelers, a social construction directed by the Senate's new bill which will, as it operates, shape how we interpret and value the past. Here, a politics of sameness with a specific, historically rooted, view of mobility is operationalized. Quite another view was in evidence in 1882 when the Exclusion Act was framed, and in 1910 when the barracks on Angel Island opened for business. One moral geography of mobility revolves around a banal imagination of totalizing mobility while the other rests on notions of essentialized difference where one mobility has to be carefully distinguished from another.

These two points in history should not be read as a simple linear and progressive transformation from one imagining of American mobility to another. In 1882, a mythology of American national mobility was already well established in notions of the frontier and of manifest destiny. It had been used to boost the construction of the very rail-roads that Chinese immigrants had been instrumental in building. And now, even as the Act that helps to assure the future of Angel Island Immigration Station as a heritage site operating under the metanarrative of sameness is put into place, the idea of racialized and differentiated mobility is still very real.

In November 1994, California voters approved an initiative, Proposition 187, that would bar illegal aliens and their children from access to healthcare, social services and education:

PROPOSED LAW *SECTION 1. Findings and Declaration.*

The People of California find and declare as follows:

That they have suffered and are suffering economic hardship caused by the presence of illegal aliens in this state. That they have suffered and are suffering personal injury and damage caused by the criminal conduct of illegal aliens in this state. That they have a right to the protection of their government from any person or persons entering this country unlawfully.

Therefore, the People of California declare their intention to provide for cooperation between their agencies of state and local government with the federal government, and to establish a system of required notification by and between such agencies to prevent illegal aliens in the United States from receiving benefits or public services in the State of California. (Immigration and Naturalization Service website)

Although subsequently declared unconstitutional in the Federal Courts, public approval of this initiative has inspired an increase in policing and harsh treatment of new immigrants within California. For the purposes of our argument, the text of this proposed law is illustrative of similar discursive constructions of immigrants employed in the 1882 Chinese Exclusion Act. In this more recent example, groups are classified in terms that are somewhat more severe in classifying the "people of California" as victims requiring "protection" from immigrants committing "criminal" acts of "damage" and "personal injury." In both cases, a discursive definitional tool is used to differentiate mobilities in order to project socio-political meanings onto bodies and pronounce the characters alien or citizen as a frame of reference for action. In this process, the State imposes meaning on the movement of the individual, which is then deemed legitimate, or not. Such meaning is always political and derived from questionable perceptions of health, class, race and gender. Significantly, enforcement proceeds by means of abstract generalizations attaching attributes to the individual by their association to an imagined group. At the same time, such an individual becomes isolated as a body, understood as "different" even "alien" to the extent that constitutional rights and moral obligation do not apply. Labeled as "non-persons" they are left to reside outside the generally accepted boundaries of justice and welfare provision.

What the Peopling of America Act attempts to combat is not the negative value of difference ascribed to the Chinese in America during the late nineteenth century but the existence of difference itself. This is performed by means of the articulation of a universalizing discourse of mobility that removes difference by positioning it under an umbrella of sameness. The intentions of this Act are to enfranchise those Chinese groups previously excluded from stories of the nation's past by highlighting their role in its development. But framing these objectives using traditional models of American pluralism, those that place the nation at the center inevitably divert attention away from a popular acknowledgement of imposed difference and its exclusionary material effects. Just as in 1882, the Chinese Exclusion Act inscribes a negative value onto the difference of Chinese that is taken for granted as a natural fact intrinsic to the group; in the same way the Peopling of America Theme Study Act 2001 constructs an idea of similarity that is equally unquestioned.

To adequately represent Chinese immigrants of the late nineteenth century means not to follow a strategy that simply includes their story in a bland epic that perpetually fails to reflect their experiences. Inclusion in this sense, as if a mislaid episode added to the embellishment of the whole, does little to establish resources for the articulation of self-authored histories where difference can be non-hierarchical, emancipatory and progressive. Neither do we see the benefit of including a banal superficial difference by restoring trails, buildings and workplaces of the Chinese as part of an enhanced but still traditionally patriotic heritage landscape. On the contrary, we argue for the benefits of providing resources to the disenfranchised so that they may be better equipped to uncover and present their own pasts and thus provide the means to a self-definition of difference that is so necessary.

The achievements of Asian-American activists and other advocates at Angel Island Immigration Station illustrate that there is indeed an intention to disrupt "traditional" national myths and put forward an anti-essentialist, relational account of the Chinese immigrant experience in America. What is also clear, however, is that the intention is disrupted by the dictates of policymaking and the necessity of encouraging a positive and patriotic history of the nation as a requirement for the restoration project's success.

Like a postmodern novel, this story has many endings. What we have been writing about here is the socio-geographical construction of Chinese immigrants to the United States by means of two pieces of legislation. Both of these texts touch upon the place where we began – Angel Island. The discourse surrounding current attempts to make a prison into a museum is deeply strategic – designed to gather funds to memorialize a previously hidden set of histories. This plays on notions of totality in order to make the case for funds and preservation. These texts resonate with still more texts – a whole genre of American historiography, which places mobility at the center of an overarching sense of Americanness. Akaka's inference that everyone is a traveler would be already established in the minds of many, as it is part of the mythology of the nation. Similarly, the older text – the 1882 Act – played on pre-established notions of the Chinese and the alleged threat that they posed to the good order of localities.

If one expression of an American postmodern culture is embodied by the desire to include diverse groups within a new movement of multiculturalism, its translation into Federal policy works only to incorporate more groups of people into hierarchical sameness. Perhaps, then, what we are witnessing with the Peopling of America Theme Study Act can be explained as a reaction against the loss of unity experienced in postmodernity and a desire to maintain the metanarrative for solidarity; a strategy to defend the idea of the nation against perceived fragmentation. This takes us back to the postmodern politics of difference proposed by Lyotard and Young. While some may see bland, inclusive multiculturalism as postmodern in itself, insofar as it is attentive to the multiplicity of identities that formally fell outside of the umbrella of "politics," we believe that such a strategy inevitably involves the production of a metanarrative and that, following Lyotard, incredulity might be the correct response.

Our use of the politics of mobility in this case is employed to interrogate the production of social metaphors (mobility as essentially American, on the one hand, and mobility as an essential threat, on the other) and make known the situatedness of the supposed universal perceptions derived from them. The universalizing discourse of mobility may, however, not be the one that gets played out in Angel Island. It is possible, after all, that the museum will become a space that does reveal its process of production and take difference seriously. Perhaps it will become a site where the kind of postmodern politics of difference proposed by Young intersects with heritage to display, clearly and unequivocally, the earlier politics of (essential) difference that produced it in the first place. If nothing else, the words of an anonymous Chinese immigrant detained at Angel Island will be there for all to see, problematizing any simple celebration of American mobility: "I will not speak of love when I level the immigration station."

Notes

1. The term "moral geographies" refers to the expected and "appropriate" connections between geographical entities such as place and mobility, on the one hand, and particular people and practices, on the other. Some people and the practices associated with them are thus considered appropriate in some instances and not in others.

Works Cited

Akaka, Daniel. "Akaka Calls for Interior Study." Official Press Release. 27 Apr. 2000. 3 March 2003 <http://www.senate.gov/~Akaka/speeches/>

—. "Akaka proposes interior study on the peopling of America." Official Press Release. 14 Feb. 2001. 3 March 2003 <http://www.senate.gov/~Akaka/speeches/>

Anderson, Kay J. Vancouver's Chinatown: Racial Discourse in Canada, 1875–1980. Montreal, McGill: Queen's UP, 1991.

Baudrillard, Jean. America. London: Verso, 1988.

Boorstin, Daniel. The Americans: The National Experience. London: Weidenfeld and Nicholson, 1966.

California Secretary of State's Office General Election 1994, California voters' information Proposition 187, text of proposed law. 5 Sept. 2002 <http://www.altenforst.de/faecher/englisch/immi/proptxt.html>

Castells, Manuel. The Rise of the Network Society. Oxford: Blackwell, 1996.

Charlesworth, Andrew. "Contesting Places of Memory: The Case of Auschwitz." Environment and Planning D: Society and Space 12 (1994): 579–93.

Cooke, Steven. "Negotiating Memory and Identity: The Hyde Park Holocaust Memorial, London." Journal of Historical Geography 26. 3 (2000): 449–65.

Craddock, Susan. City of Plagues: Disease, Poverty, and Deviance in San Francisco. Minneapolis: U of Minnesota P, 2000.

Cresswell, Tim. "The Production of Mobilities." New Formations 43 (Spring 2001): 3–25.

—. The Tramp in America. London: Reaktion, 2001.

Daniels, Roger. Not Like Us: Immigrants and Minorities in America, 1890–1924. Chicago: Ivan R. Dee, 1997.

Grunebaum-Ralph, Heidi. "Re-placing Pasts, Forgetting Presents: Narrative, Place and Memory in the Time of the Truth and Reconciliation Commission." Research in African Literatures 32. 3 (2001): 198–213.

Hacking, Ian. "Making Up People." Reconstructing Individualism: Autonomy, Individuality, and the Self in Western Thought. Ed. Thomas Heller, Morton Sosna and David Wellbery. Stanford CA: Stanford UP: 1986. 222–36.

Hoelscher, Steven. "Conserving Diversity: Provincial Cosmopolitanism and America's Multicultural Heritage." Textures of Place: Exploring Humanist Geographies. Ed. Paul Adams, Steven Hoelscher and Karen Till. Minneapolis: U of Minnesota P, 2001. 375–402.

Hyndman, Jennifer. "Border Crossings." Antipode 29.2 (1997): 149–76.

Immigration and Naturalisation Service. 5 May 2001 <http://www.ins.usdoj.gov>

Jasper, James M. Restless Nation: Starting Over in America. Chicago: U of Chicago P, 2000.

Kirshenblatt-Gimblett, Barbara. Destination Culture: Tourism, Museums, and Heritage. Berkeley: U of California P, 1998.

Kraut, Alan M. *Silent Travelers: Germs, Genes, and the "Immigrant Menace."* Baltimore: Johns Hopkins UP, 1995.

Lai, Him Mark, Genny Lim, et al. *Island: Poetry and History of Chinese Immigrants on Angel Island, 1910–1940.* San Francisco, HOC DOI; distributed by San Francisco Study Center, 1980.

Loewen, James. *Lies Across America: What our Heritage Sites Get Wrong.* New York: Touchstone, 1999.

Lyotard, Jean-Francois. *The Postmodern Condition: A Report on Knowledge.* Trans. Geoff Bennington and Brian Massumi. Minneapolis: U of Minnesota P, 1984.

Lyotard, Jean-Francois and Jean-Loup Thébaud. *Just Gaming.* Trans. Wlad Godzich. Minneapolis: U of Minnesota P, 1985.

Massey, Doreen. "Power-Geometry and Progressive Sense of Place." *Mapping the Futures: Local Cultures, Global Change.* Ed. Jon Bird, Barry Curtis, Tim Putnam, George Robertson and Lisa Tickner. London: Routledge, 1993. 59–69.

Paris, Erna. *Long Shadows: Truth, Lies and History.* London: Bloomsbury, 2001.

Pierson, George W. "The M-Factor in American History." *American Quarterly* 14 (1962): 275–89.

Sibley, David. *Outsiders in Urban Society.* New York: St Martin's Press, 1981.

Solnit, Rebecca. *Savage Dreams: A Journey into the Landscape Wars of the American West.* Berkeley: U of California P, 1994.

State of California Constitution. 1879. 26 January 2005 <http://www.leginfo.ca.gov/const-toc.html>

Tocqueville, Alexis de, Harvey C. Mansfield, et al. *Democracy in America.* Trans., Ed. and with an introduction by Harvey C. Mansfield and Delba Winthrop. Chicago: U of Chicago P, 2000.

Torpey, John. *The Invention of the Passport: Surveillance, Citizenship and the State.* Cambridge: Cambridge UP, 2000.

Turner, Frederick Jackson. *The Frontier in American History.* New York: Holt, Rinehart and Winston, 1947.

U.S. Government 1882 Chinese Exclusion Act. Forty Seventh Congress, Session 1. Chapter 126: An Act to execute certain treaty stipulations relating to Chinese. Approved 6 May 1882. 26 January 2005 <http://www.civics-online.org>

U.S. Government Peopling of America Theme Study Act 2000. (S.2478) 79–010. Calendar No. 636. 106th Congress, 2nd Session. 27 June 2000.

Ward, David. *Poverty, Ethnicity and the American City, 1840–1925.* Cambridge: Cambridge UP, 1989.

Young, Iris Marion. *Justice and the Politics of Difference.* Princeton, NJ: Princeton UP, 1990.

—. *Intersecting Voices: Dilemmas of Gender, Political Philosophy, and Policy.* Princeton, NJ: Princeton UP, 1997.

Zelinsky, Wilbur. *The Cultural Geography of the United States.* Englewood Cliffs, NJ: Prentice Hall, 1973.

Thamyris/Intersecting No. 12 (2006) 87-99

Land to Light On?

Making Reparation in a Time of Transnationality	Rinaldo Walcott

Migration. Can it be called migration? There is a sense of return in migrations – as with birds or butterflies or deer or fish. Those returns which are lodged indelibly, unconsciously, instinctively in the mind. (Brand, A Map to the Door of No Return 24)

Origins. A city is not a place of origins. It is a place of transmigrations and transmogrifications. Cities collect people, stray and lost and deliberate arrivants. (Brand, A Map to the Door of No Return 62)

This essay takes its title in part from Dionne Brand's collection of poetry *Land to Light On* (1997). In the title sequence of the poems the narrator declares that she is giving up on land to light on. The narrator of the poem states:

> *I don't want no fucking country, here*
> *or there and all the way back, I don't like it, none of it,*
> *easy as that... . (48)*

The refusal of country is also a quite specific refusal of forms of history that bind to original and imagined homelands. The unspoken of "all the way back" signals Mother Africa as central to a chain of refusals. However, it is safe to say from reading the entire volume of poems that the narrator does not give up on responsibility to and from nation-states, nor from history, and that, therefore, the narrator is intent on the ethicality of human relationships. Instead, the refusal of nation, of country if you will, and specific articulations of history is premised upon an analysis of nations as spaces of tremendous human troubles, especially when national claims are at stake and history is addressed as a kind of bind that can blind one to continued injustices. In this regard, Brand attempts to articulate an internationalist stance infused with what Bruce Robbins would call "global feeling."

In the final section of the volume titled "Every Chapter of the World," Brand writes of the upheavals of late capitalism and the intensified global traffic of finance, war, propaganda and the terror that has been wrought on human beings across the globe. In this regard, in terms of resisting the troubling sides of nations, nation-states, nationalisms and history, Brand articulates a diaspora consciousness and sensibility. This particular diasporic sensibility does not pay allegiance to an original homeland. It signals a connection to another geographic space, but that geography is a political geography related, in various resistances and responses, to an internationalist ethic and solidarity that refuses current transnational capital's organization of our lives.

The poems of *Land to Light On* roam the globe, finding too few places where the ethical and responsible poet, and by extension human being, might take a rest or reprieve. It is often, in fact, within some notion of the ethical that many choose refusal of nation and nation-state as the only responsible response to the world we live in. In such a regard, I want to read for the spaces and places of an ethical diasporic criticism in two of Brand's other works: a novel, *At The Full And Change Of The Moon* (1999), and a collection of essays, *A Map to the Door of No Return: Notes to Belonging* (2001). In each of these works, I want to read for a refusal of nation and nation-state that is infused with a transnational or diasporic sensibility and ethic of care; and, simultaneously, a desire to make reparation with numerous imaginary homelands. Finally, I want to suggest that Brand's project is not a pessimistic one but rather a project that provokes us to rethink the terms of belonging from merely those of a multicultural recognition to those of an ethic of hospitality.

In this essay, the work of the ethical is crucial in making sense of the ways in which Brand's writing occupies a pivotal place in diasporic, multicultural and postcolonial conversations. Throughout this essay, the ethical is invoked both to signal the different moral and political stances it appears difficult to take in the post-1989 world and, simultaneously, to stake the claim for taking a stance concerning questions of justice without simplifying what might be at stake in any given claim. Thus the ethical and the political lie together in an effort to memorialize the past, fashion a future, engage in practices that might approach the realm of justice and forgiveness and thus, in Jacques Derrida's terms, fashion a "democracy to come" (*On Cosmopolitanism and Forgiveness* 55). To conceive of the ethical without the political is to unhinge the very difficult but necessary question of what justice might look like. As we know, justice is always a work in progress that can only be made sense of by those who understand themselves to be on the receiving end of it, thus making the attempt for its accomplishment always a question or an unfinished project. In this essay, I move towards the notion of hospitality as the source for a possible utterance of justice. Hospitality might require us to think the ethico-political as a relation of ongoing negotiations and desires of the unfinished project of achieving justice.

To make sense of Brand's writing, one must situate it between a series of social, political and cultural movements of the 1960s and after – the continuing impact of transatlantic slavery in the lives of black people in the Americas and Canadian multicultural politics, both official and everyday. All these various moments that I identify in the broad strokes for reading Brand's work, are involved in a project of articulating what a moment of coming to achieve or "sight" justice might mean. Brand's writing spans at least two decades of engagements with histories of racism, colonialism and imperialism in the Americas, Africa and elsewhere; feminist and lesbian politics in North America; a multicultural and cross-cultural intellectual conversation concerning poetics and politics; and, most importantly, an internationalist Left political commitment, even as such commitments have come under Left fatigue and stress. Such is the basis of her ethical stance in the world as it is articulated in the texts I will discuss. Brand's critique and assessment of our world is positioned *vis-à-vis* some twenty or more years of official multiculturalism in Canada. Official multiculturalism has not brought to marginalized Canadians any real and sustained national involvement. Thus giving up on land to light on is to give up on the promise that nation building can ever be an ethical project in the context of the contortions of late global capitalism as the subaltern seeks justice.

Brand's oeuvre sits somewhere between the borderlands of what we in the academy call multiculturalism, on the one hand, and postcolonialism, on the other, both interacting but also signifying different theoretical and ethico-political implications and relations. Additionally, nation-state policies like multiculturalism belie the ways in which those marked as different are imagined and not imagined in the nation. Official policies of multiculturalism, rather than solving or adequately addressing the problem of belonging to the nation, exacerbate the problem of belonging. Brand's work, then, inhabits the space of transruption, as Barnor Hess would put it. A transruption on these terms is:

troubling and unsettling because any acknowledgement of their incidence or significance within a discourse threatens the coherence or validity of that discourse, its concepts or social practices. In one sense there is something more here than a singular interruption or an ultimate disruption. Although these qualities are sometimes apparent, a multicultural transruption is constituted by the recurrent exposure of discrepancies in the post-colonial settlement. (17)

Brand's work transrupts both the discourse of official multiculturalism and postcoloniality by articulating a decentered politics of belonging couched in an internationalist politics and desire for a just world. Brand's work is a transruption because it unsettles both nation-state and any too easy identity formation that does not articulate a politics of ethico-political relations. The ethico-political relation is an attempt both to make sense of the particular and specific conditions of the Black Diaspora and, simultaneously, to recognize how those conditions are shared by other subalterns within the vortex of global capitalist relations. In these instances, the ethico-political moves from the specific to the universal (but a universal of the subaltern) to articulate and gesture, sometimes even utter, a desire for new and different conditions of liveability.

On the question of the postcolonial, Brand's writing moves across space and time to engage the disappointments and failures of post-World-War-Two nation-states of the

Americas to produce effective forms of liberation for those who are regulatively rendered outside the ruling order. Postcolonial discourse takes as central to its concerns an ongoing engagement with forms of coloniality both old and new. Brand's writing engages forms of coloniality, both old and new, to render the conditions of anti-colonial thought as a clear and present interrogation of how the current order of the world (in particular the Americas) is lived and conceived experiencially and intellectually. In this regard, her work might be read as interrogating, critiquing and responding to the conditions of the various ways in which coloniality takes shape and fashions both psychic and material life. In many ways, multicultural discourses can be read as a subset of some of the outcomes of interrogating ongoing forms of coloniality.

Multiculturalism in Canada

It is difficult to live in Canada and to ignore the politics of multiculturalism in its official guise. Canada has had an official federal multicultural policy for over thirty years. In 1971 the Liberal government of Pierre Elliott Trudeau announced the Multiculturalism Policy, and in 1988 the Conservative government of Brian Mulroney made the policy an official Act of parliament, enshrining it in our constitution. Multiculturalism is thus a key defining element of Canadian national consciousness and, therefore, it is one of the flash points of Canadian political debate.

Michael Ignatieff, in his CBC Massey Lectures *The Rights Revolution*, states that multiculturalism in Canada, in relation to the "rights revolution," is for the liberal state:

to reassert neutrality by ceasing to observe rituals and holidays specific to the dominant group, or to recast neutrality as the encouragement of all groups (that is, to become multicultural). Most modern liberal states have taken the second option. In the multicultural response, the state subsidizes the cultural activities of a wide number of groups and designates days of the public calendar to the celebration of the heritage of as many groups as it can. Multiculturalism is intended not to subvert neutrality, but to assert it in a way that entrenches minority rights to culture against majoritarian tyranny. But this multiculturalist policy does not amount to an endorsement of group rights. It simply seeks to protect and enhance the capacity of as many individuals as possible to secure public recognition of their different cultures. (70)

For those citizens who are ambiguously positioned in the nation, individualist multiculturalism is met with a response for group rights. It is a response for group rights that poses difficult ethical questions for liberal modern nation-states like Canada. It is exactly the tension between liberal individualist ideologies of cultural difference and collective responses to cultural difference and in-difference in the Canadian public sphere that Ignatieff fails to see. Thus, the question of group rights remains a burning one in the context of how to enshrine the rights of groups within national policies without simultaneously creating homogeneous and static cultural representations of those same groups.

The tension between individualist multiculturalism and group rights is more than one of emphasis. Part of what is at stake in terms of an individualist multicultural stance is that the individual is cut off from identifying with and thus articulating a response to and desire for practices or forms of cultural expression meant to be representative of larger group concerns. When the politics of multiculturalism is played out as a set of individual concerns, what is lost is the attempt by groups to seek collective avenues to forms of political justice. In fact, what group rights pose is in many ways a refusal to concede to identity as the cultural opposite of capital in a neo-liberal economic fashion. Thus, group rights demands can often force collectivist orientations of neo-liberal propositions – affirmative action type programs is one such response.

Diaspora sensibilities always rub against multiculturalism in difficult ways. In short, racial-minority Canadians have insisted on a critique of Canadian multiculturalism not from a stance of individual desires to belong (even though one cannot too easily discount such desires) but rather from a stance of how to image whole groups of persons as integral to the national imaginary. Cast in such a fashion, the stakes of multiculturalism as official policy are much higher. For example, as Hess points out in terms of liberal democracy:

The disavowal of racism reinforces the apparition of the post-imperial phase of liberal-democracy; it eclipses any exposure of its failure to produce it. The problem is that where economically inegalitarian, racist formations are unsuccessfully concealed and subsequently exposed, the western "promise of democracy" (Derrida, 1994) is compromised by the revelations surrounding the unresolved ethnic antagonisms of its post-colonial conditions. The promise of democracy is subject to indictment as a foundational ruse by emergent multicultural transruptions. (19)

Thus, group rights, posed as a multicultural demand, expose why individualist multiculturalism is a ruse to retain a dominant interpretation of nation and citizen. In fact, in the Canadian public sphere, few suggestions exist that either Quebecers or Anglo-Canadians are "ethnic," thus exposing the particular emphasis of what multiculturalism is supposed to enforce. Subsidizing cultural activity is hardly even, if ever, thought of as subsidizing anglophone or francophone cultural practices. Such an omission pinpoints the subject(s) of multicultural discourse and its intended audience of address and restraint. Anglophone and Francophone existence, as the two founding peoples in all official documents and policies of the nation and the state, exempts them from being considered a part of the ethnic mix that the Multiculturalism Act seeks to recognize, enhance and protect in the nation. This curious relation of belonging highlights the ways in which official multiculturalism seeks to individuate, while maintaining a collective founding myth, two specially (un)marked and unethnicized groups. The multicultural contract demands that these two groups remain below the radar of ethnicity.

In this regard, Eva Mackey has written that, in Canadian public discourse concerning who belongs to the nation, there exist at least two tropes for citizenship: ordinary

Canadians or Canadian-Canadians and ethnic Canadians. "Canadian-Canadians are assumed to be white, disinterested in seeking special status of any sort and certainly their cultures (if they claim a culture at all) are neither funded nor supported by the governmental apparatus" (19-22). Such a divide has tremendous consequences for how racialized, ethnicized and marginalized Canadians actually and imaginatively see themselves as belonging to the nation. Brand's writing has been one way to bypass this divide and, instead, arrive at various ethical stances without returning to the dead ends of nationalist debate and group identities that can stiflingly reproduce a multicultural caricature of cultural representation.

Thus, official multiculturalism in Canada can, and is, positioned as an individualist posture. But when official multiculturalism meets diasporic discourses, utterances of multiculturalism are forced to contend with a collectivist ethic and sensibility. For group rights present a challenge to the unspoken group sanctity of a nationalist narrative, which positions all non-whites as outside of the nation and only accorded entrance by means of the discursive and actual policies of official multiculturalism. This politics of enterism is conditioned through the discourse and actual deployment of heritage as a significant and substantive non-white Canadian performance. Thus, diasporic group claims place official multicultural discursive rhetoric in some relief, because diaspora does drag along with it a desire for an imagined homeland – a desire for an imagined heritage. But not all contemporary discourses of diaspora are invested in homeland, as an earlier quote from Brand above infers – "I don't want no fucking country, here/or there and all the way back" (*Land to Light On* 48).

Such utterances as Brand's, which I am calling a diasporic sensibility and consciousness, detour heritage from an imaged and longed for homeland, impossible to return to, and, instead, deploy diaspora as a demand for nation-state responsibility and ethicality that reaches beyond a single nation. In this way, the nation-state is asked to move beyond the rhetoric of individual rights, to account and be responsible and ethical to group rights as well. Such a challenge within the multicultural nation is a refusal of the contemporary neo-liberal political project of claiming difference, all the while seeking to homogenize us. As Stuart Hall puts it concerning the neo-liberal discourse of globalization:

[I]t is "structured dominance," but it cannot control or saturate everything within its orbit. Indeed, it produces as one of its unintended effects subaltern formations and emergent tendencies which it cannot control but must try to "hegemonize" or harness to its wider purposes. (215)

Canada's official policies of multiculturalism work on exactly the diagnosis that Hall offers. But an ethical internationalist stance forces us to confront the enduring tension between group rights and individual rights without privileging one or the other but by taking recourse continually to the category of the human. It might, in fact, be argued that nation-state forms of multiculturalism are a Band-Aid solution to confronting the issue of rethinking the category of the human in the postcolonial moment.

Rethinking the Human after the Multicultural Moment

Dionne Brand's last two texts move decidedly beyond multiculturalism and its critique into the realm of international debates, as those debates reverberate back to the local. In Brand's texts, the local is the Americas, then Canada and, more specifically, Toronto, but Europe and Africa are deeply implicated as well. At The Full And Change Of The Moon is an excellent example of how the international and local move us beyond official multiculturalism. The novel is the difficult story of Marie Ursule, a slave woman in colonial Trinidad who commits an act that is both courageous and traumatic. Marie Ursule wakes up one morning to execute her plan of a mass suicide, which she does. But despite her courageous act of resistance to slavery, she is unable to murder her daughter Bola. Instead, Bola is dispatched to her long escaped father Kamena. The story that unfolds from this act of resistance and Bola's survival is one that verges on what is sometimes referred to as magic-realism. Bola becomes the ancestor of numerous children and their children who spread out across both the Americas and Europe.

But the narrative of the novel does not just stay tangled in the dream narrative of Bola and Kamena's escape and reunion. Instead, the novel also compresses time and social reality to offer some insights on the lives of black diaspora subjects. At The Full and Change Of The Moon is an expansive novel – by that I mean that it is wide in its scope and themes, encompassing many eras, movements, moments and conditions. For brevity's sake, I will focus on one moment or condition from the social realism part of the novel that points to the complex ways in which Brand theorizes diaspora conditions and sensibilities.

In the section titled "Soft Man," Brand develops the character of Adrian. Adrian is an excellent type, in that his composition speaks to many of the very difficult contradictions of black masculinity in the Americas and beyond it. Adrian is archetypal for many reasons. But chief among them are the ways in which he moves across space and time attaching to almost nothing as he moves. He is a decentered diasporic figure. In addition, Adrian might be read as embodying a certain kind of black diaspora suffering. It is the kind of suffering that speaks to the failures of black masculinity as it attempts to imitate dominant scripts for masculinity. Thus Adrian's drug dealing and his transnational flight and suffering is characteristic of and repeats some of the history of the black transatlantic plight both in the era of slavery and many other eras since.

I want to concentrate on Adrian's time in Amsterdam, at Dam Square. In this moment of diaspora, Brand charts its possibility, even if fleetingly so, and its pain – its utter absurdity and dreadfulness. Adrian is a failure at Dam Square, in Amsterdam. His drug-dealing enterprise comes to nothing. All this, after crossing the Americas and fleeing like a postmodern slave not back to Africa, with hope and desire, but to Europe for more pain and suffering. Adrian's character comes close to representing what Gilroy calls "the condition of being in pain" (The Black Atlantic 203). This condition of being in pain is characterized by the double negations of being both in the

West but not of the West. To confront and potentially heal this pain, reparation must be made with one's black place in the West. In Brand's characterization of Adrian, she reverses and undermines some black diaspora over-compensation with Africa as a salve for pain and suffering. This is one of those moments where Brand decenters and rearticulates diaspora, divorcing it from land, from geography, from country, from territory – all the way back. In this way, Adrian represents and puts in place the possibility for posing a series of questions and concerns around responsibility, ethicality and hospitality. Dam Square does not center anything; it, in fact, decenters; and for Adrian to return to the colonial center of former commercial enterprise as a drug dealer is not just an irony. For Brand, Adrian's difficulties in life represent the trouble with centers and origins. Thus Adrian must keep on moving as a child of the restless diaspora. The difficulty of the ethic of hospitality is highlighted here.

Derrida's reconceptualization of hospitality might be useful in making sense of Adrian's failure in Europe. Adrian's "criminal" activities violate the "home" of the dominant authority. Derrida understands violation as follows: "Anyone who encroaches on my 'at home,'" he writes, "on my ipseity, on my power of hospitality, on my sovereignty as host, I start to regard as an undesirable foreigner, and virtually as an enemy. This other becomes a hostile subject, and I risk becoming their hostage" (*Of Hospitality* 53, 55). In a reconceptualization of hospitality that moves beyond the invitation as safety, that is, one in which the host retains the power of the invitation, another understanding of hospitality would open up the host to the unknown and uncertain consequences of inviting Adrian into the "home" without restrictions. Thus, his "criminal" activities might be understood as otherwise, if a pure hospitality could be extended to him in Amsterdam. In short, how might we think differently about Adrian's drug dealing? Can his drug dealing at Dam Square and its failure, nonetheless, be read as a kind of return of the repressed?

Similarly, *A Map to the Door of No Return* begins with a story that is ostensibly about origins. In the essay "A Circumstantial Account of a State of Things," Brand writes:

My grandfather said he knew what people we came from. I reeled off all the names I knew. Yoruba? Ibo? Ashanti? Mandingo? He said no to all of them, saying that he would know if he heard it. I was thirteen. I was anxious for him to remember. (3)

The inability to name one's people is both a loss and a possibility. The possibility opens up the terrain to address the politics of what makes one's people. The possibility of making one's people beyond the context of assumed relations might be considered a gift of loss and a traumatic dis-remembering of transatlantic slavery. It is the politics of remembering and its unbearable unknowns that characterize black diasporic people's relations to nations – whether African or not. This unknowability is, in fact, the terms upon which many of the characters, especially men in *At The Full* come to live lives of much difficulty. Their inability to turn loss into promise and potentiality is their demise. But Brand's internationalism does not stop at the troubles of men. In fact, in *Land to Light On* and *A Map to the Door*, Brand's concern with women, but more generally the broader conditions of what it means to be human, is exemplary. Primarily for Brand, the concern is how to belong. Yet Brand is not articulating an easy and assumed humanism. Instead, her articulations are more akin to Fanon's "new humanism." As Fanon states: "make of me a man who always questions" (232).

Fanon's articulation of a new humanism is crucial, I believe, for making sense of the conditions of modern life. In particular, I believe that his new humanism has many insights to offer postcolonialism and multiculturalism. Fanon's declaration "The Negro is not. Anymore than the white man" is the utterance of a new universality (231). Such a new universality – which Gilroy has recently, drawing on Fanon, termed a strategic universality (*Against Race*) – does not throw out the category of the human as too tainted to rescue but, instead, attempts to resignify the category of the human by denuding it of its troubled history. It is so that the traumas of that history might be lived differently, with different implications. To attempt to make a new subject in the postcolonial and multicultural contexts requires that we think differently about the category of the human and what it might and can mean. As Fanon states elsewhere: "To understand something new requires that we make ourselves ready for it, that we prepare ourselves for it; it entails the shaping of a new form" (95). Both the conditions of postcoloniality and multiculturalism, as articulated material and discursive lived experiences, are partial attempts to prepare us for new shapes yet to come.

Making Reparation: Towards New Forms of Human Life

Following Fanon's new humanism and the desire to move beyond the constraints of historical bondage, we might turn to Melanie Klein and Sylvia Wynter to make sense of the new context for thinking the human differently. Melanie Klein and Sylvia Wynter offer us ways to conceptualize and move towards some kind of resolution in terms of black diasporic desires for home and homelands. To move beyond calls for a certain kind of maturity, we might call that maturity "the break." Klein proposes that the problem of separation for the child from its parent is one founded on guilt but, if worked through properly, love is possible. The outcome of love is only possible when reparation concerning the guilt is made. The guilt is constituted through the relation of the emotions involved in making the separation possible in the first instance. Klein's analysis has much to offer an analysis of how new world black peoples might adequately and lastingly come to terms with their traumatic removal from Africa.

On the other hand, Wynter tells us that the traumas which gave birth to the Americas have led to a constitution of new forms of human life not seen before 1492. These new forms of human life, born of the trauma of the Americas' colonial condition, are transnational and global traumas with global implications and repercussions. Forging an alliance between Klein's theory of reparation and Wynter's new forms of human life can bring us closer to making sense of what is at stake for black diasporic peoples in the Americas. Forging an alliance between Klein and Wynter can help us to mediate between group rights and individualism, and move towards an ethic of hospitality.

I want to spend some time remaking Klein's theory of reparation because I think that, metaphorically, it serves as a bridge towards making sense of New-World black peoples as a new form of human life. In Klein's essay, wherever mother or parent appears, replace it with Mother Africa and, wherever child appears, replace it with New-World black. In this way, Klein's insights can offer much to a theory of reparation for New-World blacks. Klein writes that:

feelings of guilt and the drive to make reparation are intimately bound up with the emotion of love. If, however, the early conflict between love and hate has not been satisfactorily dealt with, or if guilt is too strong, this may lead to a turning away from loved people or even to a rejection of them. (321)

This insight, applied to New-World blacks, runs the gamut of hatred and rejection of Africa to extreme identifications with Africa which reject outright five hundred years of black life in the Americas. The disidentification with Africa and Eurocentric distortions of continental Africa has produced a rejection of the "Motherland" by many New-World blacks. Such a rejection is often expressed as guilt and shame by many other New-World blacks and over-compensated for by way of glorification of a heroic African past by yet many others.

So how might New-World blacks come to terms with their new form of human life in the Americas? Klein writes:

Only if we have successfully dealt with our hatred and jealousy, dissatisfaction and grievance against our mother, and have succeeded in being happy in seeing her happy, in feeling that we have not injured her or that we can repair the injury done in the phantasy, are we capable of true identification with another woman. (332)

This insight of Klein's goes a long way towards revealing the ways in which New-World blacks' over-compensation with regards to representations of Africa also impact on how they understand their relation with their new home in the Americas. It is only by making reparation with Africa, that is, guiltlessly separating from Mother Africa, that the Americas can become a true home. For New-World blacks to accept the Americas as a true home, they must acknowledge the new forms of human life that they have become. The fundamental expression of this new form of human life is in its creoleness. By this I mean that New-World blacks live lives of cultural borrowing, sharing and cultural retentions, all based upon the traumatic encounters of the violent formation of the Americas as we have come to know them. This violent poetics of relation, as Édouard Glissant (1997) has put it, opens up an opportunity for acting and thinking beyond nation-state boundaries. It means coming to terms with a diasporic sensibility. Brand's writing enacts this diasporic/creole consciousness, not as forms of hybridity that coolly celebrate racial and cultural crossings, but as an imperative to think beyond the self and to think beyond the nation. This ethical vision is at heart a critique of the modern nation-state, a form of disciplining citizens in which black diasporic peoples have always been less than citizen.

Thus diaspora/creole consciousness is not embodied in the coolness of racial crossing but rather in the acknowledgement that, as human beings, we can do no more than borrow and share. In this regard, the contexts of borrowing and sharing in the Americas, violent as it has been, has produced new ways of seeing and living the life of the human. Thus, to borrow two phrases from Glissant, the Americas have furnished us with "the creative criticism of political thought" (*Caribbean Discourse* 102) and a "new economy of expressive forms" (106). These new moments require different perspectives on the histories that bind us to each other. In an essay on trauma and pedagogy, in which I attempt to think about the difficulty of the binds of history and what they might potentially hold for rethinking the category of the human, I discuss the necessity to live more actively with the possibility of "risking failure" (*Caribbean Discourse* 150). Such a risk means that we throw nothing out but we attempt to work and rework the contexts and conditions that we find ourselves in so that we eschew a politics of the corrective in favor of the politics of ongoing negotiation and ethical relationality. An ethical relationality means that we engage in forms of "conversation" which acknowledge that it is only possibly through the coherence of numerous singularities that anything approaching a community of consensus might be had (Nancy). Thus, relationality is an important element of desiring "a democracy yet to come" because it is through the conditions of relationality that the possibilities of identification might produce terms upon which an approach to a pure hospitality, or put another way, a pure justice might be had.

Conclusion: Multiculturalism Revisited in a Time of Transnationality

Following Stuart Hall, the imperative here is not to throw away multiculturalism. Rather "we have no alternative but to go on using and interrogating it" so that we might "rescue a new multicultural political 'logic' from the debris of existing political vocabularies which the eruption of the multi-cultural question has left in its wake" (209). I am calling this new political logic of multiculturalism "hospitality." Jacques Derrida's *Of Hospitality* tells us that hospitality immediately brings with it movement and transgression. By transgressing all the laws (limits, powers, rights, duties) of hospitality as we have come to know the term, we do justice to "the law of hospitality, the one that would command that the 'new arrival' be offered an unconditional welcome" (77). To offer an unconditional welcome or unconditional love is to place oneself in a place of paradox (thus refusing the laws of hospitality while extending them unconditionally) and simultaneously opening up the terrain of ethical relationality. Anne Dufoumantelle, in conversation with Derrida on the question of hospitality, writes insightfully that: *"But to reject the family (and any structure in which it is continued – civil society, the state, the nation) is to confirm pure hospitality in its impossibility"*

(Dufourmantelle 96; italics in the original). Thus, the practice of a pure hospitality in our time is a refusal of the regulating apparatus of nation-state directives. What is more, pure hospitality short-circuits practices and discourses of multiculturalism, leaving them empty moral claims devoid of an ethics. A new multicultural political logic requires us to think contrapuntally within and beyond the nation and to fashion a citizenship that moves through and across national and transnational space, articulating a global feeling and ethicality that, from Dionne Brand's suggested perspective, requires us to think non-territorially and still demand something of nation-states. Such a request is located in what Paul Gilroy suggests of "diaspora":

An alternative to the metaphysics of "race", nation, and bounded culture coded into the body, diaspora is a concept that problematizes the cultural and historical mechanics of belonging. It disrupts the fundamental power of territory to determine identity by breaking the simple sequence of explanatory links between place, location, and consciousness. It destroys the naïve invocation of common memory as the basis of particularity in a similar fashion by drawing attention to the contingent political dynamics of commemoration. (Against Race 123)

In Brand's terms, "diaspora," then, is not a desire or wish for a homeland, since such a wish can not be fulfilled. "Very few family stories, few personal stories have survived among the millions of descendants of the trade. Africa is therefore a place strictly of the imagination – what is imagined therefore is a gauzy, elliptical, generalized, vague narrative of a place," Brand writes (*A Map to the Door of No Return* 25).

By coming to terms with the "vague narrative of a place," New-World blacks must come to terms with the violent and immediate narrative of another place – the Americas. Such coming to terms requires a form of hospitality that exceeds contemporary everyday invocations of the term hospitality. First, a new logic of multicultural hospitality banishes the notion of black peoples as perpetual outsiders to the Americas, Europe and ultimately the West. To go further, a new logic of hospitality problematizes contemporary official multiculturalism by forging a rethinking of how, what and who does the welcoming.

Brand's *At The Full* and *A Map* positions New-World black peoples in a strategic place both to rethink and re-practice, metaphorically and materially, the terms of hospitality in modern nation-states. Such a rethinking and re-practicing would lead to a reconsideration of the foundational claims of modern nation-states and their contemporary understanding and multicultural logics as a necessary site of containment and exclusion. It would also entail a rethinking and re-practicing of the modern nation as a site of multiple and conflicting open-ended ethical demands, desires and commitments. Brand's oeuvre encourages us to think about what this would mean for a renewed category of the human.

Works Cited

Brand, Dionne. *Land to Light On*. Toronto: McClelland & Stewart, 1997.

—. *At The Full And Change Of The Moon*. Toronto: Alfred A. Knopf Canada, 1999.

—. *A Map to the Door of No Return: Notes to Belonging*. Toronto: Doubleday Canada, 2001.

Derrida, Jacques. "Foreigner Question" and "Step of Hospitality/No Hospitality." *Of Hospitality*. Jacques Derrida and Anne Dufourmantelle. Trans. R. Bowlby. Stanford: Stanford UP, 2000.

—. *On Cosmopolitanism and Forgiveness*. Trans. M. Dooley and M. Hughes. London: Routledge, 2001.

Derrida, Jacques and Anne Dufourmantelle. *Of Hospitality*. Trans. R. Bowlby. Stanford: Stanford UP, 2000.

Dufourmantelle, Anne. "Invitation." *Of Hospitality*. Jacques Derrida and Anne Dufourmantelle. Trans. R. Bowlby Stanford: Stanford UP, 2000.

Fanon, Frantz. *Black Skin White Mask*. New York: Grove Press, 1967.

Gilroy, Paul. *The Black Atlantic: Modernity and Double Consciousness*. Cambridge: Harvard UP, 1993.

—. *Against Race: Imagining Political Culture Beyond the Color Line*. Cambridge: Belknap Press of the Harvard UP, 2000.

Glissant, Édouard. *Caribbean Discourse: Selected Essays*. Trans. J.M. Dash. Charlottesville: U of Virginia P, 1989.

—. *The Poetics of Relation*. Trans. B. Wing. Ann Arbor: U of Michigan P, 1997.

Hall, Stuart. "Conclusion: the Multi-Cultural Question." *Un/settled Multiculturalisms: Diasporas,* *Entanglements, Transruptions*. Ed. Barnor Hess. London: Zeb Books, 2000. 209-41.

Hess, Barnor. "Introduction: Un/settled Multiculturalisms." *Un/settled Multiculturalisms: Diasporas, Entanglements, Transruptions*. Ed. Barnor Hess. London: Zeb Books, 2000. 2-30.

Ignatieff, Michael. *The Rights Revolution*. Toronto: Anansi, 2000.

Klein, Melanie. *Love, Guilt and Reparation and Other Works 1921-1945*. London: Virago, 1994.

Mackey, Eva. *The House of Difference: Cultural Politics and National Identity in Canada*. London: Routledge, 1999.

Nancy, Jean-Luc. *The Inoperative Community*. Trans. Peter Connor. Minneapolis: U of Minnesota P, 1991.

Robbins, Bruce. *Global Feeling: Internationalism in Distress*. New York: New York UP, 1999.

Walcott, Rinaldo. "Pedagogy and Trauma: The Middle Passage, Slavery, and the Problem of Creolization." *Between Hope and Despair: Pedagogy and the Remembrance of Historical Trauma*. Ed. Roger Simon, Sharon Rosenberg and Claudia Eppert. Lanham: Rowman & Littlefield Publishers, Inc, 2000. 135-51.

Wynter, Sylvia. "The Pope Must Be Drunk, the King of Castile a Madman: Culture as Actuality, and the Caribbean Rethinking of Modernity." *The Reordering of Culture; Latin America, The Caribbean and Canada in the Hood*. Ed. Alvina Ruprecht and Cecilia Taiana. Ottawa: Carleton UP, 1995. 17-41.

—. "Columbus, the Ocean Blue, and Fables That Stir the Mind: To Reinvent the Study of Letters." *Poetics of the Americas: Race, Founding and Textuality*. Ed. Bainard Cowan and Jefferson Humphries. Baton Rouge: Louisiana State UP, 1997. 141-63.

Relocating the Idea of Europe

Keith Piper's Other Headings	Ginette Verstraete

Navigating Europe with Derrida

This essay takes its lead from Derrida's *The Other Heading: Reflections on Today's Europe* (1992), a booklet written at the time of the Treaty of Maastricht (installing the European Union based on monetary and economic cooperation) and of the rising tensions in ex-Yugoslavia. In it, the philosopher seeks to generalize the ethnic and national conflicts that have emerged since the fall of communism in such a way that they can become the responsibility of the whole of Europe. Rather than an exception to be neglected, the pending Balkan war is exemplary of Europe. To that purpose, Derrida reflects on the *aporia* that has always internally riveted the idea of Europe: the more the union becomes concrete, the more fragmented it gets. Derrida introduces the idea of exemplarity to explain this contradictory logic. Time and again Europe has been presented as the ideal example of everything that is pure, authentic, spiritual; as at once a particular instantiation and a teleological model for everybody else, or as at once a specific place and the "universal heading" for all the nations and peoples of the world. There is, indeed, a whole tradition of articulations of Europe as this place of universality: from Hegel to Husserl, Heidegger, and Valéry, Europe has been represented in such a way that the particularity of its place of positing – indistinguishable from the idiom of the philosopher – becomes idealized as the epitome of *the heading toward* universality. The French and the Germans have always believed their languages and cultures to be exemplary instances of Europe understood as the *telos* of universal spirit. Consequently, Europe naturally looks white, Franco-German and male: "'I am (we are) all the more national for being European, all the more European for being trans-European and international; no one is more cosmopolitan and authentically universal than the one, than this 'we,' who is speaking to you.' Nationalism and cosmopolitanism have always gotten along well together, as paradoxical as this may seem … 'Europe looks naturally toward the West'" (Derrida 48-49).

Dominated by this law of exemplarity inscribing the universal in the proper body of a singularity – remember that the singular bodies that have been projected as universal have always been white, Franco-German, male – the idea of Europe is structured like a metaphor in its Aristotelian definition, "as the application of an alien name by transference (epiphora)" (Van den Abbeele xxii). It implies an elementary transference between the one and the other, between singularity and universality, between the particularity of a place and its horizon somewhere else. One of the recurrent metaphors used by intellectuals (in a variety of forms) to evoke this permanent movement of displacement, this metaphoricity underlying the presentation of Europe *as exemplarity*, is, according to Derrida, that of "capitalization," "navigation" or, especially, "heading." In fact, Europe-as-a-heading emerges as the metaphor of metaphoricity *par excellence* and hence of an *exemplary* movement beyond that of the simple metaphor, that is, ultimately, the movement of "another heading" and of "the other of the heading." And so Derrida sets out

from a Europe where the metaphor of navigation [or heading] has always presented itself as a mere metaphor, where language and tropes have been ventured in the expectation that they would return with an even greater value attached. If such Eurocentric biases are not to be repeated, Derrida warns, the question of Europe must be asked in a new way; it must be asked by recalling that 'the other heading' is not a mere metaphor subject to capitalization, but the very condition of our metaphors, our language, and our thought. (Naas xiv-xlvi)

It is in the philosophers' repetitive usage of exemplary metaphorical figures of Europe (as this headland or heading or *cap, telos,* even *captain, chef* and *phallus*), at once mere samples and ideal instantiations, that Derrida traces the contradictory and inherently multiple logic of particularizing and universalizing at work in the idea of Europe. Derrida calls it the logic of exemplarity through which Europe as an ideal has always been presented, always again and always differently, as at once unique and repeatable, looking to the future and the past. "The other (of the) heading" that Derrida is reclaiming from and for Europe is the excessive nature of this logic of exemplarity, according to which the equation of Europe with universality coincides with its displacement through the (French, German) exemplary figures by which it is embodied or accumulated. Since exemplaries always exist both inside and outside of what they exemplify, they put aside what they illustrate; leave without representative what they represent; make improper the proper. Thus, the singularity of Europe – what constitutes its unique identity – is excessive and finite, signaling nothing other than the endlessly repeated (exemplified) law of exemplarity according to which "an" example is "the" exemplary instance of something else. The capital figure of Europe attests to its repeated absence as well, and to that political possibility that emerges when the limits to presentation and presentability are exposed.

Since Europe is at once infinitely repeatable and unrepresentable, since it occurs as a mode of setting an example of what remains without example (in reserve), what is singular about Europe is that its manifestation is not only limited but also different from itself: it is heading toward the other of the communal, universalized "we, Europeans," through which European identity becomes internally divided, one among many others. It is in this direction (*cap*) that is "not ours" that Derrida asks "the question of the *place* for a capital of European culture ... the question of at least a symbolic place: a place that would be neither strictly political ... nor the center of eco- nomic or administrative decision making, nor a city chosen for its geographical loca- tion" (46). The new topology of this capital (*la capitale*), this symbolic place, of Europe is, according to Derrida, intimately linked to the idioms of the English and French lan- guages – the two languages vying for cultural hegemony in Europe – according to which "capital" also means something totally different: *le capital*, the market, capi- talism. After all, Europe is traditionally seen as both the birthplace and the product of capitalism, as the Treaty of Maastricht affirms once more. "To say it all too quickly, I am thinking about the necessity for a new culture, one that would invent another way of reading and analyzing *Capital*, both Marx's book and capital in general. ... Is it not necessary to have the courage and lucidity for a *new* critique of the *new* effects of capital (within unprecedented techno-social structures)?" (56-57). Derrida's question about the new symbolic *place* for a capital of European culture not unexpectedly opens up a divisive point with two genders: *le capital, la capitale*. The connection between city and money, place and flow, matter and spirit constitutive of Europe tra- ditionally (at least in the English and German idioms) goes by way of a sexual divi- sion, whereby the former is female while the latter is male. The universal here appears by way of a division of functions between male (mobility, transcendence) and female (immobility, immanence). Thus, we are again concerned with at least two exemplary figurations of the universal and the marks of difference between them: the flesh and the spirit, the place and the heading, which, taken together, point at the sin- gular and time-bound cultural constructions of the collective body of "we Europeans," at its local idioms, its histories of belonging, but also of sexual exclusion.

So what are today's exemplary tropo-topological sites, at once concrete and sym- bolic, at which the new Europe gets produced and deferred? What cultural idioms within which "unprecedented techno-social structures" make it possible today for Europe to be present as absent other, thereby connoting something different from itself in a movement of alterity, difference and infinite responsibility towards the other? One way to begin to answer that question is by conceiving of Europe as it is actively "taking place" today, in the event as it were: place as an allegory of time, the place that, by marking its own occasion or historical-material accumulation, is already being dis-placed, scattered. This historicized and materialized place points to a different mode of location, an elsewhere, an otherness that does not quite fit the immaterial distance and disembodiment that has endowed Europe with universal authority. Ultimately, what Derrida has in mind is a discursive-performative space held together by (sexual, national) differences (*le/la capital(e)*), entertaining a privileged relation to profane and hence time-bound and scattered mediations; in Valery's words: "*things, material objects – books, pictures, instruments etc – having the probable lifespan, the fragility, and the precariousness of things*" (67). Seen from the perspective of its materiality, historicity and contingency, Europe's social-symbolic space begins to function in a different way, away from the monolithic immanence-transcendence dichotomy and *in the direction of* scattered places and their instantaneous means of connecting. It is in this movement of dispersal and contraction of that other, infinitely mediated and capitalized, space, that the crisis of capitalist accumulation gets a spatial "form." Derrida speaks of:

this extreme capillarity of discourses. Capillarity: one need not split hairs to recognize in this word all the lines that interest us at this moment, at this point [point], at the point or end [pointe] where their fineness becomes microscopic; cabled, targeted [cablée, ciblée], as close as possible to the head and to the headman [chef], that is circulation, communication, an almost immediate irrigation. Such capillarity crosses not only national borders. ... [also those between the public and the private, GV]. (42)
The late-capitalist European social space targets, subjects and objects (money, goods, cars), the private (internal) and the public (external), the particular and the universal as well as the various nations and sexes. Europe emerges here as a scattered interface that disperses and momentarily connects its local subjects to the globe.

Now it is clear that the claiming of a worldly space from a Europe that never simply existed in the first place raises questions not only about the Eurocentrism of that stance, but also about its validity. Can such claims be made within the explicitly European intellectual tradition here evoked, if its Europeanness is precisely what needs to be questioned? Can we rethink its discursive space, and the global reach thereof, outside the parameters of Eurocentrism or anti-Eurocentrism? Derrida is the first to acknowledge the urgency of these questions: as he says, every attempt to think Europe anew and differently falls into the traps of:

another well-known program, and one of the most sinister, a "New Europe" ... Is there then a completely new "today" of Europe beyond all the exhausted programs of Eurocentrism and anti-Eurocentrism, these exhausting yet unforgettable programs? (We cannot and must not forget them since they do not forget us) ... Beyond these all too well-known programs, for what "cultural identity" must we be responsible? And responsible before whom? (12-13)
If we remain responsible for remembering and envisioning a particular cultural identity *vis-à-vis* a particular, yet unknown, audience – an audience perhaps "in" but not "of" Europe, "here" but also "there" – what is important is to articulate a momentary address, the idiomatic features of which open up a particular identity in the act, still to come. It is an idiom inseparable from the social nexus, yet not reducible to the

familiar (European) notion of community. Europe would then be radically contained – (dis)located – by the particularities of that style of address and the immediate effects and responses it may elicit at the occasion. But this means, among other things, that "I" need to invent a "we" without a priori reducing the impression "I" make on "you" to the philosophical idea of Europe or the impossibility thereof (the way Derrida does). Hence, let me repeat my critique of Derrida otherwise: are Europe's radically limited idioms, its singular cultural features, to remain those of continental philosophy or can we leave behind the abstractions of French thought and look for other "capillatory" mediations and addresses instead? How do we reconceptualize the grand universality that Europe has always claimed in such a way that its headings become locally specific and culturally differentiated, its generalities a task of translation across irreducible cultural (more than simply sexual and national) differences?

Postcolonial Diasporas

Many postcolonial theorists (Stuart Hall, Chandra Mohanty, Gayatri Spivak) have done exactly that: they have dislodged the universal from its exemplary residence in the (rhetorical) movements of the white European male and mobilized the concept of "diaspora" to shift the direction of the debate and trace the circulation of capital and its symbolic forms in different locations and (besides sexual also ethnic and racial) embodiments. Let me briefly explore this term, its circulating idioms if you wish, and see how some of its most recent transfigurations enable us to rephrase the questions raised so far such that they can address the *particular* cross-cultural operations of late-capitalist mediations and the communities they instantiate, much beyond Derrida's philosophical idea of (a sexually divided) Europe.

"Diaspora" has its etymological roots in the Greek: "dia" (through, across) and "sporein" (scatter, sow). It refers to a scattering process that, according to Gilroy, is closely associated with the sowing of seed (294). Unpredictable natural process, sexual reproduction or kinship, seeds taking root in different places: these are some of the term's bodily-organic connotations which are relevant to the process of forced Jewish displacement and affiliation at a distance that it also signifies. To the extent that in most encyclopedias and dictionaries, "diaspora" is said to designate both the general breaking up and scattering (in its Greek sense) of a people and the specific "physical dispersal of Jews throughout the world" (Britannica), it reinscribes a general movement of migration within a particular European cartography and history of displacement. Diaspora interpreted as a Jewish phenomenon thus gets "emblematically situated within Western iconography as the diaspora *par excellence*" (Brah 181). Yet, as Avtar Brah also notes, this conjunction between the general meaning and the particular reference recurrent in the definition of the term requires that we keep both in mind, as mutually implicated, without either simply conflating or absolutely opposing them. Thus seen, diaspora designates a concept as well as a particular experience of displacement and the ongoing transformative articulation between the two. Put differently, diaspora here emerges as a scattered interface between the individual and the collective, the singular and the plural, between the local and the global. We could say that in diaspora the global phenomenon of deterritorialization, characteristic of late capitalism, gets particular features with particular effects: national or religious ones (Jewish or otherwise), but also much more than that. Ultimately, diaspora is a traveling concept as well as experience that sustains a movement across various idioms, locations and groups of people without reducing the differences between them.

According to Naficy, diaspora originally

referred to the dispersion of the Greeks after the destruction of the city of Aegina, to the Jews after their Babylonian exile, and to the Armenians after Persian and Turkish invasions and expulsion in the mid-sixteenth century ... myriad peoples have historically undergone sustained dispersions – a process that continues on a massive scale today. The term has been taken up by other displaced peoples, among them African-Americans in the United States and Afro-Caribbeans in England. (13)

Steven Vertovec and Robin Cohen, James Clifford, Paul Gilroy, Caren Kaplan, Stuart Hall and Avtar Brah belong to those intellectuals that have reflected on the transcultural transference that the term designates and undergoes, each time with different resonances. While for Paul Gilroy "diaspora" is a mode of linkage that enables him to rethink the commonality of the black atlantic displacement without falling back on an essentialist black experience or consciousness, Stuart Hall has used the term to emphasize the hybridity of the Afro-Caribbean (rather than simply black) identity, i.e., its being caught up in a variety of African, European, and American histories: "The diaspora experience as I intend it here is defined, not by essence or purity, but by the recognition of a necessary heterogeneity and diversity; by a conception of 'identity' which lives with and through, not despite, difference; by *hybridity*" (235).

James Clifford, in turn, has pointed out the gendered dimension of our focus on diaspora in terms of movement alone. By relating it to place and dwelling as well, he brings women's experiences into view, thereby differentiating between specific gendered histories of displacement and the relations between them. How this linkage between travel and location inherent in diaspora enables us to resituate a white feminist politics of location (practiced by Adrienne Rich and Nancy Hartsock) within a transnational context of movement and migration is further elaborated by Caren Kaplan:

Location is, then, discontinuous, multiply constituted, and traversed by diverse social formations. One becomes a woman through race and class, for example, not as opposed to race and class. ... One's citizenship and placement in relation to nation-states and geopolitics formulate one's experience of gender when the threat of deportation, the lack of passport, or subaltern status within the nation as an indigenous "native" place limits on or obstruct mobility. (182)

In a similar vein, Avtar Brah launches the concept of "diaspora-space" to foreground the gendered but also ethnic and economic "entanglement of genealogies of dispersion with those of 'staying put'" (16). To her, diaspora is always about collectively leaving a place under certain conditions to settle elsewhere under different historical circumstances and within particular regimes of power. What interests Brah are the ways in which departure and arrival, journey and settlement are related, and how individual and collective narratives are mobilized along the way to relate the past and the future and construct an imagined diasporic identity. She says:

Diasporas, in the sense of distinctive historical experiences, are often composite formations made up of many journeys to different parts of the globe, each with its own history, its own particularities. Each such diaspora is an interweaving of multiple travelling; a text of many distinctive and, perhaps, even disparate narratives. This is true, among others, of the African, Chinese, Irish, Jewish, Palestinian and South Asian diasporas. ... I would suggest that it is the economic, political and cultural specificities linking these components that the concept of diaspora *signifies. (183, emphasis in the original)*

Despite some crucial differences pertaining to nationality and religion, gender and sexuality, class and age, race and ethnicity, all of these articulations of diaspora have certain things in common: they link theory to political practice, generalities to situated histories, and emphasize the need for a transcultural but locally specific and materialist approach to the universal (the global). Also, in contrast to exile, which, according to Clifford, tends to carry the promise of a return to the homeland, the "local" connected with diaspora references not a given place but one constructed in multiple circulation (of people, goods, images), in movements of placement and displacement, of projections and remembrance. At best, it is concerned with a contradictory relational positioning within historicized, transnational configurations of power that have to do with class, race, gender, nationality, and so on.

Digisporas

While most theories of diaspora introduce the concepts of race and ethnicity that are sorely lacking in Derrida's notion of Europe's "Other Heading" as differential (dis)placement, they rarely pay attention to the complex technological developments mediating current experiences of mobility and placement worldwide. Let me, therefore, reflect for a moment on what forms these diasporic movements could possibly take within the context of the technological mediations that Derrida has explicitly focused on. New spaces of dispersal are produced by instantaneous technologies of communication, as these transform spatial distance into a function of time, and physical dislocation (travel, labor migration) into virtual presence and social networking (for instance via *chatting* boxes) but also differentiation and stratification (for instance the gap between the digital literates and illiterates). Manuel Castells has described

the current transformation of the symbolic realm by means of new communication systems as the "culture of real virtuality" (372), by which he means a computer-
generated symbolic environment in which the material existence of people and goods
(reality) can no longer be dissociated from the economy of the virtual image setting,
and in which the appearances on-screen do not simply communicate experience but
become the experience itself. This does not simply mean that local cultural experiences are homogenized according to the logic of the global communication system.
According to Castells, "it is precisely because of the diversification, multimodality,
and versatility of the new communication system that it is able to embrace and inte-
grate all forms of expression, as well as the diversity of interests, values, and imagi-
nations, including the expression of social conflicts" (374). This implies, among
other things, that the new complex interrelationships between locality and globality,
between the particular experience and the general flow of images and information
mediating experience in the network society, are also socially and materially differentiated. One only has to be reminded of the military and profit-oriented uses made
of the new technologies and of the cheap labor by Third-World women in the elec-
tronics industry (Escobar). The tensions that are generated in and across those differences give rise to the formation of oppositional identities and social movements
in those contexts where people feel excluded from the globalization process (e.g.
feminist and environmental movements). Once these groups organize themselves by
means of existing technologies, the media that they use are at once internally inte-
grative or particularistic on the one hand, and resistant *vis-à-vis* the whole of society,
on the other.

John Durham Peters has re-articulated this hybrid and conflictual experience in/of
the network society (and its cultures of real virtualities) in private terms by focusing
on the receiver's mental state, especially on the particularizing function of the media
targeting (creating) a specific audience at a distance, thereby fragmenting "the public" into a series of displaced spectators. He has called this movement of displacement "diasporic" and has this to say about how diaspora helps us to understand the
interconnection between the realities of physical displacement and the virtualities of
its symbolic mediation:

*The notion of diaspora is quite suggestive for media studies. First, diaspora sug-
gests the peculiar spatial organization of broadcast audiences – social aggregates
sharing a common symbolic orientation without sharing intimate interaction. Indeed,
broadcasting stems from the same line of sowing imagery as diaspora. Second, the
German term for diaspora, Zerstreuung, also means "distraction." Hence, in German,
diaspora has a double relevance for media studies: scatteredness describes at once
the spatial configuration of the audience and its attitude of reception. To indulge in
popular entertainments, as the great theorists of Zerstreuung, ranging from Heidegger
to Adorno, have argued, is to go into a kind of exile from one's authentic center. The*

classic complaints of vicarious participation, sociability-at-a-distance, and pseudo-community that accompany mass-cultural critique are also, in a sense, the features that describe diasporic social organization. Such terms as can sustain a variety of readings. (24)

Thus taken as a trope for the experience of distraction – the scattered, already repro-duced, experience of mass-entertainment by a "broadcast" audience – "diaspora" links spatial (real) to psychic (symbolic) movements, the collective to individual expe-rience, the orderly to the random, presence to absence, "here" to "there." Moreover, the *Zerstreuung* that Peters introduces is typically one that concerns both the object and the subject. To speak with Benjamin, who interpreted *Zerstreuung* more posi-tively than Adorno: the technologically reproduced work of art loses its auratic status as an autonomous object, while the shock effect generated by the disjointed con-catenation of reproduced images calls forth an unfocused audience, a distracted and centerless collective subject receiving the reproduced artwork in incidental fashion, as if by habit. Through technological reproduction and distribution the (scattered) art-work meets the (distracted) beholders halfway. Benjamin goes on to compare this "inter-active" distracted state of habit to the way we respond to architecture:

Buildings are appropriated in a twofold manner: by use and by perception – or rather, by touch and by sight. Such appropriation cannot be understood in terms of the attentive concentration of a tourist before a famous building. On the tactile side there is no counterpart to contemplation on the optical side. Tactile appropriation is accomplished not so much by attention as by habit. ... For the tasks which face the human apparatus of perception at the turning points of history cannot be solved by optical means, that is, by contemplation, alone. They are mastered gradually by habit, under the guidance of tactile appropriation. (240)

What is important about Benjamin's and Peters' definitions of distraction is that they relate physical movement through space (by means of buildings in Benjamin's case and geographical space in Peters' examples) to the (re)production and reception of moving images. According to Benjamin, that reception is of an optical and tactile nature, at once distant and close by, absent and present, passive and inter-active. The diverse (*zerstreut*) material-economic linkages producing the literal and figural diasporic experience are here translated in terms of the global (dispersed) mass media and their differential productions of social symbolic orders as well as the incidental-habitual-interactive receptions thereof by a collective audience at a distance. We are back at Derrida's culturally idiomatic and performative address of the "we" received by an immanent addressee at the distance, not yet there, lacking a presence of mind, within "unprecedented techno-social structures." It concerns a tele-communicated discursive space marking the advent and event of another (more than simply European) community, an inter-active "we" present in distance, absence of mind or accumulated "reserves." Let me illustrate with an example.

Keith Piper's Other Headings

The British-Jamaican multimedia artist Keith Piper (born in Malta in 1960) has explicitly connected the theme of the "other headings" of Europe to the experience of the black diaspora, on the one hand, and the movements of interactive but distractive navigation on the other.[1] Since the 1980s, Piper has explored the limits of verbal and visual media as well as the possibilities of translation between them in close conjunction with a far-reaching reflection on diasporic identity. Central to his work are the politics of placement and displacement inherent in artistic mediation: at the same time that certain media present and make present in particular ways, they also exclude and make absent. The development of the new media introduces new modes of representing, archiving and unconcealment even as they are accompanied by new modes of forgetting and concealment. Old borders are transgressed while new exclusions are installed. Piper's online exhibition *Relocating the Remains: Three Expeditions* (1997) reflects on, and performs, the act of locating what has been dislocated.[2] The "remains" of the title refers to the capital reserves that Europe has generated over the years: the excess of material goods, money and technologies. But it also references the excluded "others" – the ethnic and sexual minorities – without whose expulsion Europe could not have projected itself as a community or collective identity. Finally, and closely related, the "remnants" are Piper's personal belongings: the forgotten history of his Caribbean forefathers who were first shipped from Africa to Europe's colonies in the 16th century and who then, many centuries later, migrated to Europe in search of better living-conditions. It is an "unrecorded history" within the annals of Europe conceived of as the capital of culture and civilization, which Piper now wants to record by making his previous artworks digitally accessible. For the greater part, this oeuvre consists of a violent collage of words, objects and images from African, American and European popular cultures. We may, then, say that the personal is also political, the local also global, the historical always already an uncertain translation between media. But this transition from the individual (artist, artwork, medium) to the collectively global is not unproblematic since it goes by way of the remains of history. More particularly, Piper is here, in the act of digitalization and globalization, producing the leftovers of an unpresentable history that colonizer and colonized share, albeit in radically different ways. Rather than claiming to tell the truth about a transparent and accessible past, the artist raises questions about the ontological status of his archive, the way it appears at the juncture of space and time, past and future, identity and alterity, one medium and the other. The position of the artist here has much in common with that of Benjamin's angel of history (Klee's "Angelus Novus"): with his face turned to the ruins of the past he is carried forward into the future with great speed. Seen thus, technological "progress" begins to look like an accumulation of ruins (capital reserves) while the memory that is needed to guarantee a continuity with the future emerges out of time's passage, if not destruction.

Figure 1   Keith Piper, *Relocating the Remains* (screenshot), 1997.

At every moment of the present, the colonial past is recalled in a movement of shattering and scattering (cabling) and thus made – problematically – accessible to the future. It is Piper's way of extending the limits of our (European) re-collection in another direction, through "another heading," so that it can address a larger, unknown, audience and refer it *en masse* to what has been left unsaid. This referral to what remains unsaid is what Kobena Mercer has called an "ethics of answerability integral to the call-and-response dialogue that enacts his political commitment" (Tawadros and Chandler 5). Piper's multimedia collage wants to be not only diasporic but also interactive in radically new ways. This needs more explanation.

The website "Unrecorded History" presents some of Piper's early works in the form of two paintings. [Figure 1] The digital disclosure at the same time thematizes the old frames of the medium paint: what has been incorporated, what has been left out of the margins? What has been "concealed" (left below), what is "present" (right below)? The painting at the bottom, a triptych, concerns the relation between a white court and the black servants that do not belong there (left) and between Christianity, aristocracy and colonization (right): hence the black crusaders, who possibly refer to the theme of the Black Church in Piper's early works, i.e., the religious fundamentalism of Christianity that the black population has appropriated as a means of resistance *vis-à-vis* the colonizer. The central focus of this tryptich is clearly the middle panel.

But that center is hardly visible: the only thing we can recognize is a *collage* of two men with beards, the left one of whom is drawing or counting. In front of him is jewelry. This richness seems a product of the colonial expedition/deportation evoked in the upper painting, right there where the men's heads are. Is the slavery depicted on top perhaps the result of their imagination? If so, does the lower painting evoke the court of Elisabeth I who gave the ship "Jesus of Lubeck" to John Hawkins in 1564 to deport the first African slaves to the Caribbean? A picture of a ship dominates the upper canvas and recalls Piper's ode to that famous first Middle Passage of his ancestors in his installation "A Ship Called Jesus" (1991).

Whatever the interpretation may be, the movement between the right and left panel, between presence and absence concealed in the lower painting, is linked to the movement of the upper canvas. And what is most important is that the interactive surfer is the connection between the two. It is in the movement of the surfer that the connection between upper and lower images, between black diaspora and European kingdom is made. But the relation between above and below, and between the spectator and the screen is not unproblematic. If we move the cursor at the bottom to the *right* then the image on top moves along so that we get to see the *left* side of the upper painting (this part concerns a reference to an earlier photomontage called "Go West Young Man" (1987), the West being the Americas). And *vice versa*: a movement below to the *left* takes us to the *right* in the upper canvas (called "The Fictions of Science" (1996)). The interactive spectator may be the crucial chain in the in-between-space (the *Middle Passage*), between top and bottom, presence and absence, here and there. At the same time, the surfer does not fully control the movements on-screen. Neither does she control the text ("Unrecorded Histories") in the upper part. The movement of the cursor generates unintended effects on the screen.

On Piper's website the diasporic movement of the black artist is indissociably linked to the – optical and tactile – experiences of the interactive but distracted surfer. The spectator, who navigates the screen interactively in order to learn about the capital reserves of European history, gets incidentally immersed in a movement she does not fully control. While she appropriates the interactive space *here and now* via the movement of the mouse, she witnesses something strange: "another heading" turning her proximity, even complicity, into an act of distancing; presence into absence; here into there; concentration into dispersal and distraction. Keith Piper's "real virtuality" generates an *unheimlich* expedition that is difficult to place, let alone identify. It is as if *others* have preceded us while the cursor lets us touch something that remains strange, untouchable.

The next website, "Exhumation of an Unmapped Body," is concerned with the black body as it is mapped by the "Fictions of Science" (anthropology, sociology, biology, craniology etc.). [Figure 2] Piper mobilizes the images of the "primitive" body that were launched by nineteenth-century scientists and massively reproduced in European

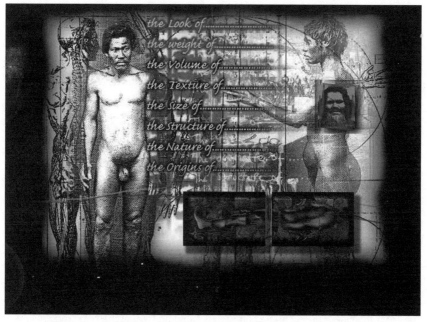

Figure 2   Keith Piper, *Relocating the Remains* (screenshot), 1997.

popular culture. Central to the nineteenth-century debate was the question of how the black body differed from the universal anatomy depicted by Leonardo da Vinci and which is here reproduced in the background. The norm by which all bodies were judged was that of the white male. What deviated from this norm was considered backward, at the bottom of the evolutionary ladder. The "others" were made into animal-like bodies, reduced to their sexual organs. Especially black women, here on the right, were registered as having big vaginas and protruding thighs. Piper depicts the Western scientific gaze as pornographic; only through the labeling in terms of "volume, weight, structure, nature ..." (in the middle of the site) can the gaze claim to be scientific. Again the artist excavates what has remained absent and unrepresented in western history, while at the same time demonstrating how his own strategies of representation cannot but reproduce those exclusions as well. What is made visible always takes the place of, and thus displaces, what is invisible; the "here and now" carries the traces of "then and there." Hence the question emerges: whose (sexual) body do we actually get to see on Piper's websites? Do his images not also speak of the sexual desires of the invisible European spectator? And since the dominant sexual figure on-screen is male, is the ideal spectator perhaps a heterosexual woman, or a homosexual man? Thus, the surfer finds herself literally situated in an ambiguous, all but innocent, space in-between a man and a woman. We are part of an interactive third space of real virtuality marked by racial, gendered and sexual differences. It is a site for which we carry responsibility as well. With the cursor we can make the pictures of "native" men and women in the middle appear and disappear at will. But the freedom that seems to go with this act of navigation is radically limited. We can only conjure up time and again the stereotypical pictures that the artist has selected from his archive.

And there is more: our interactivity is brought to a complete stop once we move our cursor to the flickering body *autonomously moving* at the bottom of the page. It is a reproduction of one of Piper's video-installations called "Cargo cultures" (1993), which parodies Hans Holbein's "Dead Christ in the Tomb" (1521). Rather than a divine body giving way to transcendence in its death, we see a fragmented body decomposing into physical pieces which do not quite fit: parts of white feet, dark hands and hips, no sexual organs, and a head that gives way to material things such as coins, maps and coffee-beans. It is a scattered, hybrid body that, to speak with Derrida, carries the marks of *le/la capital(e)* and the irreducible (sexual, ethnic, economic) differences that go with it. As an unmapped body with a movement of its own, it belongs to no-one but archival and accumulated history; let's call it the Other of the heading forward. In that sense, we are dealing with an archeological body reminding us of the fact that the "new" media reinscribe the content and form of the "old" media, just as Derrida's "new" Europe cannot but incidentally carry the traces and habits of the "old" Europe he wants to leave behind. Here and now is also there and then. We, the navigators of the 21st century, are always already distracted, subject(s) to other headings.

The final website I would like to introduce is called "The Observation of an Unclassified Presence" and deals with the themes of technological surveillance and strategies of identification: Big Brother is Watching You. [Figure 3] The "you" addressed here is the fugitive body targeted by the radar on-screen. Once the diasporic body is hit by the needle of the radar it turns into all that is non-white: a collage of African, Asian, Indian faces. To be non-white means to be "other" and hence not welcome, even excluded, in Europe's digital space. Hence "No Go." Don't enter this space or you get marked, tracked, localized, criminalized and thus made into a dangerous "remnant" by all kinds of tele-visual, tele-detection technologies, such as the radar, the reproduced fingerprints in the background, the photographic negatives on the left. But also the tele-communication in front of us plays a crucial role in addressing and thus situating "you": the surfer is asked to "mark this site." Add your marks, for instance by accelerating the fugitive body by means of the mouse; or by touching and thus filling in the negatives on the left so that we can identify the "criminal" faces. To mark this site, then, means to participate in the process of exposure, demarcation and identification. *Show yourself* that the unwanted foreign bodies in virtual space are mostly black males. Of course, this says more about us *here and now* than about those

---

Figure 3   Keith Piper, *Relocating the Remains* (screenshot), 1997.

strangers *over there*. For, by coloring in the negatives, we first and foremost expose our own racial and sexual prejudices, focused as they are on black men. In this manner we situate ourselves. In the marks of the criminalized "others" we find traces of ourselves. *Those there* are also *us here*. "Mark this site" stages an interactive address in which the physical dislocations and non-belongings of the diasporic artist and his predecessors and the distracted-incidental-habitual moves of the surfer are intertwined. What remains is a space in-between you and me, self and other, producer and consumer, reality and virtuality in which "we" are made to carry the responsibility for another heading, in the sense of a transcultural movement across irreducible sexual, racial and economic differences. It is Piper's way of relocating "us Europeans" elsewhere, in a locally specific and culturally differentiated heading that marks the advent and event of another community, no longer characterized by the immaterial distance and disembodiment that has always endowed Europe's community with universal authority.

Notes

1. For a good introduction to Keith Piper, see *Relocating the Remains: Keith Piper*.

2. Piper's work can be found at http://www.iniva.org/piper/3xp1.html.

Works Cited

Abbeele, Georges Van Den. *Travel as Metaphor: From Montaigne to Rousseau*. Minneapolis and Oxford: U of Minnesota P, 1992.

Benjamin, Walter. "The Work of Art in the Age of Mechanical Reproduction." Trans. Harry Zohn. *Illuminations*. Ed. Hannah Arendt. New York: Schocken, 1969. 217-51.

Brah, Avtar. *Cartographies of Diaspora: Contesting Identities*. Gender, Racism, Ethnicity. London and New York: Routledge, 1996.

Castells, Manuel. *The Rise of the Network Society*. The Information Age: Economy, Society and Culture.Vol. One. Three vols. Oxford: Blackwell, 1996.

Clifford, James. *Routes: Travel and Translation in the Late Twentieth Century*. Cambridge: Harvard UP, 1997.

Derrida, Jacques. *The Other Heading: Reflections on Today's Europe*. Trans. Pascale-Anne Brault and Michael B. Haas. Bloomington and Indianapolis: Indiana UP, 1992.

Escobar, Arturo. "Welcome to Cyberia: Notes on the Anthropology of Cyberculture." *The Cybercultures Reader*. Ed. David Bell and Barbara M. Kennedy. London and New York: Routledge, 2000. 56-76.

Gilroy, Paul. *The Black Atlantic: Modernity and Double Consciousness*. Cambridge: Harvard UP, 1993.

Hall, Stuart. "Cultural Identity and Diaspora." *Identity: Community, Culture, Difference*. Ed.

Jonathan Rutherford. London: Lawrence and Wishart, 1990. 222-37.

Kaplan, Caren. *Questions of Travel: Postmodern Discourses of Displacement*. Post-Contemporary Interventions. Ed. Stanley Fish and Fredric Jameson. Durham and London: Duke UP, 1996.

Naas, Michael B. "Introduction: For Example." *The Other Heading: Reflections on Today's Europe*. Trans. Pascale-Anne Brault and Michael B. Haas. Bloomington and Indianapolis: Indiana UP, 1992. vii-lix.

Naficy, Hamid, ed. *Home, Exile, Homeland: Film, Media, and the Politics of Place*. New York & London: Routledge, 1999.

Peters, John Durham. "Exile, Nomadism, and Diaspora: The Stakes of Mobility in the Western Canon." *Home, Exile, Homeland: Film, Media, and the Politics of Place*. Ed. Hamid Naficy. New York & London: Routledge, 1999. 19-41.

Relocating the Remains: Keith Piper. London: Institute of International Visual Arts, 1997.

Tawadros, Gilane and David Chandler. "Foreword." *Relocating the Remains: Keith Piper*. London: Institute of International Visual Arts, 1997. 4-5.

Vertovec, Steven and Robin Cohen. *Migration, Diasporas and Transnationalism*. The International Library of Studies on Migration. Ed. Robin Cohen. Cheltenham (UK) and Northampton, MA: Edward Elgar, 1999.

III. Mobilizing the Theory of Politics

Ambient Fears

Nikos Papastergiadis

At the precise midpoint of Gillo Pontecorvo's *The Battle of Algiers* (1966), the ultimate revenge is exacted in a cafeteria on Rue Michelet. It is late afternoon and the French colonial middle class has gathered to relax. Couples are having coffee, children are enjoying ice creams and hopeful men hang at the bar. A young woman in a white dress enters and approaches the bar. A man moves to the side, offers his seat and smiles. She orders a coke, places a bag beneath her feet. She looks sexy and cool. Midway through her drink she gets up. "Leaving?" He inquires. "Yes." She replies. "Pity." He adds. No sooner has she crossed the road than the bar explodes. Within minutes two other bombs are detonated.

Who can you trust? The enemy could be anyone and anywhere. Prior to the explosions in *The Battle of Algiers*, three women had met up. They had removed their veils and burka. They had dyed their hair, dressed like Europeans, assumed an aloof appearance of enti-tlement and subsequently passed every security checkpoint, pausing only to take a nervous breath, or flirt with the soldiers. The colonizer's greatest fear is not the con-frontation with otherness within the enemy but the unexpected danger in intimacy. The intimate enemy can not only do greater harm than the visible foe but can also sus-tain a state of perpetual anxiety that undermines any relief found in conquest (Nandy).

Ever since the attack on the World Trade Center on September 11, 2001, the per-ception of risk has not only escalated but the meaning of fear has changed. At a per-sonal level people have been speculating about their exposure to danger and about institutions revising their security measures. Their capacity to cope with threats has been undermined by a loss of trust and morale. Fear has saturated every aspect of life. The American government has had to measure its ambition for global domination against the simmering prospects of revenge and sabotage occurring within their own locale. This level of anxiety is different from earlier forms of fear. It was easier to gain a sense of ironic distance from the earlier renditions of an invasion. For instance, shortly after Reagan "warned" that the Sandinistas were closer to Texas than the

Texans were to Washington, a cartoonist drew a picture of paranoia. It showed two men, a father and a son, sitting on a veranda with shotguns on their laps. Against the background of a clear night, the moon and the stars shining, the son turns to his father and suggests: "It's a bit quiet out there." The father replies: "Yeah, a bit too quiet!"

Ultimately, this state of being – when even silence seems pregnant with danger, and where every stranger is also a potential enemy – is precisely the goal ascribed to the avenging colonized. Their aim is to disperse fear and to make anxiety ubiquitous and unlocatable. Another scene from *The Battle of Algiers* illustrates this level of fear. The French Commander reflects on the difficulty of distinguishing the terrorist from the ordinary citizen. "Our enemies have great mobility.... They have their anonymity. They are everywhere in the Casbah and in the European sectors." Part of the difficulty, he admits, is the method of parallel recruitment that isolates the different teams from each other. "The reason we do not know our enemy is because they do not know each other." Or in today's jargon, the fear lies in the awakening of the "sleepers." The terrorist is not a discernible outsider, but one of the many long-term residents with ordinary jobs, valid identity papers, a conventional social life and a secret mission.

In the weeks after September 11th, almost all the world leaders spoke in calm voices, but adopted the language of hyperbole. Their initial response was couched in a discourse that vacillated between the apocalyptic and epiphany. The events of September 11th were immediately perceived as symbols of the end of a previous world, and the beginning of a new and as yet unknown and unnamed world. After September 11th, the fear of the other could not be contained within either a single territorial entity, or confined to a given place of origin. Fear was ambient. Initially, war was not waged against an enemy with a conventional army, but against the very concept of terror. The original code name for the conflict was "Operation Infinite Justice" – it was replaced by "Enduring Freedom" because, as Muslim clerics noted, only God could execute infinite justice. The boundlessness of the "war against terror" sent out a chilling message, not only in the context of the ambiguities of place and identity within global politics, but also with regard to the suggestion that a world with infinite terror implied that vigilance and war would never end. The twenty-first century began with the re-mobilization of the emancipatory metaphor of "permanent revolution" as a slogan of dread.

Attack on America?

Bush declared that the terrorist assault of September 11th was an attack on the American way of life. If that was its target, then who would be next? Or perhaps, more crucially, what are the other vulnerable symbols of the American way of life? Accepting the logic of this response could only lead to a new national paranoia. An alternative response would require earnest self-reflection and a revised scrutiny of world affairs. But the promise to engage in such critical thinking was short-lived in the public imagination. For instance, within a month of *Vanity Fair* pronouncing the end of the age of cynicism, it returned to promoting trivialities, with Tom Cruise on its front cover. The complex challenges of contemporary times were not communicated with the same dramatic force as the initial "Attack on America." Public sentiment was bombarded with political rhetoric that stressed the new forms of boundless threats and justified open-ended acts of retaliation. Both the terrorist strikes and the political responses to September 11th globalize fear. In America, fear spread not just because of the insecurity over the invisibility and unpredictability of the enemy but also because it resonated with pre-existing anxieties about the loss of social control and the realization that it was not exempt from the new global disorder.

The terrorist strikes on September 11th were not aimed at the "American way of life" in America, but rather at its dominance within global power and culture. Resentment against America had escalated while its role as global policeman and sole super-power was consolidated. Increasingly, the new forces of globalization became conflated with the spread of the "American way of life." Due to the fact that American cultural products saturate global markets, the US administration demonstrates a preparedness to act outside of the framework of international law, and dedicate a budget to its military division that exceeds that of the combined pool of the eleven next-largest countries. This translates into the awareness of a growing general sentiment that the pursuit of a national way of life has already spread itself over many borders. However, this external image of global authority and unrivalled power does not correspond with internal perceptions of social control and its place on the world stage.

Since the 1990s, Americans were experiencing a new sense of social unease. According to Mike Davis the collective consciousness of America was already gripped by "inexplicable anxiety" (Davis 36). He claimed that the susceptibility for paranoia had been foreordained by television programs such as *The X-Files*; the appearance of diseases like AIDS, unpredictable flare-ups of road rage, and had climaxed with the "millennium bug." The fear of fear became the oxygen for a new kind of authoritarianism within political rhetoric but it also drew on the existing history of anxiety and fear within the American psyche.

Slavoj Zizek argued that although Hollywood, by means of its extensive list of catastrophe movies, unwittingly prepared the American unconscious for this event, it was the performance by American leaders via the media that created a further blurring of the boundary between reality and fiction. With the compulsive replaying of the passenger planes crashing into the World Trade Center, "it is not that reality entered our image: the image entered and shattered our reality" (Zizek 16).[1] Comparisons with blockbusters such as *Independence Day, Escape from New York*, and *Matrix* only heightened the sense of confusion. It was these escapist films that were meant to be unreal, but, as Zizek claimed, the representation of September 11th did not conform to the catastrophe genre. In the representation of annihilation there is usually the underlying promise of renewal. Subsequent to depicting disaster within this genre, the hope is ignited that the founding spirit of the American pioneer will accomplish regeneration. The repeated telecasting of the news on September 11th not only heightened the feeling of dread within the American psyche but also introduced the image of the monstrous brought closer to home. In the words of Adam Carter, a funeral director in Madison: "It's not something I thought I'd ever see, our country invaded like this. You're used to that stuff going on in the Mid-East because it's always going on there, but you don't expect to see it coming home" (qtd in Tomkins 2).

Americans had become accustomed to witnessing violence on their screens, but the victims usually remained either foreign or fictional. On September 11th the image of horror became more familiar to American viewers while, at the same time, the reality of the horror was more foreign than ever before. Without the boundary of fiction, it was no longer possible to imagine invasion, and, with the reality of the explosions, it was impossible to maintain the illusion of separation. Americans felt stunned by the attack and surprised to be so close to the horror that was meant to take place on the other side of their screens. The image of the "Empire's" financial center crashing and the US military command center in flames sent shock waves across the world. Even people who were not related to the victims felt a surprisingly high level of empathy. The report of Seth Morris phoning his wife as the plane loomed large outside his window motivated the following response from a British journalist called Blake Morrison: "My elder son is called Seth and almost shares his surname. That's how this tragedy gets you. Even if you're lucky and lost no one, it feels like family" (Morrison).

The capacity for strangers to feel empathy for victims does not always take the form of a pure response based on inter-personal connection. The outpouring of grief in Europe and Australia was as much an indicator of the power of the media to stimulate sentiment as it was a result of the terrorists' deliberate scheduling of the strikes to maximize attention for their grievances and mobilize support for militant Islam. Both sides were conscious of the dominance of screen culture in contemporary life. In these increasingly mediated representations, the technique of "othering" the adversary reached new forms of distortion and vilification. If the "war on terror" were to be a battle for dominance in the public imaginary, it would have to be fought on-screen.

To argue that the primary site of this conflict is the imaginary is not to ignore the tragic death and destruction that was caused by the terrorist attacks. Rather, it is to demonstrate that the physical damage was not an end in and of itself, but a means to a more "spectacular" kind of destruction. These strikes did not seek to weaken the military power of the enemy, or hamper its civil infrastructure. The intended target was accomplished only in the form of symbolic reverberation that could be amplified by the media. Psychological warfare has always been one of the weapons of the military weaker party in modern battles. In the current scenario, "weakness" has become a weapon. The proliferation of media forms has opened up channels of representation that those in power would rather foreclose. From Al Jazeera to google searches that link George Bush to "miserable failure," the new networks of information exceed the regulative powers of any state. The reverberation between the virtual and the real increased the sense of insecurity over America's place in the world and the growing sense of global chaos.

In the hiatus between the period of the "Cold War" and the current "War on Terror" there were numerous ethnic and civic clashes. According to Philip Stephens, the threat to international stability was no longer imagined in terms of a collision between rival super-powers or the deliberate guile of a known adversary, but from the reckless chaos of collapsed national sentiment, the spill-over from states that can no longer control their own territories, and the violent revenge that stems from cultural humiliation:

Another conceptual shift is required. Hitherto, the west's security framework has been embedded in the assumption that the risks lay in the ambitions of over mighty or rogues states. Russia, China, Iraq, and North Korea: these were the potential enemies. Now the US and its allies are obliged to recognise the distinct threat from the spreading chaos of failed and broken states. (Stephens 21)

The spread of these new forms of threat expanded the frontiers of fear. With the end of the Cold War there was no comfort to be found in America's elevation as global super-power or any certainty that its authority would be universally welcomed. Opposition had not diminished with the collapse of the Soviet Union. After the fall of the "Iron Curtain," and the so-called triumph of capital, there was a dispersal and redefinition of opposition to American dominance. Where opposition was once concentrated within geo-political boundaries, it has now fragmented into pockets of resistance. There is a growing perception that the threat to US supremacy is no longer identifiable as a single entity but is, instead, made up of a complex amalgam of different forces that strike on multiple fronts and follow a lateral form of political leadership.

Such loss of certainty was also evident in the way enemies of the US articulated their grievances. For over a decade Western commentators have been struggling to fathom the rationale manifest in the new wars that were spreading across the world. Hans Magnus Enzensberger claimed that anxiety and insecurity spread in the world after the collapse of the colonial structures and the demise of the ideological battle between communist and capitalist states. In the absence of explicit struggles that were defined by the need to gain independence, or the desire to promote a new social vision, Enzensberger argued that the motivation behind contemporary conflicts was either pointless or incomprehensible:

What gives today's civil wars a new and terrifying slant is the fact that they are waged without stakes on either side, that they are wars about nothing at all. This gives them the characteristics of a political retrovirus. We have always regarded politics as a struggle between opposing interests, not only for power, for resources and for better opportunities, but also in pursuit of wishes, plans and ideas. And although this power play results in bloodshed and is often unpredictable, at least the intentions of those involved are usually obvious. (Enzensberger 30)

Enzensberger's nostalgia for the old ideological battles not only clouds his ability to perceive any force other than a death drive operative in warfare, but is also symptomatic of the lack inherent in Eurocentric perspectives on ethnic conflicts and in the formation of new transnational cultural ideologies. From the self-destructive race riots in LA to the rampages in Rwanda, there was a growing anxiety over the spread of chaos. Each outbreak may have its own specific logic, but in the eyes of Western commentators it was just another example of the loss of control. In this context, if it was impossible to locate the source of fear, then there was also little chance in developing a dialogue that brings hope.

Even before September 11th the "American way of life" was under threat. The loss of internal social control was compounded by a profound sense of insecurity within the new world disorder. The American way of life became increasingly entangled in the contradictory forces of globalization. In one sense, it became a victim of its own success. The initial expression of grief and sorrow was quickly turned into widespread contempt and anger. Bush's assumption of the right to unilaterally launch pre-emptive strikes and the increasingly dubious propaganda campaign to legitimate the necessity of war fractured the nascent global solidarity. The unilateralism of the invasion may have inspired greater support if it did not reflect a broader trend that had been set by the administration when it refused to sign the Kyoto Protocol and exempted itself from the recently established International Criminal Court. While Bush ranked the enemy under the slogan "Axis of Evil," few were convinced that this correspondingly implied that America was "Home of the Good." The wars in Afghanistan and Iraq dismantled two objectionable regimes, but Osama bin Laden escaped and the forces of terror have segmented and dispersed. It was a hollow victory, which has left a moral vacuum and a credibility gap in the American administration. Far from feeling safer, Western society is not only more vulnerable to future acts of terror, but also more aware of the deceit and incompetence of Western leadership.

In What Name?

What changed on September 11th? Was the scale and form of the terrorist attack a unique historical event? Did we witness an act of unspeakable evil that could only be comprehended in terms of mixed metaphors: part political and part biblical? For other victims around the world this was not the first time that they had witnessed a brutal attack on innocent civilians. The way in which the moment was captured and then replayed by the global media, however, was unique. Despite the endless televisual replays, American commentators remained in a state of stunned incomprehension. It was unclear to the American mainstream whether this was "the work of the devil" or, as Colin Powell noted, "the dark side of globalization."[2] The struggle of naming the conflict after September 11th was nowhere more palpable than in George W. Bush's speech to the nation. At first he sought to draw a link with the previous "righteous" wars in which America fought against fascism and communism. By comparing the terrorist attacks to Pearl Harbor he sought to awaken a spirit of defiance and create a sense of an enemy that must be conquered.[3] But who is the enemy now? In what sense can there be a war if no opponent reports for fighting? In what sense is it a war if the field for battle and the territory to be conquered cannot be identified?

This was not a war that would fit into any of the available categories of territorial conflict. It was neither a national war nor a class war. There was nobody that lurked on the fringe of national space that represented either a liberation struggle or a guerrilla insurrection. There was no preparation for conflict or previous warnings that were part of the public culture. The grievances of the attackers were known but the attackers were never given the status of a rival or adversarial opponent. Prior to September 11th, there was a hiatus; the world was no longer divided into the antagonistic spheres of the Cold War. If there were enemies out there, they did not have a uniform identity. Their place in the public imaginary was not supported by a clear set of ideological or territorial claims.

Hugo Young, a seasoned commentator on international affairs, was quick to recognize that while Blair and Bush were comparing "the war against terror" with the invasion of Kuwait, or to the intervention in Kosovo, this conflict was different because the moral outrage could not be neatly attached to an obvious political entity (Young 22). In the week after the attack, the Bush government invoked the rhetoric of war against terror, but failed to legally interpret the events within the context of the numerous treaties on territorial invasion or international terrorism.[4] To legitimate its own point of entry into the conflict, the USA needed both to blur the categories of retaliation and self-defense, and expand the field of engagement. Young noted that, as the name of the enemy eluded easy categorization, the terms of military engagement could not be clearly defined. How could it be known when victory has been achieved? At what point would the enemy be defeated? Where else will the battle be fought if satisfaction was not accomplished in one field? In this sense we are confronting a war without horizons. Thus the war on terror was also the first ambient war.

The subsequent translation of the "war on terror" into "regime change" did not produce greater clarity over the terms of military engagements and the agency of terror. Even the most senior advisor in the US Army War College's Strategic Studies Institute claimed that the "global war on terrorism is dangerously indiscriminate and ambitious." The war in Iraq was described as a "war-of-choice distraction from the war of necessity against al Qaeda."[5] Motivations for attacking Afghanistan and Iraq blurred the connection between internal repression and the sponsorship of global terrorism. By dispersing the frontier of terror and folding the regimes that were now identified as the "axis of evil" into this psychic domain, the American administration attempted to bring the ambient warfare into a more conventional focus. However, just as the terrorists distorted the logic between causing humiliation and imperial responsibility, the administration also exaggerated the connections between sovereign states and global chaos. When Bush adopted the policy of unilateralism, he found justification for war not on the basis of combating a known aggressor but on the basis of fear of terror. War could be unleashed at any place or time. The linkage between terror and invasion twisted into deeper levels of anxiety as each side exploited the ambiguous connections and origins of their own fears.

The panic over the placelessness of fear has served as the pretext for Western leaders to redefine their "right" to initiate pre-emptive strikes on other states: in Bush's words, "to strike before they emerge." The logic of "forward defense" has recently been extended by the Australian Prime Minister John Howard, or, as he is now known in the region, "deputy sheriff to the US." Howard proclaimed that a pre-emptive strike against terrorists in a neighbor state was a reasonable act of self-defense. Such an incursion, he argued, did not qualify as an invasion because we now live in a "borderless world" of terror. The circularity of this argument is given another spin when the contradiction between pre-emptive strikes and the UN Charter is presented as evidence of the need for international law to "catch up with the new reality." "When the charter was written, the idea of attack was defined as an 'army rolling across the border'," Howard said. "Now attacks are different. You're getting non state terrorism which is just as devastating" (qtd in *Herald International Tribune* 1).

An ambient war is a war with an identity problem. It is not a war that can be won with precision guided bombs. The authors of the "war on terror" are not sovereign leaders or revolutionaries who declare their position and engage their enemy in open conflict. The US quickly learnt this basic lesson and translated the "war on terror" in the context of Afghanistan and Iraq into a "regime change." It was an attempt to shift the countenance from ambient to conventional warfare. But the US administration continued to miss its target. The links between the attacks on September 11th and the wars in Afghanistan and Iraq have never been proven. A victory over the wrong opponent does not bring satisfaction but only breeds more confusion, as ambitions for further conflict and absolute justice collide. The campaign for "regime change" perhaps sought to focus the symbolic resonance of September 11th by attributing agency and identifying a zone of conflict. But this confused the point of the initial attack. The attacks on September 11th were not symbolic acts in the conventional sense of delivering a message person-to-person, or state-to-state. Who was the real sender? Who was the intended receiver? It is worth remembering that Taliban leader Mullah Mohammed Omar denied any Taliban involvement; that the links between the bombers and Iraq are tangential at best, and that Osama bin

Laden never directly claimed responsibility for September 11th or the subsequent anthrax attacks. The US began their response by identifying an enemy with no territorial basis and lacking coherent social context. The original profiles of the attackers were so primal and vague that it only enhanced the fear that they would strike back anywhere, anytime, without reason or provocation.

The "war on terror" needed an ambient figurehead, and if Osama bin Laden did not exist, then one would have been invented. The "war on terror" could not commence without an original "author of terror." In spite of this the location, let alone arrest, of this author has brought no finality. For over seven years the CIA has been tracking Osama bin Laden's movements, resulting in what one journalist called the "world's deadliest goose chase" (Allen-Mill 6–7). Even with the most sophisticated surveillance operation and the most experienced British and American "henchmen" at their disposal, and in spite of elaborate inducements for local betrayal, nothing led to the capture of bin Laden. "The monster has become a ghost and he is beginning to scare American planners" (Allen-Mill 6–7).

Osama bin Laden could be elevated to an ambient figurehead, but at no stage has he been represented as a symbolic leader, who stands for a known body of people. None of the prisoners illegally held in Camp X-ray in Guantanamo Bay, Cuba, have publicly confessed an allegiance. He is an author without a stable text, a symbol without a clear referent. World leaders were quick to deny him any representative status of a specific national or ethnic community. Even Western leaders acknowledged that he was not heir to the civilizational claims of Islam. Every effort to identify him resulted in a further exile into an unknown conceptual terrain. He was routinely referred to as a millionaire madman, driven by anti-Western and anti-modern ideology, and as possessing a vision of the future that was already buried in the past (Friedman, "One War, Two Fronts" A25). Rather than seeing him as outside the time frame of global politics, it would in fact be more useful to place him within a specific milieu of the disaffected Saudi middle class and regard him a conspirator that surfaced in the aftermath of the cold war machinations between the US and USSR power plays in Afghanistan. However, US complicity and the precise configurations that link members of a national elite with a pan-Islamic crusade are seldom acknowledged as being internal to the dynamics of global politics.

The global media have failed both to communicate Osama bin Laden's vision, and to demonstrate his direct control over the networks of terror.[6] Colin Powell promised to present a case proving that Osama bin Laden was the mastermind of global terrorism. The only statement of fact that Powell issued was a mere assurance that the case against bin Laden was "not circumstantial."[7] When the Taliban offered to hand over bin Laden to a third country on condition that evidence of his involvement in September 11th were made public, Bush replied: "There's no need to discuss innocence or guilt. We know he is guilty" (Buncombe 1). This authoritarian disdain for legal process reached its zenith in the responses of the White House to the UN's weapons inspectors' failure to find evidence of the so called "smoking gun" of weapons of mass destruction: "We know for a fact that there are weapons there. The problem with guns that are hidden is you can't see their smoke."[8] In the absence of a factual debate, the US had constructed its enemy out of ambiguous innuendo and uncertain presumption.

Osama remains an ambient figurehead because his location and his destiny are still unknown. Where is he? What else is he responsible for? When will he strike again? Fear looms in these unanswered questions. In this context, the ambience of fear is all the more penetrating because the associations of risk are not affixed to a single entity but defined in abstract terms. The fear of Osama bin Laden within the public imaginary proliferated like a virus. This generalized fear was accentuated when it was coupled with the outbreak of anthrax. Part of the panic over the danger of anthrax was that attackers were able to strike without leaving an obvious trail. Anthrax became the new index of ambient fear. In one instance, when a newspaper's building was put on alert, the phobia was extended to a fear of contact with the newspapers. In a state of ambient fear the time and place of danger is uncertain. Risk can appear everywhere and in anything. The fear that followed in the wake of September 11th was not for a military invasion but rather, as Zizek noted, was based on fear of a more insidious threat – anxiety attacks: "On the level of visible material reality, nothing happens, no big explosions; yet the known universe starts to collapse, life disintegrates" (Zizek 37).

The experience of fear is now more pervasive. For when war can be conducted without being declared, then the sense of the origin and finality of a conflict are also dissipated. War is now caught within the promiscuous rhetoric of globalization that overrides the principles of national sovereignty and ignores the standards of international law. War always makes use of bellicose rhetoric, however, in this instance, the language shifts from the defense of national values into a more boundless form of authoritarian pragmatism. As Nancy observed, the ambience of war in the context of globalization pulls the concept away from its original purpose of defending national sovereignty and pushes fear into every dimension of life:

Nowhere, then, is there war, and everywhere there is tearing apart, trampling down, civilised violence, and the brutalities that are mere caricatures of ancient, sacred violence. War is nowhere and everywhere, related to any end without any longer being related to its supreme end. (Nancy 135)

War in the Age of Globalization

The fact that the enemy within this conflict could not be identified within the conventional categories of international warfare might have provoked a re-thinking of the binary codes of belligerence. However, the investigation into the legitimacy of an ambient war was blocked by the pervasive fear that the enemy was beyond rationality and reason. The Taliban were referred to as "bearded fanatics" and the Iraqi leadership as a "band of criminal psychopaths" (Hoagland, "Terrorists Can't Be Kept in a Box"). The orientalist tropes for demonizing the enemy not only glossed over any linkage between the geo-political power of America and the socio-economic damage of globalization, but also reduced the debate to a crude loyalty test between the "civilized West" and the "barbarous rest."

To oppose democracy to fundamentalism and compel the world to choose between them not only establishes a false basis for deciding, but also presumes a level plane, upon which there is another implicit claim that they possess something in common. This oppositional strategy was evident in editorials such as the one in *The New York Times* on September 16th that claimed: "the perpetrators acted on the hatred of values cherished in the West as freedom, tolerance, prosperity, religious pluralism and universal suffrage" (Kennedy). Such determined self-righteousness and disdain for the other, barely camouflaged the complicities of the West and its false claims of a monopoly over democratic principles. Western leaders such as Gerhard Schroeder, interpreted this conflict as a "clash between civilization and bar-barism." Silvio Berlusconi made this exhibition of racism, implicit in Schroeder's adoption of the Huntington thesis, explicit when he reformulated the equation as a battle between the West and Islam. Yet love of democracy and obedience to the rule of law continue to suffer as a result of the US administration's preference for a uni-lateralist policy. Bush's 2002 State of the Union address, during which he first named the "axis of evil," clearly established the US's "right" not only to attack "rogue states" but even to launch strikes against friendly states that harbor terrorists. Most recently, Richard Perle, as chairman of the Pentagon Defense Board, has stated that the US should not feel constrained by international democratic outcomes that con-tradict their interests. Consensus is, in his view, not a point of resolution, but a bur-den: "It would be a great mistake to become dependent on it, and take the view that we can't act separately" (qtd in Goldman). Throughout the public debates Western politicians have made use of ambient fears of terror to justify the recourse to author-itarian practices. By claiming that the terrorists operated outside the rule of law they defended the legitimacy of their claim to suspend "normal" rights and obligations.

This confusion was only extended by the demand that Western governments expand their powers of domestic surveillance and limit their compliance with inter-national laws. When intellectuals and civil rights lawyers refused to fall for this new authoritarian loyalty test, politicians did not just attack their moral integrity by accus-ing them of treason, but, rather, struck an even cruder blow. They viewed these argu-ments as virtual pedantry in the face of real and empirical threats. As Bob Carr, the Premier of New South Wales, in a moment of self-righteous anger declared during a media interview shortly after Bali:

We had the slaughter of innocent Australians in Bali … We've had warnings that Australia might be targeted … So John (Dowd, New South Wales Supreme Court Judge) wake up to yourself. The threat is real. (Morris)

Opposition was now not just heresy but sheer stupidity. The classical balancing act of civil society – the weighing up of public safety against personal liberty – has been overturned by fear. This displacement of critical judgment is a hallmark of the new authoritarianism that uses the exceptionalism of barbaric terrorism, not only to exempt itself from following the civilized procedures of law and ethics, but also to make the additional emotive appeal of victimhood.

The war against terror was increasingly legitimated by emotive appeals to both pre-existing fears and a regressive stereotyping of cultural differences. Both the threat of "alien" cultures and suspicion towards internal critics fuelled exaggerated claims about the causes and consequences of terror. Edward Said observed that the political rhetoric of war and the vocabulary of "gigantism" in the press were a means of avoiding a deeper understanding of the turbulent interdependence of our times:

A unilateral decision made to draw lines in the sand, to undertake crusades, to oppose their evil with our good and to extirpate terrorism doesn't make supposed entities any easier to see. Rather, it speaks to how much simpler it is to make bellicose statements for the purpose of mobilising collective passions than to reflect, examine, sort out what it is we are dealing with in reality, the interconnectedness of innumerable lives, "ours" as well as "theirs." (Said)

Edward Said suggested that at the heart of this terrorism are the uncertain consequences of globalization. Osama bin Laden is not the first CIA operative to turn against his former master. Despite his puritanical accusations of the abuse of power in the Gulf States and the corrupt core values of global capital, his own political ideology cannot be defined as something that is external to the dynamics of globalization, but rather as a product of its own distortions and excesses.

By contrast, Thomas Friedman argued that the Arab-Muslim states have kept "the soil for bin Ladenism ever fertile," not because of the excesses of globalization but because they have not allowed for sufficient cultural penetration (Friedman, "Foreign Affairs: Breaking the Circle" A25). He claims that while they willingly imported the luxury commodities of the West, they also systematically blocked the cultural process of innovation and transformation. This argument again shifts the blame onto the other. There is no suggestion that globalization would encourage equivalent forms of exchange at both ends of the spectrum.

Globalization has introduced changes that go beyond new modes of commerce and thus need to be understood beyond the conventional frameworks of international relations. The boosterist ideology on globalizing opportunity and innovation has concealed the attendant tensions associated with the elevation of the neo-liberal market economy and the dispersal of fear and discontent. Globalization is more than economic transformation, it is also a political project: stimulating the dissemination of ideas that dislodge the authority of traditional values, distributing people along

new directions and relocating communities in foreign places. The disruption of traditional social structures, the displacement of vast numbers of people, and the great
ecological disasters, are all part of the underbelly of globalization. If globalization
is spreading discontent through the world, then what institutions can accomplish
security?

Nation-states were founded on the belief that they were the best socio-political
systems for creating and regulating security. Globalization, however, threatens the
nation state not just because of the loss of political power through economic and
legal concessions to transnational corporations, but also due to the destruction of
institutions embedded within a national culture. When civic and national leaders
plead with global capital for inward investment, offer financial incentives, relax
labor laws, reduce tariffs or remove ecological obligations, are they not also undermining their own regulatory powers? A cartoon by Michael Leunig, the finest satirist
in Australia, illustrates the contradiction between globalization and what he calls
its ensuing "privatised, free-enterprised, cannibalistic democratic consumerism."
It depicts two men, one in a gray suit with a saltshaker in his hand asking, "Do
you need salt?" The other, up to his neck in a boiling pot, replies: "It's up to you"
(Leunig).

In economic terms, globalization is primarily defined by the enhancement of cross-
border connectivity and the extension of trading relations across the globe. Global
trade rose from 18% of world gross domestic product in 1990 to a record 26% in
2000 (Roach).[9] In the wake of September 11th there are fears that the increasing
levels of scrutiny as well as the increasing numbers of regulations across physical
borders will retard this global trade. Added to this insecurity is the fear of a backlash
that is driven by awareness of the profound inequalities between the first and the
third worlds. For, despite promises of connection and integration, globalization
accentuates historic patterns of polarization and the widening of the gulf between
rich and poor.

Research by the International Monetary Fund has shown that "the richest 25 per
cent of the world's population experienced a six fold increase in real GDP per capita
during the last century. By contrast the lowest quartile of the world population enjoyed
less than half that gain" (Roach).[10] The promise that globalization would assist the
development of the poor, moreover, has been sharply contradicted by a recent study
commissioned by the United Nations. This report not only alarmingly warns that an
additional one hundred million people will be living on less than a dollar a day by the
middle of the next decade, but also observes that international trade is "part of the
problem, not the solution":

Contrary to conventional wisdom, persistent poverty in poor countries is not due to
insufficient trade liberalisation. ... The problem for the least developed countries is not
the level of integration with the world economy but rather the form of integration. ... For

*many LDC's external trade and finance relationships are an integral part of the poverty
trap. (qtd. in Denny)*

This ever-widening chasm between winners and losers even threatens to destabilize
the alliances on which America relies for greater global economic penetration. Part of
the new global instability is that globalization lacks a visible regulative force. In the
absence of a defined framework that supersedes earlier models of international relations, there is considerable confusion over the geo-political institutions that can control globalization. While the US has grasped the mantle of global domination in
geo-political terms, it has not only been reluctant to legitimate its authority within the
parameters of an international consensus, but also continues to be parsimonious in
its compliance with the UN. As Bush warned the United Nations General Assembly in
September 2002, the US was prepared to make Iraq disarm with or without the UN's
mandate (Bush).

Like all complex systems, globalization produces counter-reactions. If conclusive
evidence is ever given regarding a global network of terrorists, it is unlikely that this
structure will conform to the anachronistic metaphor of "an axis of evil." A number of
commentators have argued that terrorists do not work in consort with nation states.
Despite the stereotypical representation of fundamentalism as espousing cultural
values that are locked inside a frozen image of the past, the political motivation of
terrorists appears to be more complex and there is no doubt that they are prepared to
utilize the most sophisticated forms of contemporary technology. Terrorists have
demonstrated that they can exploit the technical resources and adapt the communicative structures of globalization. Throwing slurs at the intelligence of the enemy not
only risks underestimating their capacity, but also eschews the task of identifying the
emergence of any new methods of organization. Many Western commentators have
ridiculed the rhetoric of vengeance but also failed to grasp the complexity of the formation of a political mechanism that has dispersed and segmented the units of its
membership. They failed to track the complex ways in which the terrorist structures
have mimicked the new "parallel systems" within communication technologies and
camouflaged their activities by adopting a fragmented command system. Their structure is not integrated into a centralized body of command and execution but dispersed
along multiple nodes, each with the capacity to form its own dynamic; respond to evolv-
ing shifts in its specific terrain; and articulate an improvisational decision-making
process. Umberto Eco has argued that, in order to understand these new forms of
resistance, political discourse needs to adopt new non-linear models (Eco 11).

These models would move discussion away from one-dimensional stereotypes
and suggest that terrorists now organize themselves in clusters that resemble a
capillary system. Their formal structure does not resemble a monolithic command
center. Units are, at best, loosely connected, with some sections hidden and unaware
of their own partners. According to Osama bin Laden's biographer, Roland Jacquard,

it is in the "nature of bin Laden's organisation to plan attacks in advance, to choose the commandos who will carry them out and give them the ability, technology and financing so that they can act without needing orders or having to return to their bases" (qtd in Gibson). To recognize that terrorists not only adopt the technologies of globalization but also adapt its logic to their own ends demands a deeper understanding of the processes of change and of the complexity of contemporary life. The debate on fear and hope will have to go beyond the thesis of a clash of civilizations. It will require new forms for conceptualizing both the survival of belief systems and the processes for cross-cultural exchange.

The first step towards confronting fear is to "know thine enemy." This would involve understanding their principles, examining the causes of their grievances, identifying their method of organization and evaluating their capacity to do harm. It is becoming clear that terrorists are not just cowardly fanatics who hate the West, but also agents who have defined their own values of courage and integrity in opposition to Western forms of decadence and greed. Even conservative scholars like John Carroll have recognized that, through his own example of austerity and conviction, Osama bin Laden has both challenged the materialism of the West and taunted the indulgent "boyish president" with the question: "What do *you* believe?"(Caroll). The public debate on terrorism has focused a great deal of attention on the likelihood of harm, but done little to advance our understanding of the metaphysical claims, historical injustices and political structures that have sustained the belief systems of the terrorists. Globalization will bring about its own downfall if it continues to promote the material benefits of an elite and fails to address the other sources that confer a sense of ontological security.

Ethics after Outrage

In the past decade, economic and cultural debates have increasingly promoted the progressive features of mobility. Economists have championed the cause of free trade, celebrated the innovations of "just-in-time" delivery systems, calculated the benefits of outsourcing and urged companies to develop new collaborative practices. Artists have also seized the new communicative technologies to transform the modes of production, interaction and reception of their work. They have argued that neither the context of their practice, nor the meaning of their work is bound to an exclusive locale. The common desire to reach a broader audience or gain access to more markets does not mean that all contemporary artists have uncritically embraced the logic of global capital. The events of September 11th have sharpened the ethical demands on cross-cultural communications and re-fuelled the political function of art in a transnational context.

Artists have often identified new trends long before they are articulated in mainstream debates. Artist collectives like *Multiplicity* and the collaborative projects initiated by Fareed Armaly have both mapped the complex movements of people in contested spaces and identified the way that geo-political power is now focused on the control of spatial flows rather than on the occupation of territory. In a prescient video installation, "3-minute survival attempt" (2000), Anna Jermolaewa simulated both the destabilizing effects of conflict and the anxiety over the faceless aggressor. The fragile balance of the social order is played out by means of the interaction of toys made in the shape of pendulum figures. Accompanied by an ominous sound-track of jackboots, one piece suddenly falls onto another, precipitating a cascading effect. As the pieces begin to tumble into each other and fall in a multitude of directions, it is never clear in which order they will ultimately fall; the only certainty is that disaster is imminent. Although each toy is uniform in shape, and at first appears to be stable, their movement leads towards a chaotic fall. The displacement effect is compounded by another unseen force that creates a swirling motion. The toys spin and fall into a vortex. Eventually, even the surface tilts and everything falls off the edge. But the "aggressor" who precipitated the fall is never shown.

September 11th provided a stark reminder of the need to reinvigorate the connections between art and politics. Artists and theorists were urged to examine the function of art in relation to its capacity to reflect, anticipate, clarify and expose social problems. The aesthetics and ethics of art were no longer abstract debates but were brought into focus by being articulated through the conceptual parameters of one or more of the four forms of social knowledge: analysis, revelation, explanation and prediction. In a flurry of exhibitions and special issues of art magazines, artists and theorists sought to comprehend how different parts of the world relate to each other; examine the consequences of cross-cultural contact; explore the drive towards destruction in human nature; and speculate over the possibility of alternate visions. There was a renewed self-confidence that art could expand our consciousness of the political and psychic dimension of tragedy. By means of exhibitions that mounted powerful photo narratives of "ground zero," comparisons with other disasters, and symbolic vessels that could convey the act of mourning, artists urged the public to re-think the event.[11] Unlike political economy, cultural theory and psychoanalysis, art does not proceed from within a singular or totalizing theoretical framework. The language of art is always hybrid. It is composed of a multiplicity of theoretical and experiential sources. After September 11th, artists did not seek to construct an answer to the complex questions of our times by following the steps of logic but rather by reworking the layers of fear and desire in everyday events and experiences. While artists have stressed the utopian dimensions of mobility and celebrated the encounters with strangers, this runs in opposition to the new authoritarian stand taken by politicians across the world.

After September 11th, the moral balance of the ideological representation of globalization could have altered. The US could have reflected on the causes of global discontent and the consequences of their own hegemony. It was a timely moment to consider the US's consistent opposition to a global consensus in relation to climate control, bio-diversity plans, bans on land mines, the creation of an International Criminal Court, and the anti-ballistic missile treaties. There was a historic opportunity for the US to reconsider its status as a global superpower. "Ordinary Americans," who were interviewed shortly after September 11th, expressed both confusion over why anyone would want to hurt a peace-loving nation, and fury that anyone would dare to challenge its unparalleled authority. In response to the question that was repeat-edly broadcast ("Why do they hate us so much?"), there was both blank incompre-hension ("we never did anything to anybody") and ruthless vengeance ("an eye for an eye") (qtd in Tomkins 2). In the mainstream press, there was barely a voice that acknowledged that the US was not on a journey of global altruism but acting as a neo-imperial asset stripper. Studs Terkel risked pariah status when he warned of the need to re-think the conditions that made Americans the ones that are "always looked on badly" (Terkel).

The unanswerable question of "why should this thing happen?" could have been universalized to encompass all victims, but Bush immediately enjoined a sense of collective outrage and nationalized the desire for vengeance into a summons for patriotic defense. Armed guards marshaled the public transport system, jets pat-rolled the skies, and children were reminded to double their daily pledge of alle-giance. America was in no mood to accept either its vulnerability or its responsibility. The political response was reduced to restoring the American dream by avenging the dead. America, by way of Microsoft and Hollywood, may have colonized every screen in the world, but over 85% of Americans do not own a passport. After September 11th, the majority of Americans were said to have experienced greater levels of depression but also an intensified feeling that their country would emerge stronger than before (Alcorn 3). And when George W. Bush wanted to inspire a sense of secu-rity and serenity in the world, he said to his fellow Americans, "fight evil, go out and shop ... don't give in to the terrorists, take a plane, go to Disney Land, enjoy life."[12] How could the ordinary American feel the moral contradictions inherent in globaliza-tion when they are told to go forth and be good shoppers and happy tourists?

The real challenge of September 11th was in facing the causes of fear. Rather than submitting to a new culture of fear that stressed the perils of other cultures and the threat of foreign people, there is a need to develop new ways of relating to strangers. It is no longer acceptable to assume that everyone will assimilate into a single model or that different cultures can simply exist in isolation from each other. We can gain an insight into this challenge by considering the place of art within contemporary society. Today's artists do not presume to operate from a pedestal, or imagine themselves as lonely figures living on the fringes of society. They are immersed in the production of the images, symbols, perspectives and values of everyday life. This gives them an intimate awareness of the intensity of information flows. Images are coming towards us in greater numbers and from more different directions than at any other time in history. This does not only mean that we are faced with a greater volume of images to decipher, it also involves a transformed understanding of the different codes and contexts from which they originate. Complexity is found at all levels.

The challenge is compounded by the absence of an over-arching or unifying framework that can accommodate the different images and allocate a place to different perspectives. They all jostle up against each other with no clear order. On the one hand this creates a dynamic field for cultural interaction; on the other, it allows for the pre-existing power relations to operate in a more covert manner. In the absence of a unifying framework, artists are still experimenting across the boundaries of aesthetic forms and questioning the ethical dimensions of cultural representations. This practice is increasingly being conducted in cooperation with (non-artistic) people from diverse backgrounds. These collaborative techniques and improvisational strategies are important tools that could be applied in further areas. There is an urgent need to extend these aesthetic and social experiments into a broader political framework.

Force can be employed in making people surrender; and logic has the power to persuade; but only desire makes people want to relate to each other. Artists have the capacity to trace the lines of desire that connect different cultures. Their task is not confined to celebrating the purity of beauty, but found in the exploration of the parallels between different perspectives and the creation of new paradigms that enable a feedback between the different cultural systems. The interplay of differences cannot be pre-judged by any of the earlier models that privileged one set of values over all others. It requires a new kind of openness to cultural difference, rather than the reinforcement of the boundaries of political correctness. When artists engage with such social issues it does not reduce their art to mere propaganda. Art is not political from the outset but is politicized as it responds to the social circumstances in which it is embedded. Similarly, artists do not announce their ethical standpoints on banners, but allow them to emerge from within the reactions and decisions that they make when faced with conflict.

Culture, according to Jacques Derrida, is born from the tensions within difference – between what he calls the competing needs to be both hospitable and colonial. Every culture has the capacity to be both hospitable to the other (to receive them without question), and also to colonize the other by receiving them as a guest (to confine their admission to ways which confirms the authority of the host). This tension cannot be resolved in an absolute way, and Derrida recognizes that "unconditional hospitality" is impossible. However, he also insists that to lose sight of the principle of hospitality is to risk losing the marker of justice (Derrida).

Today the politics of hospitality, and the general strategies for cross-cultural dialogue, are threatened not just by the prospects of global war, but also by the placelessness of the other and the loss of boundaries for defining social responsibility. In the "War on Terror," the vilified other was not located in a specific place. The enemy could be anywhere and their identity could be anyone's. By stressing the placelessness and facelessness of the enemy, the risks of mobility and the fear of strangers were intensified. When the enemy is not merely on the other side of the battle line but in every neighborhood, then the strategy of defense infects the fibers of everyday life. From the pulpit of the national Cathedral at the memorial service for the victims of September 11th, Bush announced: "This conflict was begun on the timing and terms of others, it will end in a way, and at an hour, of our choosing." This day of reckoning is now an open rendezvous with the horizon. The battle for *Enduring Freedom* is not only global but, as US Defense Secretary Donald Rumsfeld announced, extended into the foreseeable future and, in the reactionary mind of one commentator, it is code for the eternal vigilance that is now necessary so that it may never happen again (Hoagland, "The Lifting of the Afghan Curtain of Horrors" 15).

The ethical choices are not confined to revenge and prevarication. We must resist both the development from the prosecution of the criminal to the persecution of communities and the conflation of the innocence of the victims with the culpability of the system. Paranoia and anger blur these boundaries but justice insists upon them. The pursuit of the global terrorist networks has already instilled a state of terror in the collective psyche. Increasingly, strangers are treated as suspects; curiosity is trapped inside the cage of anxiety; and civil freedom is left in ruins. Welcome to Hotel California, where we are all prisoners of our own safety, and children match gas masks to suit their casual clothes. The hollow promise of finding peace after war confuses annihilation with resolution. For, as Gayatri Spivak observed, the suicide bomber is an example of the absolute failure of hospitality. In this act of self-annihilation the bomber is both the object of destruction and destroyer of the self. Suicide explodes the possibility of communication, and, "if we cannot hear the message, then we will not be able to alter the hospitality" (Spivak). Peace is not found by means of conflict but only by means of the ability to prepare a space for dialogue. Peace is the life force that precedes and pre-empts conflict. War only disperses more fear.

Notes

1. Hollywood was quick to adopt self-censorship and happy to be part of the defensive endeavor. The shooting of other catastrophe movies was not only suspended but, between October and November 2001, Hollywood directors were "recalled" to the Pentagon for advice on future "unimaginable" scenarios and to help co-ordinate the messages on the "war on terrorism" (Caterson 7).

2. Or, as MacKenzie Wark noted in relation to the growing flows of illegal migration, a form of "globalization from below." See Wark.

3. Thomas Friedman extended this analogy even further by suggesting that the "war on terror" should be executed with the same nuclear force with which the war in Japan was concluded ("Foreign Affairs: Smoking or Non-Smoking" A27).

4. The absence of debate on the definition of terrorism, including the US's own Congressional code on terrorism, may have been designed to distract attention from what Noam Chomsky has described as a long history of state-sponsored terrorism, coercive diplomacy and illegal invasions. See his interviews in Chomsky.

5. Professor John Record (qtd in Ricks 6).

6. Robert Fisk, one of the few Western journalists to have interviewed Osama bin Laden, reported that he takes a rather simplistic form of opposition to US hegemony and has a burning desire to avenge the perceived humiliation of Islam (qtd in Chomsky 32).

7. Colin Powell. *New Speak Times* 3 Oct. 2001 (qtd in Boyle).

8. Ari Fleischer (qtd in Goldman).

9. Stephen Roach is Chief Economist of Morgan Stanley.

10. According to Michael Dumment, the differential in the ratio of real income per head between the richest countries and the poorest is even more startling. He cites a ratio of 3:1 in 1800, 10:1 in 1900, and the explosive figure of 60:1 in 2000. See Dumment.

11. Two exhibitions are illustrative of this global response: *Fall Out*, VCA Gallery, Melbourne, November 2001 and *Slanting House*, Museum of Contemporary Art, Tokyo, November 2002.

12. This was in response to reports that retail sales for September 2001 were the lowest in 30 years. Perhaps the commercialization of patriotism was meant to reboot the economy. Examples of the new range of nationalist kitsch varied from plastic wrappers stamped with "Freedom! Bravery" to eagle-shaped dish sponges. See Riley.

Works Cited

Alcorn, Gay. "How America Changed." *Sydney Morning Herald* 29 Dec. 2001: 3.

Allen-Mill, Tony. "Why Can't They Find Him?" *Sunday Times* 28 Oct. 2001: 6-7.

Boyle, Francis. "No War Against Afghanistan!" 18 Oct. 2001, Illinois Disciples Foundation. 10 Oct. 2001 <www.ratical.org/ratville/CAH/fab112901.pdf>.

Buncombe, Andrew. "Bush Rejects Taliban Offer to Surrender bin Landen." *Independent* 15 Oct. 2001: 1

Bush, George W. Address to the United Nations. CNN. 12 Sept. 2002. 31 Oct. 2002 <http://archives.cnn.com/2002/US/09/12/bush.transcript/>.

Carroll, John. *Terror*. Melbourne: Scribe, 2002.

Caterson, Simon. "The Words on Terror." *The Age* 15 Dec. 2001: 7.

Chomsky, Noam. *September 11*. Sydney: Allen & Unwin, 2001.

Davis, Mike. "The Flames of New York." *New Left Review* 12 (Nov/Dec 2001): 34-50.

Denny, Charlotte and Larry Elliott. "100 m More Must Survive on a Dollar a Day." *Guardian* 19 June 2002. 21 June 2002 <http://www.guardian.co.uk/business/story/0,,739876,00.html>.

Derrida, Jacques and Anne Dufourmantelle. *Of Hospitality*. Trans. R. Bowlby. Stanford: Stanford UP, 2000.

Dumment, Michael. *On Immigration and Refugees*. London: Routledge, 2001.

Eco, Umberto. *Five Moral Pieces*. Trans. A. McEwen. London: Secker & Warburg, 2001.

Enzensberger, Hans Magnus. *Civil War*. London: Granta, 1994.

Friedman, Thomas. "Foreign Affairs: Smoking or Non-Smoking." *New York Times* 14 Sept. 2001: A27.

—. "One War, Two Fronts." *New York Times* 2 Nov. 2001: A25.

—. "Foreign Affairs: Breaking the Circle." *New York Times* 16 Nov. 2001: A25.

Gibson, Nikla. "West Warned of Lasting Threat from bin Laden." *Irish Times* 3 Oct. 2001. 20 Oct. 2001 <http://www.ireland.com/newspaper/world/2001/1003/wor10.htm>.

Goldman, John. "Iraq Gets Mixed Report Card." *LA Times* 11 Jan. 2003. 12 Jan. 2003 <http://www.theage.com.au/articles/2003/01/10/1041990097141.html>.

Herald International Tribune 3 Dec. 2002: 1.

Hoagland, Jim. "The Lifting of the Afghan Curtain of Horrors Should Concentrate Minds on the Consequences of the Neglected." *Washington Post* 17 Nov. 2001: 15.

—. "Terrorists Can't Be Kept in a Box." *Washington Post* 18 Nov. 2001. 12 Dec. 2001 <http://www.ljworld.com/section/diary_111801/story/73878>.

Leunig, Michael. Cartoon. *The Age* 17 Feb. 2004: 4.

Kennedy, David M. "Fighting an Elusive Enemy." *New York Times*. 16 Sept. 2001, late ed., final, sec. 4: 11.

Morris, Linda. "Backlash Building Over Anti-Terror Laws." *Sydney Morning Herald*. 27 Nov. 2002. 20 Jan. 2002 <http://www.smh.com.au/articles/2002/11/26/1038274303898.html?oneclick=true> .

Morrison, Blake. "We Weren't There for Troy or the Burning of Rome, This Time There Were Cameras." *Guardian* 14 Sept. 2001. 16 Sept. 2001 <http://www.guardian.co.uk/g2/story/0,,551553,00.html>.

Nancy, Jean-Luc. *Being Singular Plural*. Trans. R.D. Richardson and A. O'Byrne. Stanford: Stanford UP, 2000.

Nandy, Ashis. *The Intimate Enemy*. New Delhi: Oxford UP, 1984.

"President Bush's address to the United Nations." CNN, September 12, 2002. 31 Oct. 2002 <http://archives.cnn.com/2002/US/09/12/bush.transcript/>.

Ricks, Thomas. "US Army College Attacks Bush Terror Policy." *The Age* 13 Jan. 2004: 6.

Riley, Mark. "Anxious Nation Faces New Terror Alarm." *The Age* 11 Oct. 2001: 25.

Roach, Stephen. "Back to Borders." *Financial Times* 28 Sept. 2001: 20.

Said, Edward. "Two Civilisations, Deeply Entwined." *The Age* 23 Oct. 2001: 13.

Spivak, Gayatri. Keynote Lecture. Congress CATH on *Translating Class, Altering Hospitality*. Leeds. 23 June 2002.

Stephens, Philip. "Chaos That Cannot Be Tolerated." *Financial Times* 28 Sept. 2001: 21.

Terkel, Studs. "Have We Learnt Our Lesson?" *Guardian* 14 Sept. 2001. 14 Sept. 2001 <http://www.guardian.co.uk/g2/story/ 0,,551556,00.html>.

Tomkins, Richard. "Fortitude in a Fearful New World." *Financial Times* 29 Sept. 2001: 2.

Young, Hugo. "A New Kind of War Means a New Kind of Discussion." *Guardian* 27 Sept. 2001: 22.

Wark, MacKenzie. "Globalisation from Below: Migration, Sovereignty, Communication." e-mail to the author. 5 Dec. 2001.

Zizek, Slavoj. *Welcome to the Desert of the Real*. London: Verso, 2002.

Thamyris/Intersecting No. 12 (2006) 141-158

On the Road with *Lamerica*

Immigrants, Refugees and the Poor	Marcia Landy

What's in a Name?

If there is a consensus concerning critical constructions of "postmodernity," it resides in a reaction against the "grand narratives" of Western culture inherited from the "Enlightenment" and invested with notions of progress, national identity, rationality, universalism, and belief in the power of representation to approximate the "real" conditions of existence.[1] This critique insists on multiplicity and difference, the constructed and not the essential or "true" character of belief systems, and the fragmented, not unified, character of the psychological/social subject. The productive aspects of such thinking can be seen in the introduction of concepts and methods of analysis that have challenged longstanding discourses and practices of patriarchy, sexism, racism, and colonialism, contributing to emergent social movements in the 20th and 21st centuries. However, in the context of this critical engagement with the legacy of modernity, social class has been transformed into a "transient, omnipresent, mobile subject, a testament to the irrepressible aleatory character of existence" (Hardt and Negri 156). But who are these "mobile" subjects, and how adequate (or, for that matter, how new) is the metaphor of mobility for understanding contemporary economic and ideological conditions identified by many theorists with postmodernity?

While it can be conceded that traditional conceptions of social class and class-consciousness may be inadequate for understanding forms of late capitalist production with its advanced technologies of warfare and consciousness commodities in the age of information, it does not follow that social class has disappeared within the landscape of postmodernity. In fact, global capital has discovered new opportunities for exploitation. As Hardt and Negri argue, "The proletariat is not what it used to be, but that does not mean it has vanished. It means, rather, that we are faced again with the analytic task of understanding the new composition of the proletariat as a class" (Hardt and Negri 53). Therefore, rethinking the conditions and the specific composition of social class in relation to configurations of postmodernity is mandatory for distinguishing the emergent and residual conditions of subalternity, and, therefore, the potential for trans-individual action. The "unemployable," the "poor," the "refugee," and the "immigrant" offer a different, more distinct, sense of mobility tied to the state's power over life and death.

For my analysis I rely on Italian filmmaker Gianni Amelio's 1994 film *Lamerica*, which dramatizes the thwarted exodus of large numbers of men, women, and children from Albania in the early 1990s. I discuss the style and many-layered perspectives of the film to expose the current forms of power expressed in the monetary flows of international capital. New, deregulated, constantly changing and intensified economic conditions are inextricably fused with the character and conditions of mobile populations in transnational spaces. In seeking to provide a contemporary and sobering view of social class in the context of postmodernity, I draw on the writings of Michel Foucault and Giorgio Agamben and their elaboration of the concept of "bio-power." Both writers acknowledge demographic, juridical and institutional forms of control that establish sovereign power over life and death. As I shall argue, "bare life," rather than labor, underpins the character of social class, uniting the various mobile and contingent elements of postmodernity: the economically dispossessed, immigrants and refugees who disjoin "the continuity between man and citizen, *nativity* and *nationality* ... [and] put the originary fiction of modern sovereignty in crisis" (Agamben 131). *Lamerica* introduces manifold questions concerning the nature and fate of national identity, historical parallels between and differences from the present economic and political situation and the Italian Fascist past, and an exploration of the composition and destiny of social class as expressed in bio-political terms that render it exploitable, stripped of rights, and expendable.

The Journey to *Lamerica*

Lamerica begins with reminiscences about relations between two countries – Italy and Albania – early on in the 20th century. Newsreel footage from the Fascist era produced by LUCE, the organization responsible for propaganda during Italy's Fascist regime, is accompanied by a sonorous voice-over extolling the Italian conquest of Albania in 1939, coupled with images of the arrival of Mussolini and Italian troops. The propaganda celebrates the abdication of King Zog and pledges a new reign of peace and economic prosperity through the draining of swamps, rural health reform, the building of hospitals, schools, roads, and the creation of employment under the aegis of Mussolini's Italy.

By means of the newsreel footage, accompanied by the title credits, the film invites the viewer to entertain significant parallels between the earlier Italian conquest of Albania and the present involvement of Italy in Albanian economics and politics. The propaganda newsreel from the Fascist era raises the question of whether the contemporary treatment of Albanians by Italians is another permutation of Italian imperialism with equally dire effects on the Albanian nation. By introducing this earlier film footage, *Lamerica* indicts past and present media for misrepresenting and mystifying present conditions. The presence of the newsreel as prologue is a reminder that Italian media was a significant factor in the Fascist conquest of Albania in the mid-20th century. *Lamerica*'s focus on media also anticipates the current situation whereby Italian television, like US TV, creates illusory images that promise economic prosperity, entertainment, and political transformation. In contrast, the film's dramatic ending is not newsreel footage. It offers a different and deliberately fictionalized version that juxtaposes past and present, inviting a questioning of connections between fiction and non-fiction in the cinematic uses of history and in the construction of images of social class.

While the film is set in Albania and is based on an actual event – the turning back of the ship Vlora bound for Italy with its cargo of would-be immigrants in 1991, – its portrait of Albania is specifically calculated to provide images of that country that are transposable to other parts of Eastern Europe, if not Africa – countries that have seen the exodus of peoples to Western Europe. In the film, the Vlora is renamed "Partizani," a name that further evokes memories of Italy, in particular of post-World-War-Two Italy, the Resistance, and further the dashed hopes for a society rejuvenated after Fascism but enthralled by the US. Coming as it does at the end of the film, the images of the immigrants bound for "Lamerica" are not only a counterpoint to the numerous allusions to contemporary Italian media situated throughout the film but also to the failed expectations of the immigrants.

The filmic narrative begins in 1991 in Durazzo, Albania, with the arrival of two Italian venture capitalists, Fiore (Michele Placido) and Gino (Enrico Lo Verso) who are greeted by an Albanian bureaucrat, Selimi (Piro Milkani), who acts for a time as intermediary in the men's plans to bilk the government of funds for the phony shoe factory "Alba Calzature," which they do not plan to establish. As the men climb into their shiny Italian car, the camera captures throngs of people swarming in the streets and seeking entry into the government compound. The three men travel by car on their way to meet candidates for the role of a local chairman for their company, and, thus, the spectator is witness to two different kinds of "mobile" subjects in the film: the Italian entrepreneurs who are "on the road," having traveled to Albania to exploit the workers with the assistance of state bureaucrats, and the unemployed and impoverished populace who are itinerant because they are homeless, and harassed by the state. Later on in the film, Gino, abandoned by Fiore, will find himself on the road in a similar class position. Gino's turn of fortune thus reinforces the contingent character of social class central to the film's investigation.

The camera captures images of a bleak landscape and Fiore, oblivious to these miserable conditions, expounds his economic "philosophy." He complains about the lack of initiative and resourcefulness of Albania in terms reminiscent of contemporary supply-side economics and its elevation of work, and not state support, as a means of restoring productivity to the economy. Accusing the Albanians of "lacking brains," Fiore insists that, given the vast and, to him, unpopulated terrain, the abundance of land, oil, and water are there to be exploited and, if they are not, the failure of economic development can only be attributed to laziness and improper management on the part of the Albanians. His opinions recall the language of Fascism, its racism, and its false promises of invigorating Albanian production as presented in the LUCE newsreel at the beginning of the film. These sentiments, couched in the language of the colonizer, are also suggestive of the language of underdevelopment, as articulated by major Western powers in the age of global capital.

Most importantly, Fiore's descriptions of the Albanians prefigure the film's preoccupation with the politicization of human life, its transformation into "bare life," a life that is regarded and treated as devoid of value. In Agamben's terms and following Foucault, this politicization is expressed through political and social mechanisms that involve the state's direct and indirect sovereign power over life and death. This form of control either takes the form of violence perpetrated by the state upon the bodies of the socially unfit or of the seemingly benign legal apparatus of judgment by means of incarceration, institutionalization, medicalization, or juridical procedures, all affecting an individual's and a group's "right to live." The film introduces its depiction of *homo sacer* when, launching their quest for their "straw" chairman, Gino and Fiore are taken by Selimi to a former labor camp where enemies of the regime had been incarcerated. This episode further reinforces the film's attentiveness to connections between Fascism and biopower. In this episode, the camp is not a mere throwback to an earlier moment in time but, as described by Agamben, it is "the hidden matrix and *nomos* of the political space in which we are still living" (166).

The stark images of the inhabitants offer a further perspective on the film's political and class analysis – a reminder that social class as a sign of differential relations between exploiters and exploited still exists and has power over decisions governing life and death. The male inhabitants of the camp, suffering from malnutrition and numerous diseases, surround the two Italians who are repelled by the sights of horror that confront them. Deprived of rights and privileges, committed to a place where they are excluded from social life, these men confirm the existence of what Agamben has characterized as bare life, life deemed as valueless, dispensable, regulated by the state and its denizens, and excluded from the protection of the law. In the inhuman conditions of this milieu, Gino and Fiore select the man, "Spiro Tozai," presumably an Albanian and presumably an anti-communist dissenter, to become the "straw chairman" of their non-existent company. Only later does Gino learn that Tozai is, in fact, not an Albanian but Michele Talarico, an Italian from Sicily, who arrived with other Italians during the war when Albania was "Mussolini's colony." After the war, when the country became communist, he, like many Italians, was imprisoned in this camp.

In light of the complex state mechanisms necessary to establish their company and the limited economic and industrial resources available, Fiore abandons Gino and returns to Italy, leaving Gino with the impression that he is to finish the bureaucratic work. From this point onwards, the film becomes a road film, a genre appropriately associated with Americanity and with an escape from social, familial, and class constraints, a contest between the traditional and the new, and an expression of the discontents of modernity, identity, and cultural dislocation (Cohan and Hark 3). This film genre often involves a traveling couple that interacts with each other antagonistically, romantically, sexually, or in filial fashion, thus enabling a focus on the nuances of their relationship with each other as well as with their milieu. While *Lamerica* shares some of these characteristics, it diverges starkly from many films of the genre in that the road is associated with the movement of refugees and labor immigrants rather than merely with socially disaffected couples, involving the two men in encounters with large segments of Albanian workers, and with institutional, familial, and generational aspects of Albanian life.

The contingent nature of social class is manifested by means of highlighting Gino's physical metamorphosis as he travels on the road with Michele. For example, at the outset of the journey, Gino's appearance has stood in stark contrast to that of the Albanians. Dressed in the latest fashion, sporting Italian dark glasses, carefully groomed, and driving a jeep of the latest vintage, he stands out as the incarnation of Italian advertising and prosperity. By contrast, the villagers he encounters are poorly dressed and seem to spend their time in village squares or on the road. There is no mistaking Gino for an Albanian early on in the film but, as he travels on the road, he loses the appurtenances that identify him as a prosperous Italian and comes to resemble contemporary Albanians as well as an earlier historical image of the Sicilian immigrant as exemplified by Michele.

First, Gino loses the wheels of his jeep and is forced to travel by bus and truck. Next, he loses his sunglasses. His clothes become shabby and dirty. Finally, he loses his job, and, after his arrest, he loses his passport, becoming indistinguishable from the Albanians. "No one has passports here," he is told by the police. Gino, an Italian, becomes an Albanian once he is divested of his passport. A number of motifs coalesce: national identity is not a matter of birth but a matter of documents and hence political status, and identity can be conferred and also withdrawn by the state, revealing the vulnerability of the subject. In what will become a counter-narrative of the postmodern tourist or internationally mobile entrepreneur, Gino, like the other "mobile" Albanians, becomes another victim of the state's power over life and death and another reminder of the persistence, not disappearance, of social class.

The film increasingly turns on the interactions between Michele and Gino. Their relationship is quite unlike the action film genre, that is, the spaghetti western or the war film, where two men are indissolubly linked in camaraderie and in life and death

situations. Michele is an archaic remnant of another world and time. His role is connected to the newsreel footage that opens the film, since he was one of the soldiers
conscripted into the Italian army during the Fascist regime. A deserter from the army,
he remained trapped in prison in Albania for half a century. As he begins to confide
in Gino, the viewer learns that both men are from the south of Italy, from Sicily, historically a less developed region of Italy and a locus of massive immigration to the
United States. Hence, the old man and the young Italian share a common national
and regional identity. But it quickly becomes evident that they are from two different
Sicilian and Italian worlds, and while Michele is lost in the past, Gino is oblivious to
the present. Gino's treatment of Michele is condescending, even cruel, punishing,
and rejecting. He treats him at first in a paternalist fashion, as if Michele is a way-
ward child, but in no way does he acknowledge the bond that Michele claims they
share as Sicilian Italians. Michele, by contrast, first behaves in childlike fashion
toward Gino, but then, later, assumes a paternal role. On the one hand, their interactions highlight their shared, national paternity and their new situation of homeless-
ness, and on the other hand, their differing responses to and inability to understand
their past, present, or future.

The Ruins of the Past
Gino and Michele are the film's instruments for creating a narrative that invites
the viewer to speculate on points of contact between past, present and future. The
roles of Gino and Michele, the old and the new Italian, the era of fascism and the
contemporary moment, the earlier movements of Italian immigration, and the present
moment of Albanian immigration, bring layers of past and present into confrontation.
The film is invested in exploring questions of history and national identity. This investment is not in the service of a seamless or progressive narrative from past to present or of a nostalgia that reinstates earlier conceptions of social class, but is
heuristic and even pedagogical. The film offers critical versions of the past to invite
comparisons with the present and specifically to produce contemplation about
the nature of the "people" and questions relating to the transmogrification of social
class.

Lamerica's uses of the national past do not celebrate national unity, technology,
populism, and human progress but subject them to questioning. This pedagogy
involves the introduction of memory – what has been forgotten or elided. Indeed, the
persistence of the past in the present is invoked everywhere in the film by means of
the numerous images of and allusions to physical and political ruins. The landscape
and characters portrayed in Lamerica are a reminder of violence, war, and abuse of
state power that contradict any sense of linear progress and present the viewer with
a historical and philosophic reflection on time and on the importance of distinguishing repetition in the interest of difference and change.

In a reflection on the ruins of time, Pier Paolo Pasolini, commenting on transformations in Italian culture in 1975, wrote:

The Italy of today has been destroyed exactly as was the Italy of 1945. Indeed the destruction is much more serious, because we do not find ourselves among the ruins, however distressing, of houses and monuments, but among the ruins of values, humanistic values and what is more important popular values. (57)

Pasolini's comments join the literal and figurative ruins from the past with present cultural and political destruction. Michele and Gino were born at different moments, but each man is a sleepwalker, unable to come to terms with the passage of time. Michele is the ghost from the fascist past, the spiritual "father" of this offspring of the New Italy. He is also an embodiment of an earlier form of hope in the prospect of the immigrant.

Gino is caught in the fantasy of the "easy life" of prosperity and consumerism, a scion of Italy's post-industrial and consumerist culture. Each character is a "prey to a vision, pursued by it or pursuing it, rather than engaged in an action" that could awaken him from this dream (Deleuze 3). Michele still believes or pretends that it is 1939 and that it is possible to return to his former life, despite Gino's cruel taunt that "The war ended fifty years ago! Your wife's probably dead." Michele clings tenaciously to the fantasy of his coming reunion with his family in Italy. Similarly, Gino clings to the pragmatic and immediate realization of the company without any sense of the fraudulent character of the enterprise and the absurdity of making Michele a company "president."

In this context, Albania serves as more than a portrait of a nation underdeveloped industrially and with high unemployment: the country is a reminder of pre-World-War-Two Sicily, a country of emigration, not immigration. The parallel, however, functions not to create an equivalence between past and present so much as to underscore significant differences between that earlier world and the present. In an interview for *Cineaste* and echoing Pasolini's melancholy reflections on Italy, Amelio stated that his film is a film "about two Italies really – the Italy of my father and the Italy of today in which I live. My father's Italy was poor but full of hope. Today my Italy is very cynical and arid" (Crowdus and Porton 7). This "cynical and arid" Italy involves the status and condition of global immigration not only relevant to the Albanians but also to large segments of the world population displaced by development as well as war. The title of the film – *Lamerica* – echoes the earlier aspirations of Italian immigrants to escape poverty and find economic security in the United States or in Latin America. These new immigrants look toward Italy, for them the new America, as their means of escape.

Encountering each other again on the ship bound for Italy with its "illegal" cargo, Michele talks to Gino of his own father's emigration to America, which he describes as "a big place" where one could find work. The image of the crowded ship at the end of the film also looks back and forward in time. On the one hand, it conjures up images of the earlier immigrant ships headed for a new life in America. On the other, it is a reminder to the viewer of a different journey in the present that ends in harsh internment and return to Albania. The film does not include these episodes, ending on an ambiguous note. The camera scans the faces of the men, women, and children without the benefit of dialogue to "explain" their situation. Mostly youthful, with the exception of Michele, the passengers seem to capture a sense of anticipation and hope. They will not reach "Lamerica," or answer the question posed by the film to the viewer about their collective character and their fate.

Narrating an Aesthetics of Difference

The film's strategy of constructing the narrative around movement through space and time is consistent with the direction taken by the European cinemas in the post-World-War-Two era from neorealism onward as a means of challenging the continuity of the classical realist narrative. Films produced by such filmmakers as Rossellini, Antonioni, Pasolini, and Amelio are critical of classic realism, strict lines between documentary and fiction films, narrative continuity, and self-conscious protagonists who act to alter events. Instead, their narratives, or rather anti-narratives, are built on discontinuities, wanderings through emptied spaces where situations are "not extended directly into action" (Deleuze 4). The characters are no longer determinants of the situation, they are incapable of action. But this incapacity need not extend to the viewer, who is presented with a form of narration that is founded on resistance to easy assimilation and interpretation.

Within classic realist cinema, the spectator is given the possibility of situations requiring series of actions and reactions, conflicts and resolutions. In the post-World-War-Two cinema, beginning with neorealism, the image "becomes a space for reading: seeing and hearing as decipherment rather than following an action" (Rodowick 75). The disconnected and emptied spaces, the hallucinatory dimension of character, give rise to "weak connections that are capable of releasing huge forces of disintegration" (Deleuze 19).

While critics might be inclined to identify *Lamerica* with a restrictive conception of neorealism because of the use of location shooting, non-professional actors, and "an accurate accounting of social conditions" (Bondanella 454), I believe that the film is not a return to this formulation of neorealism with its familiar "accounting of social conditions" but a means of reconfiguring character, milieu, action, and narration as delineated by Gilles Deleuze in his examination of the time-image. The trajectory of the narrative and its means of treating agency, conflict, and conflict resolution are shifted onto the spectator who is offered a different relation to the images projected onto the screen. The strategies associated with post-World-War-Two cinematic theories and practices are evident in the opaqueness of character, the sense of the openness and threat of time, the elliptical and multivalent nature of events that

transpire, and the emphasis on failure rather than success, all of which invite not solutions, nor unified meanings, but questions that pertain to an investigation of social
life and class.

In short, *Lamerica* flouts the assumption that the cinematic image leads either to
organic and universalizing interpretations of situation and character, associated with
earlier forms of classic realism, or to simplistic conceptions of neorealism that focus
on its technical adherence to location shooting and non-professional actors. Amelio's
film raises the possibility that there is another route toward a critical treatment of the
cinematic image, one that introduces the possibility of thinking differently about culture
and politics through a use of characters that foregrounds their inability to act and,
thus, to ameliorate their steadily deteriorating condition. As described by Deleuze in
his characterization of post-World-War-Two cinema, character is "no longer subject to
the rules of a response or an action. He is prey to a vision … rather than engaged in
an action" (Deleuze 2, 3). Because of Gino and Michele's blindness to their situation,
it becomes possible for the viewer to focus on events, to contemplate their complexity, and to realize that the film does not offer a solution so much as enact a philosophic and political pedagogy.

In its portrait of post-Communist Albania, the film mounts a critique of its economic
exploitation by European entrepreneurs; its continued existence as a police state;
and the presence of the hungry, unemployed, and the devastated poor who prey on
each other but who are capable of altruism as well. It portrays subaltern life in terms
that reveal unrealistic expectations of a life in Italy that involve finding employment
and gaining citizenship. The final moments of the film provide not only a contrast to
images of earlier immigrants but a rare depiction of the plight of today's homeless,
stateless, unwanted, and economically exploited populations. If anything, these
images are an invitation to locate a critical alternative, an aesthetics of difference that
takes into account "the way subject positions do not come into being in a void but are
in themselves the interpellated roles offered by this or that already existing group"
(Jameson 345).

These "subject positions" are not abstract counters of the hyper-reality of the
"postmodern condition," but indications of the collusion between postmodern thinking
with the politics attendant on late capital logic in transforming people into "populations" and assigning them with new and ephemeral identities as "asylum-seekers,"
"refugees," and, most abstractly, "mobile" postmodern subjects. The challenge *Lamerica*
poses is how to identify what is "mobile" and "new" and what is long-standing about the
character and existence of social subjects in relation to the permutations of money
and capital. Mobility, it turns out, involves the unimpeded movement of capital,
whereas the movement of populations is subject to economic and political constraints, and this is where questions of social class arise concerning its composition
and its viability as a category of analysis.

Lamerica does not produce a sentimental and militant picture of the Albanians or of the two Italians, creating through them an image of warring social class in the vein of past quantitative and economistic analysis. The would-be immigrants are not portrayed as the vanguard of the revolution, nor are they all cut from the cloth of an earlier "working class." They are victims and also exploiters of each other in their struggle to survive, caught in the confluence of a number of determinants that have been identified by Antonio Negri with capitalism in its post-World-War-Two manifestations (Negri 61-75). These workers exemplify the qualitative and quantitative changes attendant on the transformations from Fordist, social welfare, and socialist economies to a monetary economy that crosses national boundaries with political consequences expressed in redefinitions of work, citizenship, and national belonging.

As *Lamerica* explores the dire effects of these transformations, it also visualizes the possibility of comprehending their effects, a necessary precondition for redefining the "mobile subject" in terms of class considerations. Inherent to this redefining process is, as *Lamerica* dramatizes, the role of technology and the media. In the case of many commercial films, videos, and television, narratives of refugees and immigrants are geared to producing liberal, sentimental, and politically correct images of human rights and multiculturalism. In fiction films and newsreels one also finds a presentation of the homeless, the immigrant, and refugees, as part of a climate of fear. They are stigmatized through the language of criminalization, connected to numerous and dramatic instances of terrorism, moral degeneracy, drugs, and underworld activities. Images of "the people" are increasingly delivered over to this mode of double thinking, something that the Amelio film recognizes and problematizes by means of its critical treatment of the role of the media and its own recasting of this role as a form of what Deleuze has described as "creative storytelling" in contrast to "information." Countering the "radical ineffectiveness" of information, Deleuze suggests the necessity of going beyond:

all the pieces of spoken information; to extract from them a pure speech act, creative storytelling which has as it were the obverse side of the dominant myths, of current words and their supporters; an act capable of creating the myth instead of drawing profit and business from it. (269-70)

The storytelling in *Lamerica* is the "obverse side" of dominant myths: the film unsettles relations with the past; it also disturbs conceptions of national identity. The two Italian men become the film's instruments for exploring the fictive character of nation, a fiction that has material consequences for them. Though both men claim Italian identity, the film will use this claim to delicately dissect the fictive and historical character of national belonging so as to establish different grounds for an analysis of their present situation. The film situates their plight as belonging to the modern category of the stateless, the asylum seeker, the refugee, and the economic immigrant, a condition that is usually considered in a legalistic and political rather than a nuanced historical, economic and ideological fashion. Through the stripping away of Gino's possessions, his confidence in his superiority, and finally his Italian citizenship after the loss of his passport, Lamerica exposes the illusory character of beliefs in the solidity of economic investment, state protectionism, and citizenship in the nation. Gino's situation comes to parallel that of the Albanians whom he scorns, and his reversal of fortune enables the spectator to reflect on the conditions that have brought Gino to share the Albanians' fate. By means of the degradation of Gino's position, the spectator cannot but be aware of, even empathize with, the turnaround of his fortunes and its implications for others in this situation. Moreover, this trans-formation can forge the terms for the spectator's comprehension of the slipperiness, that is, the mobile character of social class and national identity in a global context.

Images of Immigrants, Refugees, and the Poor
Dina Iordanova distinguishes Lamerica from such films as Before the Rain (Manchevski, 1994) and Ulysses' Gaze (Angelopoulos, 1995), where one witnesses a "demi-Orientalization" of the Balkans, focusing on the area as a site of primitivism, and where a Western European figure is the filter through which events are seen, privileging the Western European gaze – the "foreigner's point of view" (263-70). By contrast, Lamerica focuses on Gino's limited perspective and on his progressive marginaliza-tion by means of staged contrasts between Gino's "blindness," his lack of insight and the viewer's contact with images of the landscape and people that elude Gino's gaze. Throughout the film, the spectator is made aware of different perspectives on the situation of the Albanians involving the gaze of Fiore, the women at the factory, the villagers on Gino's journey to find Michele, the police, the immigrants on the bus and on the ship, and the gaze of the camera. These multiple spectatorial positions undermine the exoticism and primitivism alluded to by Iordanova.

Despite its severe critique of contemporary society and politics and its portrait of the bleakness of many aspects of Albanian existence, the film conveys moments and ges-tures that temporarily reveal the presence of a recognition of life and vitality on the part of people in the face of hardship. One such moment, commented upon by many review-ers of the film, is the image of the young female child in the midst of puddles of water in the run-down and overcrowded hotel, dancing, absorbed in the music and oblivious to her surroundings. This episode complicates, though it does not erase, the starkness of the portraits of exploitation, violence, and death presented in the film. The film's focus on youth is emblematic of the people's uncertain and threatening future, but also of their resourcefulness in the struggle to survive. Such moments invite a reconsidera-tion of forms of life, of gestures that counter the bare means and ends of survival.

The film also complicates its uses of history, drawing its images of the landscape from different sheets of past and present. Important to the film's uses of the past are reminders of the intervening time between 1939 and the present – in the form of the ubiquitous bunkers dotting the landscape; the monumental architecture of the government buildings belonging to the era of the Hoxha regime (1944-1985); the labor camp where Michele was imprisoned; the slogans and signs plastered throughout the countryside as propaganda for and against Hoxha; and even in graffiti invoking the war in Vietnam. The landscape has its own history to narrate. Interestingly, Michele asks Gino about the significance of the name of the dictator Hoxha etched on a hillside, confusing it with the name of Mussolini.

By far the most important aspect of the film's use of history can be traced in its treatment of immigration: its allusions to earlier Italian immigration and its portrait of the present exodus from Albania to Italy. Through the character of Michele, the film introduces memories of Italy as a country of emigrants, as he reminisces about his father's earlier immigration to the "L'America." The present situation involves economic and political changes that were responsible for emigration from the Balkans to Southern Europe in the 1990s. While some modest gains toward industrialization were made in Albania, they could not provide "sufficient jobs for all of its citizens. Approximately 20 percent of the work force was employed abroad and 20 percent was unemployed" (Perlmutter 206). Certainly, conditions in Albania have become a major issue for Italians today who are both unprepared for and unwilling to confront their new situation as a country of immigration.

Italy's treatment of refugees has had a checkered history. Following the unification of Italy in the mid-nineteenth century, known as the Risorgimento, the new nation had been liberal in its conduct toward refugees and, as a country that had experienced successive waves of emigration, Italy was not averse to granting foreigners "the same civil rights enjoyed by the Italians" (Sciortino 234-35). While this situation changed during the Fascist era, during the years from 1945 to the mid-1970s "the very idea of immigration to Italy seemed to many utterly bizarre" (235). However, from the 1980s to the present, new laws were promulgated to control the influx of domestic, construction, and farm workers, and workers involved in industry and tourism. In general, the availability of jobs in industry and in service occupations was a consequence of the declining birth rate and the higher degree of professionalization that made such work unacceptable to Italians. According to Russell King:

The model of labour immigration is based on a demand for cheap and flexible workers in the secondary and informal markets where low wages are imposed on migrants because of their illegal or semi-legal status and the lack of opportunities in their home countries. (18)
While *Lamerica* is not a sociological tract, a polemic, or a *reflection* of "real" conditions, its particularly cinematic uses of images, character, and situation offer multiple opportunities to find connections with the world outside of the frame. Through Gino's comments to the Albanians seeking to escape their country and settle in Italy, the viewer gains a sense of Italian attitudes toward its immigrants. When the men talk about their aspirations to find jobs, Gino tells them that they will be hired as

dishwashers. It is not that Gino misrepresents the future that awaits them but that he is unsympathetic, even disdainful, as he articulates that future.

Not only do the immigrants' experiences in Italy include constraining economic conditions, but immigrants are also correspondingly excluded from the rights of citizenship and socially and culturally marginalized. Generalizing on the conditions of these immigrants, Gabriella Lazaridis and Iordanis Psimmenos have argued:

One could argue that migration as a political experience today signifies not so much the triumph of economic liberalism in East and West, but rather the shrinking of workers' ability to intervene in and shape economic decision-making. The migrant is transformed into an "experimental agent" who, unable to control his/her economic environment, becomes part of a globalized unification process "free" of community, union or skill constraints. In other words, migration is the political experience of both the shrinking of social rights and the modification of labour into a political container that functions according to world market necessities. It is this understanding that turns whole regions (the ex-socialist countries in general and Albania in particular) ... into a large migratory pool of cheap and even slave-like labour. (173)

In its critical portrait of its two Italian entrepreneurs and in its portrait of conditions in Albania, Lamerica examines the social and political effects of immigration. In portraying conditions in Albania, the film provides a rationale for the Albanian men's desire to emigrate, if not a justification (becoming rich and famous). It also makes a case for the uncertain, even dire, future that lies ahead. In its emphasis on rare moments of mutuality among the characters and in its lingering visual emphasis on the common plight of the immigrants culminating in the scene on the ship, Lamerica raises the question of the necessity, if not the possibility, for considering "new kinds of proletarian solidarity and militancy" (Hardt and Negri 54).

In Amelio's portrait, one does not see the conventional equation of the immigrant with criminality. Instead, the viewer is shown how segments of the population struggle to survive by means of beggary and theft, braving the guns of the police in a desperate effort to escape. Corruption emanates from the upper echelons of government bureaucracy. In particular, unscrupulous entrepreneurs such as Fiore and Gino are symptomatic of the exploitation practiced within the country. Through Fiore's conversation with Gino, the viewer learns that this is not the first time or place that he has practiced his global predation. Earlier, he and Gino's father had schemed to set up a television company in Nigeria with used equipment. Though they profited monetarily from grants, the Nigerians did not profit at all, since the equipment never worked. Fiore's cynical comment is that, unfortunately, Nigerians did not have the ability to work with the equipment.

In Fiore and Gino's attitudes toward Albanians, the film both recapitulates earlier attitudes toward southern Italians and characterizes present attitudes toward refugees. As we have seen, early on in the film, Fiore displays his paternalistic attitude toward the Albanian workers, but, more than that, he characterizes the Albanian populace at large as lacking in initiative and resourcefulness, an attitude that analysts of immigration find in many antagonistic descriptions of the immigrant by Italians, such as their unwillingness to work so as to "improve their own living arrangements" (Perlmutter 212). In addition, the refugees/immigrants are depicted as representing:

An earlier, poorer, more barbaric version of Italians, and one that is virtually indistinguishable. Northern Italians have stereotypically resented the backwardness of southerners, and when discussing Albanians, have used a similar language to describe them. (212)

Hence, the film's portrayal of Gino and Michele as Sicilians and their metamorphosis to Albanians serve both to invoke the traditional racist animus against Sicilians and also to transfer this stereotype onto Albanians. Moreover, an exposure and critique of racism is introduced by means of the film's gradual transformation of Gino from an icon of fashionability to being "indistinguishable" from the people he disdains. His becoming like the Albanians serves a dual role. On the one hand, it undermines his sense of Italian superiority, on the other, it reveals that the differences ascribed to Albanians are a variant of racist thought couched less in terms of "natural" differences – skin color, hair texture, or physical size – and more in terms of cultural/social traits. These cultural traits are associated with the "criminalization" of the immigrant articulated as criminal disposition, lack of ambition, and likeness to other marginalized groups, justifying segregation, exclusion, and the need for legal sanctions.

The Immigrant as *Homo Sacer*

While its treatment of immigrants is tragic, *Lamerica* offers the spectator the possibility of thinking this tragedy in critical terms that might account for its existence and, therefore, provide the basis I suggest for a consideration of social class as a necessary element in undermining univalent views of the new global order with its postmodern celebrations of mobile populations, the liberating dimensions of technology, and the democratic character of multi-culturalism. The refugee, the immigrant, and the increasing unemployed or underemployed population are an affront to the *celebration* of the fragmented character of subjectivity, of mobility, and of the end of history, since this celebration of difference and hybridity often relies on suppressing vast segments of global populations that are marginalized, criminalized, impoverished, and deprived of life. More particularly, the refugee and the immigrant are symptomatic of the exclusion of large segments of groups from access to power. This exclusion can take a variety of forms involving gender, sexuality, race, and nationality but in the final analysis, distinctions between inclusion and exclusion are starker than ever. Moreover, the conditions for these distinctions become mystified if they are not acknowledged and do not become the basis for analysis and for change.

By means of its style and choice of subject matter *Lamerica* places before its spectators a vision of social class that avoids the pitfalls of reductionism and totalizing. The film acknowledges the changes that have been wrought in relation to vast segments of populations from the early part of the 20th century to the present. In its elaboration of differences, the film avoids a simple linear analysis of changes that transpired between the 1930s and the 1990s, and, especially, it avoids a sentimental and programmatic view in its portraits of the new expressions of social class that have emerged since then. For example, Gino's metamorphosis from capitalist to unemployed worker shifts the focus from a reductively binary distinction between capitalists and workers to the larger processes and effects of exploitation (Balibar 143). The film takes into account the economics that inhere in late capitalism, but the contribution of the film to a rethinking of social class resides further in its presentation of the intensified biological and social forms available for creating and controlling these "new social subjects."

Amelio's investigation of the world of the immigrant, the poor, and the stateless in *Lamerica* can be fruitfully compared to what Michel Foucault has described as modern bio-power, the power over life and death wielded by the sovereign power or the state under the conditions of globalization:

This death that was based on the right of the sovereign is now manifested as simply the reverse of the right of the social body to ensure, maintain, or develop its life ... If genocide is indeed the dream of modern powers, this is not because of a recent return of the ancient right to kill; it is because power is situated and exercised at the level of life, the species, the race and the large-scale phenomena of population. (Foucault 136-37)

Building on Foucault's commentary, Giorgio Agamben, under the rubric of *homo sacer*, regards "bare life" as the consummate condition of modern societies in the context of the increasing control and containment of populations in the modern world. The key aspects in Agamben's analysis of "bare life" involve the politicization of the notion of life (*zoë*) in terms of populations, not of individuals (*bios*). The politicization of life has dictated the erosion of boundaries between social and political inclusion and exclusion through the creation of a "state of exception." This "state of exception" operates within and outside law, determining inclusion and exclusion by rendering them indistinguishable.

The state as sovereign power defines and decides on the fate of populations, exercising power over the life and death of segments of the population through suspending the law by declaring a state of exception. According to Agamben, this "naked life" is the body that can be killed but not sacrificed ritualistically. This killing can be accomplished because the permanent "state of exception" is a zone of indistinction, a "juridically empty space" in which "everything becomes possible" (38-39). Bare life is "outside both human and divine law" (72) and, while the state of exception creates zones of indistinction in relation to the right to live and to those that are expendable, it is not only traditionally socially marginalized groups that fall under this exclusion. In fact, this biopolitics can be applied indiscriminately but expediently, including in its orbit racialized, ethnic, religious, immigrant, and gendered populations.

In the case of *Lamerica*, the image of the immigrants on the ship is a visual metaphor of the zone of exclusion. The immigrants are subject to a double exclusionary process. They are hounded, imprisoned, and detained in Albania and are banned from entry into Italy after being held hostage in the stadium in Bari. The film chooses not to portray this last episode in the story, but leaves the spectator in a similar state of suspension in order to reflect on the character and fate of these immigrants.

Speaking directly to the issue of the refugee and immigrant, Agamben states:

If refugees (whose number has continued to grow in our century to the point of including a significant part of humanity today) represent such a disquieting element in the order of the nation-state, this is above all because by breaking the continuity between man and citizen, nativity and nationality, they put the originary fiction of modern sovereignty in crisis. Bringing to light the difference between birth and nation, the refugee causes the secret presupposition of the political domain – bare life – to appear for an instant within that domain. (131)

Commenting on the consequences of the rights of man that are progressively "separated from and used outside the context of citizenship for the sake of the supposed representation and protection of a bare life that is more and more driven to the margins of the nation-states, ultimately to be re-codified into a new national identity," Agamben further asserts that the separation of humanitarianism and politics is complicit with state power (133), and this situation "cannot fail to reproduce the isolation of sacred life at the basis of sovereignty" (134).

The world becomes filled with these zones of indistinction and exclusion – camps, places of detention and of segregation, bearing similarity to the "camp" as a *nomos* of modernity. The refugee, the homeless, and the immigrant are increasingly deprived of the right to live. If the camp is no longer that established by the Nazis, it has not disappeared. The images of the prison in *Lamerica* where Fiore and Gino find their chairman, and the evocation of the stadium in which Albanian immigrants were detained in 1991 before being returned home, are variants on existing forms of the camp, exemplifying "the materialization of the state of exception … in the creation of a space in which bare life and the juridical rule enter into a threshold of indistinction" (Agamben 174). The portrait that Agamben presents of the character of "naked life" and its persistence and intensification into the twenty-first century is certainly a dire one, but one that makes imperative a reintroduction of a concept of social class, along the lines of the investigation charted in Amelio's film. Agamben's insights can serve as a justification of the need to preserve the concept of "class" albeit by re-conceptualizing it in terms of life rather than merely of labor.

In particular, the "new social subjects" of this world cannot be celebrated as a sign of the liberatory dimensions of postmodern "mobility." Nor can they be reduced to a position of constituting a faceless population, the unfortunate but inevitable victims

of the new monetary world order. They are not hyper-real, simulacra of a world completely mired in media. As *Lamerica*, itself a product of media, reveals, the "multitude" or the "people" are an austere reminder of their role in the production of value
through both their material and immaterial labor and of the imperative to examine the
conditions and terms of their exploitation, as these are manifested in concrete, bio-
political, trans-individual and transnational terms. The historical, economic, and ideological analysis of the role of the poor, the refugee, and the immigrant does not
require a return to the "totalizing" discourse of Marxist economism and its "grand
narrative" of class warfare, but an analysis of connections between economy and
sovereignty to appreciate the meaning and effects of the "mobility" of money, value,
and labor, as these reconfigure the character and the possibility for action of the
"mobile" subject.

In the 1950s, Hannah Arendt offered her critique of economistic notions of
production and consumption as life processes. Extending Arendt's observations,
Agamben indicates that, increasingly and in negative fashion, the equation between
productivity and consumption can be based on excluding those who are unproductive
along the lines articulated by Fiore in *Lamerica*. The ongoing effort to eliminate conceptions of social class can be understood as relying on a crude notion of wealth that
distinguishes between the rich and the poor on the hardly new grounds of fusing life
and labor by means of distinguishing productive and unproductive labor as the *sine
qua non* of the right to live. These are issues, I believe, that Amelio's film brings to
the fore in its treatment of the historical journey of the characters.

Lamerica offers no concrete "solutions," no answers to the questions it has posed,
but a range of significant questions about the status of history, nationalism, and citizenship, as they inflect the character and the fate of social subjects. What is clear is
that the film portrays historical, economic and political conditions that necessitate a
rethinking of the contemporary global character and implications of late capitalism.
The film does not revert to earlier forms of class analysis and to a nostalgia for the
past. In its form of storytelling that "puts everything into a trance," the film confronts
the intolerable and the impossible in contemporary cinema and politics.

Yet, *Lamerica* has, I believe, a large stake in cine-politics. It asks, more broadly, how
to understand the immigrant as a product of media but also as a reminder of the existence of differences that can fruitfully be considered under the rubric of social class.
Though it carefully undermines schematic and rigid class distinctions, the film invites
the spectator to examine the conditions of existing forms of exploitation in concrete,
bio-political, trans-individual and transnational terms. The film's reminders of a past in
danger of being forgotten and its treatment of the characters as somnambulists are
the film's instruments for creating a pedagogy, a form of creative storytelling, that
serves as a basis for re-conceptualizing social class and its connections to biopower.

Notes

1. For my comments on postmodernism I rely on such diverse sources as Lyotard, Jameson, Bertens and Natoli, Baudrillard, and Fukuyama.

Works Cited

Agamben, Giorgio. *Homo Sacer: Sovereign Power and Bare Life*. Trans. Daniel Heller- Roazen. Stanford, CA: Stanford UP, 1995.

Arendt, Hannah. *The Human Condition*. Chicago: U of Chicago P, 1998.

Balibar, Etienne. *Masses, Classes, Ideas: Studies on Politics and Philosophy after Marx*. New York: Routledge, 1994.

Baudrillard, Jean. *The Mirror of Production*. Trans. Mark Poster. St. Louis: Telos Press, 1981.

Bertens, Hans and Joseph Natoli, eds. *Postmodernism: The Key Figures*. Malden, Massachusetts: Blackwell, 2002.

Bondanella, Peter. *Italian Cinema*. New York: Continuum, 2001.

Cohan, Steve and Ina Rae Hark, eds. *The Road Movie Book*. London: Routledge, 1997.

Crowdus, Gary and Richard Porton. "Beyond Neorealism: Preserving a Cinema of Conscience, An Interview with Gianni Amelio." *Cineaste* XXI.4: 6-13.

Deleuze, Gilles. *Cinema 2: The Time-Image*. Trans. Hugh Tomlinson and Robert Galeta. Minneapolis: U of Minnesota P, 1989.

Foucault, Michel. *The History of Sexuality: An Introduction*. Vol. I. Trans. Robert Hurley. New York: Vintage Books, 1980.

Fukuyama, Francis. *The End of History and the Last Man*. New York: The Free Press, 1992.

Hardt, Michael and Antonio Negri. *Empire*. Cambridge, Mass: Harvard UP, 2000.

Iordanova, Dina. "Balkan Film Representation since 1989: The Quest for Admissibility."
Historical Journal of Film, Radio, and Television 18.2 (June 1998): 263-81.

Jameson, Fredric. *Postmodernism: Or the Cultural Logic of Late Capitalism*. Durham, North Carolina: Duke UP, 1991.

King, Russell. "Southern Europe in the Changing Map of Migration." *Eldorado or Fortress? Migration in Southern Europe*. Ed. Russell King, Gabriella Lazaridis, Charalambos Tsardanidis. London: MacMillan, 2000. 1-26.

Lazaridis, Gabriella and Iordanis Psimmenos. "Migrant Flows from Albania to Greece: Economic, Social, and Spatial Exclusion." *Eldorado or Fortress? Migration in Southern Europe*. Ed. Russell King, Gabriella Lazaridis, Charalambos Tsardanidis. London: Macmillan, 2000. 170-86.

Lyotard, Jean François. *The Postmodern Condition*. Trans. Geoff Bennington and Brian Massumi. Minneapolis: U of Minnesota P, 1984.

Negri, Antonio. *The Politics of Subversion: A Manifesto for the Twenty-First Century*. Trans. James Newell. London: Polity Press, 1989.

Pasolini, Pier Paolo. *Lutheran Letters*. Trans. Stuart Hood. Manchester: Carcanet Press, 1983.

Perlmutter, Ted. "The Politics of Proximity: The Italian Response to the Albanian Crisis." *International Migration Review* XXXII.1 (Spring 1998): 203-22.

Rodowick, David Norman. *Gilles Deleuze's Time Machine*. Durham: Duke UP, 1997.

Sciortino, Giuseppe. "Planning in the Dark: The Evolution of Italian Immigration Control." *Mechanisms of Immigration Control: A Comparative Analysis of European Regulation Policies*. Ed. Grete Brochmann and Tomas Hammar. Oxford: Berg, 1999. 233-61.

Metaphoring

Making a Niche of Negative Space	Mieke Bal

Introduction

The word *metaphor* means carrying something from one place to another, and it comes from the Greek word *meta* (which means *from one place to another*) and *pherein* (which means *to carry*), and it is used when you describe something by using a word for something that it isn't. This means that the word *metaphor* is a metaphor.

I think it should be called a lie because a pig is not like a day and people do not have skeletons in their cupboards. And when I try and make a picture of the phrase in my head it just confuses me because imagining an apple in someone's eye does-n't have anything to do with liking someone a lot and it makes you forget what the person was talking about. (Haddon 15)

This quotation comes from a novel whose narrator is an autistic fifteen-year-old boy. If the second paragraph displays a literalism that, at first sight, may seem inappropriate in a reflection on art, the first shows that the narrator is no fool. Hence I have no objection to taking him at his literalist word and taking up the challenge that that word poses: how to think metaphor in such a way that it escapes this indictment of the flight of fancy and, instead, can help a "carrying from one place to another" in meaningful, productive ways. *What* it carries over is meaning, but a meaning that includes the affective charges that all meaning-production entails. This charge, or affect, needs to be carried over from one particular situation to another so that it can reach, and have an impact on, the domain of political efficacy. Instead of the noun, metaphor, burdened as it is with a history of redundancy or falsehood (Haddon's narrator is not so far off the mark!), I will use the non-existent verb "to metaphor" to indicate this efficacy. I will explore this metaphoring from particular to particular, and with a carry-over of affect, in a work by contemporary Colombian sculptor Doris Salcedo (1958).

Salcedo's art performs research into the possibility for art to possess real cultural agency. I view such searching art as a *theoretical object*, or, as what Ernst van Alphen's book calls, following Hubert Damisch, "art that thinks."[1] In this essay

I probe a single aspect of such "thinking," philosophizing art, in an effort to locate the production of meaning that mediates, or translates, between the particularity that triggered the work and the effectivity that substantiates its claims. Between maker and receiver, something happens that cannot be of the order of under-standing only. For art to be politically effective – to have agency – the context from which it emerged, not necessarily knowable to the receiver, must, somehow, be "translated" into the context from within which the receiver might be sensitive to the work's urgency. This mediation takes place, I argue, through an activity that I call "metaphoring."

Negative Space

Sculpture works in space, and space is its primary medium. Generally speaking, Salcedo's sculptural work can be characterized by two negative modalities, modali-ties that subvert the traditions of the history of art, representation, and rhetoric of address. Both the subtle allusions to *anthropomorphism*, which stop short of becom-ing full-fledged figures or characters in, for example, her series of sculptures called *La Casa Viuda* from the early 1990s, and the extreme *slow-downs* that foreshorten

Figure 4   Doris Salcedo, *Atrabiliarios* [*Defiant*], 1991. Installation. Pulitzer Foundation for the Arts, St. Louis. DSA-92-SC-024. Photo: Robert Pettus. Alexander and Bonin, New York.

time, as in the *Unland* installation from the mid-1990s, appeal to, then refuse to col-lude with, those artistic strategies to which we have become so accustomed that they have lost their power to move. As a third strategy, Salcedo deploys metaphor as yet another form of negativity, and the semantic and narrative axis on which her sculp-tures negatively perform this engagement with metaphor is space. As with anthropo-morphism and representation, Salcedo's strategy is again used to perform negativity – that is, to refuse the traps of sentimentality, othering, and a location so specific that distancing becomes too easy. And, since space is her language, it is by means of a negative space that she achieves her effectivity.

In *Atrabiliarios (Defiant)* from 1991, a series of installations that precedes both the *La Casa Viuda* series and the *Unland* installation, shoes of disappeared people (mostly women and a few men) are buried in niches in the gallery wall, and are half hidden by animal skins roughly stitched to the wall. [Figures 4 , 5, and 6] The word "buried," of course, is chosen deliberately; it is a metaphor. There are no *literal* corpses, no burial sites, and no burial rituals being performed. We are still in the gallery, alone, facing the installation, left to our own devices, in our desire to come to

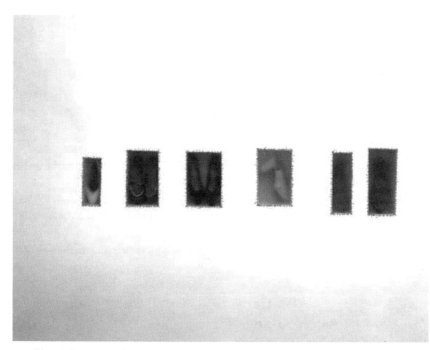

Figure 5   Doris Salcedo, *Atrabiliarios* [*Defiant*], 1991. Installation. Pulitzer Foundation for the Arts, St. Louis. DSA-92-SC-024. Photo: Robert Pettus. Alexander and Bonin, New York.

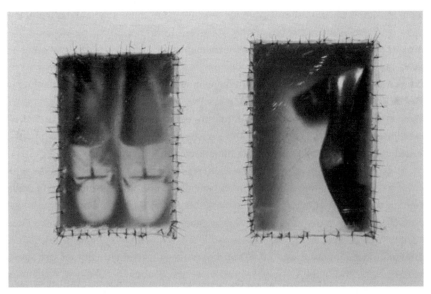

Figure 6   Doris Salcedo, *Atrabiliarios [Defiant]*, 1993. plywood, 3 shoes, animal fiber, and surgical thread. 12 ½ x 20 ¼ in 31.6 x 51.4 cm. Alexander and Bonin, New York.

terms with this work, respond to it, or even, simply, to see it. It is only by means of association that the niches recall those niches that harbor the ashes of the cremated dead, for example, in the wall of the San Michele cemetery in Venice. Hence, small as they are, they leave room for imagined, dead, human bodies. For, as distinct from the niches where urns are placed, here, in niches of the same dimensions, we actually do see a human body part, albeit in the negative – as in a photographic negative, bearing the literal, physical imprint of that body part negatively. The shape left by the disappeared foot is like a photographic negative taken literally.

Would it make sense to use the concept of metaphor here? Yes and no. Yes, because, as has been pointed out often enough, theories of metaphor cling to the referentiality of language. The very notion of metaphoricity, attached to the larger one of figurative language-use, or tropes, presupposes that its defining "other" is what is usually called "literal" or "proper" language. This clinging to referentiality may be problematic – and I will argue below, with Derrida and Deleuze, that it is – but it is not possible, as Salcedo suggests, to sever the tie between signs and reality entirely. For it is just as important to keep present, in this negative space, the absence of the foot and the body to which it was attached. Salcedo, I argue, takes issue with semiotic and linguistic theory by means of the problematic concept of metaphor; and absence, negative space, is her "argument." Thus, *Atrabiliarios* gives the lie to those who think that images cannot perform negation (Gombrich, Burke).

In the tradition of Aristotle's powerful theory on metaphor, this figure of meaning or trope tends to be construed as the transfer of meaning from one element, the evoked alien one, to another, the target element, which ordinary or literal language does not adequately describe. Various terminological pairs circulate, of which the clearest seem to be "tenor," for the element in need of description, and "vehicle," for the imported element called in to help aspects of the tenor that need illuminating. In my example, "burial" is the vehicle that helps us understand the mournful effect of the tenor, the shoes in the niches. The vehicle imports the element of death onto what could otherwise be seen, say, as a display of shoes (Richards).[2]

Indeed, this theory, like most theories on metaphor, is contingent on an overt or covert assumption of referentiality. The effectivity of a metaphor is measured through comparison with the referent. The vehicle of burial transfers the mood of mourning onto what would otherwise just be ordinary shoes. This metaphor works because the allegedly literal meaning would be inappropriate, it would miss the point entirely. The referent "shoes" does exist, they can be seen and pointed out. But, at the same time, to call these objects "shoes" would be to speak about a class of objects from which these shoes were taken, while repressing the difference between ordinary shoes and these shoes, which are laden with pastness and death. Referentiality may be the most perverse tool of repression.

Moreover, there is no coincidence between referentiality and either tenor or vehicle. The shoes are referential, but so is the death inherent in them. The distinction between "tenor" and "vehicle" is superposed on a presumed distinction between literal and figurative. This presupposes that such a distinction can be made in the first place. However, convincing arguments have been put forward that question the possibility of literal language, of which Derrida's "White Mythology" and Deleuze and Guattari's *A Thousand Plateaus* are doubtlessly the most influential. However, whereas Derrida's argument against the possibility of literal language moves towards a generalized metaphoricity, Deleuze and Guattari's thesis denies the usefulness of a concept of metaphoricity altogether.

Derrida's argument is based on the idea that language is itself already metaphorical. What seems literal is a metaphor whose metaphoricity has been forgotten. Such forgetting is the result of over-use. Nietzsche, who argued this in his essay "Über Wahrheit und Lüge im aussermoralischen Sinn" ("On Truth and Lie in a Nonmoral Sense"), compares expressions that appear literal with coins that have changed hands so often that the image and letters have disappeared. This view not only questions the distinction between literal and figurative, it also implies the need for constant innovation, and hence, paradoxically for opponents of metaphor, for the ongoing production of metaphors (Nietzsche).

For Deleuze and Guattari, speaking of metaphor already implies the representationalist view of language that they reject. Instead, they advocate the development and use of mobile concepts in order to allow language-use to be up to its task of designating, analyzing, performing and intervening in, not describing, the world. Concepts that appear metaphorical are simply imprecise. They need to be, since they designate things that are themselves not precise. As Deleuze says, this "anexactitude" is needed to "designate things exactly." These two philosophers and their followers struggle with the issue of metaphor because they resist a representational conception of language, even though no alternative is readily available (Derrida, Deleuze and Guattari, *A Thousand Plateaus*).[3]

I contend that metaphor can be reconceptualized within a non-representationalist, "performatist" view of language, and that such a conception is put forward in Salcedo's *Atrabiliarios*. Hers is a profoundly negative conception of metaphor, one that negates the distinctions on which the concept is based and, instead, proposes an activity of metaphoring. In order to grasp that position, it is useful first to go along with Richard's terminology, provided we assume that, in this theory, a hierarchy is not necessarily involved. Where two terms are somehow brought together, they interact with each other, whereby neither remains unaffected. It is only logical, then, that either term can serve the function of vehicle or tenor. Look at these niches, for example. The vehicle of burial, here, helps prevent misunderstandings that would virtually destroy the tenor if the latter were kept in quarantine from a metaphorical interpretation – for example, that these are shoe displays in a shoe store, as a critique of the capitalism that entices people to buy new clothes even if they don't need them. Clearly, this would be a misreading. Such a misreading can hardly be considered adequate, as some misreadings can, nor can it be taken to be the literal meaning. The capitalist use of shoes is not inherently more "literal," logical, or referential than Salcedo's use of mourning, memory, or art. The word "buried" has the merit of linking, interactively, the normal use of shoes, to which a violent end has been put, with the use to which Salcedo's work has put them. In this way it maintains the narrativity of violence's perversion.

But, so far, this discussion of the verb "buried" and its connotations has been a question of words, not of the artwork they are meant to designate. Hence metaphor is no less important than a possibly "literal" term. Nor is it decorative: "buried" does not add any aesthetic quality to the description. Nor is a literal interpretation adequate in itself. Moreover, as Derrida has pointed out, it is often impossible to make a distinction between literal and figurative metaphoric meaning. What other word could be used here, for example, that would avoid the connotations of "buried"? Inserted, dug, incrusted? None of these appear adequate, but, more importantly for the status of metaphor, they are also not more "literal."

The reason "buried" seems to be the most directly adequate term, even if, or perhaps because, it is clearly metaphorical, is because there is a need to implicate what is most obviously at stake in this work, but that eludes representation: death and its aftermath. Burial belongs to the realm of death. Yet to call this a metaphor would be to miss the point of the work. It is only possible to undergo the affect of this work, to relate to it, if one takes it, in a strong sense, literally. Only then does its political impact strike us as forcefully as it can, and should. Hence the work has, again, theoretical implications for the possibility of art to work politically. I contend not only that this work needs metaphor to work but, conversely, that it can only work through a recasting of metaphor. *Atrabiliarios* theorizes metaphor. It does so by recasting it in denial, so to speak. This denial is captured in my title, "negative space."

Metaphoring Negativity

As I argued earlier, metaphor, including the crux of *Atrabiliarios*'s effectivity, needs to be taken as a verb. In that neologism, it is a near-synonym of translation. Thus, "to metaphor" becomes an act that bridges. Like translation, metaphoring transfers something. This something is not meaning in a referential or representational sense, but a preoccupation that requires re-enactment in each event of occurrence. In the process, a gap is bridged at the expense of loss and with the reward of gain (Bal, *Travelling Concepts* 56-95).

But metaphor is not a mere synonym of translation. Unlike translation, its starting point is not a particular language but a situation that needs adequate expression. This situation is inherently "mobile" (Deleuze's favorite word for the dynamism at stake). This situation is particular. According to traditional conceptions of metaphor, this particular situation can be generalized. Salcedo's work holds this possibility in check, suspends it, probing it first. What are the traps? The violent death of a woman we do not know becomes exemplary for the violence that concerns us all. Or it can be essentialized as follows: the violence that is represented is a token of the shortcomings of human nature. Generalization, as this example suggests, easily misleads us into believing that states and situations are inevitable. This would be devastating for the possibility of political agency. Hence, in order to avoid the disabling abstraction that such generalization entails, a new particularity must be mobilized. This second particularity involves but does not equal the recipient of the metaphor. Through this second particularization, art can reach out across geographical distance, temporal separation, and from one individual to another. This second particularity prevents both the figurativity of the situation from being forgotten and forestalls essentializing truth claims.[4]

This second step requires agency and performance. Here the activity of the reader or viewer is indispensable. The relevance of Salcedo's work depends on its anchoring in very specific situations, an anchoring to which the stock phrase used to describe her work's thrust, "political violence in her native Colombia," even without the word "native," cannot begin to do justice. This is one forceful aspect of the shoes buried in the niches. At the same time, the work can only affectively "hit" the viewers who see it all over the world – I first saw it in Sydney, for example – and who have no access to the specific knowledge that informs the work, if it is able to "metaphor," transfer, convey, or translate this specificity without losing it.

One quite plausible, polemical intertext for this work is the well-known imagery of heaps of shoes in Nazi concentration camps. These heaps are devastating because they combine the particular idiosyncrasy of each shoe, evoking the individual who wore them, together with the de-humanizing massification of the gigantic heap. Against the backdrop of that monument to infernal violence, the niches in which the shoes are buried become shrines, homages to the individual whom violence attempted to de-individualize. In this respect, the care with which each shoe, or each combination of two shoes, has been arranged in its/their niche turns the latter into a protective home.

When considered as a translation from one particularity to another by means of the overcoming of generality, metaphor acts on a number of different levels. The metaphoricity involved is primarily negative. Moving from particularity to generality and on to the second particularity, the metaphors are denials of generalities that belong to the self-evidences by which we live. Depending on the viewer's individual baggage, any one of these metaphors can be the starting point, the first aspect one notices. I will discuss a few of these metaphors in random order and foreground their negativity, their force of denial.

First, the shoes are empty but worn: these shoes are emphatically *not* objects on display in shop windows. They are neither fashionable nor new. Hence they are not available for consumption, they are metaphors of a generalized non-availability. The niches support this metaphor. They embody a space that is not part of the gallery space, hence, that does not belong to the viewer's space. They recede beyond the gallery's wall. At the same time, by extending the gallery space, they also foreground the permeability of the latter for a world touched by art. But whereas shop windows entice their viewers to enter the shop, these niches are dead ends. There is no accessible space beyond them.

Second, the shoes are not readily available, even for visual consumption alone, for they are hard to see. The animal skin shields them from our gaze. Only a clouded vision is possible. Like consumerism, visibility is a general condition that sheds its self-evidence in this work. Covering these ordinary shoes with animal skin makes visibility a kind of "literal" meaning, which only seems literal because we have forgotten its metaphorical nature. Seeing is not a natural condition, these skins seem to say. It is an act that requires effort and that entails a transgression of some sort – an act that involves the viewer's body and being, an act for which one is responsible. From a generality, then, vision is "metaphored" into an utterly particular act for which visibility is the specific and variable condition.

Their limited visibility is, moreover, unequal. Here, a third negative metaphor comes in that again concerns the tension between generality and particularity. We cannot oversee the various constellations of shoes and build a story around them. Such a story would be a metaphorical recapturing of what we see. Narratives are particularizing versions of something that is either more general or differently particular.

This inequality of visibility posits a denial of narrative. Instead, the temporal unfold-ing that narrative implies takes place in the event of viewing itself. This event decom-poses into a series of events, because the uneven translucency of the skins not only changes the form of the shoes, but also delays the focus on them. Peering through the mist of perception, linearity is broken, and our restless eyes move randomly through the rows of niches, seeking visibility. Some shoes are immediately recognizable as shoes. Others have to be peered at in the niche for a while.

A fourth metaphor is produced at the level of the tension between surface and depth, a tension that produces overdetermined deadness. Here death shows its face in more ways than one. The niches extend into the deep recesses of the wall, whereas the skins, in contrast, close these recesses off with a rigorous boundary, like a shroud. Their surface negates the depth of the niches. Thus the skins embody yet another sense of negative space.

Because the skins are flush with the wall, the shoes look like old photographs. Ever since Roland Barthes' melancholy *Camera Lucida*, photographs have embodied our visual relationship with time passing and death. Old sepia-toned photographs foreground this relationship with temporal particularity. Old photographs show not only the past, but also a past long gone, rigorously cut off from life. This historicizing pastness easily becomes a sentimental consolation for suffered loss. Moreover, the objects on these images – not persons but shoes – turn them into still lives, still-born lives, or *natures mortes*, compounding the relationship with death through yet another layer of mortality. And, as if these three appearances of death – photography as such, old photographs, and dead objects in them – were not enough, the images shown have scars, ragged seams on which surgical violence has been performed. Thus, they look like corpses cut open and sewn shut again in a violent autopsy.

This fourth metaphor of death is particularly powerful in its quality of denial. Through its overdetermined insistence on death, it contradicts the temptation of redemption. To be sure, death is a transcendental generality, the most general of all events. Yet here death is particularized as violent. Traveling back from the surgical thread, which denotes violence performed on one who is already the victim of vio-lence, the sight that emerges for the viewer, even in the viewer's body, is an *image*. Salcedo, the sculptor, here mobilizes Salcedo, the painter, the producer of surfaces that matter. Images are representations. In the face of theories of metaphor that shun representationalist conceptions of language and, by extension, all cultural pro-ductions of meaning, the collocation of death and the image powerfully imposes an awareness of the violence of representation.

Indeed, to look at images is to accept that even violence can be represented, recast on a flat image for contemplative consumption. The metaphor moves from the particular surface we see – each piece of skin with its unequal translucency – to the resistant depth, bouncing the eye back to the surface. Once steeped in the violent death that creeps up on us through the means I have indicated, the viewer's agency and the act of looking it produces can no longer shed the sense of collusion. This is how the metaphor's negativity operates to deny the redemptive quality of art.

In these four different ways, *Atrabiliarios* metaphors negation. The polemical thrust of the work I have foregrounded here is necessary as an operation of clearance. It clears the confrontation between the work and the viewer of four fundamental operations that are so deeply ingrained in contemporary culture that removing them, stripping them of their self-evidence, is an act of violence in itself. It seems violent, indeed, to deprive viewers of what they consider most naturally theirs. This takes force. The force required resides in the intimate embrace of the metaphors, for they do not operate in isolation.

They are, instead, paired together. Two pairs of *dispositifs* have been undermined, if not altogether neutralized – which is impossible. In the first pair, the availability of goods, as in globalized capitalism, is made to appear unnatural, as is the availability of sight. Together these forms of availability constitute the fundamental conditions of art: as commodity and as visual experience. In the second pair, narrative has been turned from a passively consumed logic into an active performance, and from events happening to others into a self-inflicted struggle to see. But narrative is also a form of life that ends in death. Hence the second metaphor of this pair, death inflicted by the image, counters the unfolding of narrative with a death already in place, mute, and still. Noticing, respectively, the surgical thread of post-mortem violence, the still-ing effect of turning life into image, and the doubly deadening effect of old photographs, the viewer traverses an anachronistic narrative that could, just possibly, offer a glimpse of life in the form of agency. How can metaphor, as the indirect imposition of particularity "beyond" the generalization that must draw the art from its entrenched particularity in its own "context," fulfill the task of activating viewers into a potential political position, in ways specific to its operations?

Metaphor as Nagging

In literary theory, such a view of metaphor is not at all new. Jonathan Culler ends his analysis of metaphor with a plea for a reception-oriented conception of that trope. Rather than designating it a property either of language or of speech, he writes that metaphor is "a description of certain interpretive operations performed by readers when confronted by a textual incongruity, such as the assertion of a patently false identity" (Culler 232).[5]

While we have seen that the attempt to make a distinction between metaphorical and literal meaning leads either to a generalization or a refusal of metaphor, another distinction falls victim to the attempt to distinguish, within the domain of rhetoric, the one trope (that of metaphor) from the other (metonymy) (De Man 220). De Man associates metaphor with necessity, or essence, and metonymy with chance, while substituting the chance associations of *words* for the spatial association in the *world*.

Gérard Genette before him had declared metonymy to be at the heart of metaphor. For the latter, metaphors are motivated by semantic or even referential relations between the particular tenor (a specific church tower, for example) and the vehicle this tenor attracts (the cornfields surrounding the tower call into being the metaphor of ears of corn to describe the surface structure of the tower's roof) (Genette).

Word or sign versus world? Surely this difference would be unacceptable to art that works precisely in order to make the former an active intervention in the latter. When looking at *Atrabiliarios*, whether from afar and seeing only abstract forms, or from close by and noticing the figurativity of the shoes, it takes a while to notice that they are *worn* shoes. Hence the first negative metaphor (they are not commodities) and the second (they are not easily visually available) work together to empty the viewer of her ordinary interpretive stock of metaphors. This emptying is necessary to make new meanings available. As a preparation for interpretative performance, it corresponds with, and comments on, the need for innovation implied in Nietzsche's metaphor of used coins.

The near-invisibility of the blurred image is, however, not negative in itself. It only works by means of negativity. Instead of precluding vision, in the end it sharpens it, activating the viewer to take the risk of looking. The viewer is compelled to come dangerously close; dangerous in view of the taboo on touching art and dangerous because of the shock that approaching holds in store for the viewer. Accustomed to being, primarily, curious and eager to see, in the aesthetic sense, the viewer visiting an art gallery is enticed to come closer. As with the furniture, especially and most forcefully the tables of *Unland*, if you refrain from approaching, you don't get to see anything, whereas you came to see art.

And art is what you see: beautiful forms, unreadable shapes. Until, that is, you overcome the usual passivity of viewing – its consumerism as if before a shop window – to peer in, performing the act of looking instead of being offered a sight. Then the shock hits you. A shock bound up with the impossibility of separating metaphor from literality. A theory of metaphor is enacted at this point, through the interaction between viewer and work. This theory stipulates that the issue at stake in metaphor is not the distinction between metaphorical and literal signification but the ongoing struggle to mediate between general and particular. To make this point, this moment of the viewer's shock in seeing *Atrabiliarios* skips the indirection often attributed to metaphor. Behind the abstract sheets of animal skin, with their own variation of thick and thin that draws forms on the skin, abstraction suddenly yields to a most concrete, hyper-figurative shape.

But metaphor keeps nagging: there is no opportunity to revert to literal meaning or referentiality, nor to keep those at bay. This is not exactly a metaphor, however; it is more the experience of metaphor's primacy, its "literalness." But again, albeit in a different way, representation is insinuated between abstraction and reality, yet almost skipped. Moreover, generality – shoes as tokens of a type – yields to extreme particularity: the uniquely individual worn shoe still containing the trace and shape of the foot no longer able to walk in it. There is no transition between abstraction and an increasing clarity of figuration. From abstraction, one is thrown into reality, without the cushioning of softening figurative representation.

A worn shoe buried like an urn cemented into a wall but nevertheless visible, although with difficulty, confronts you with death and your own immodesty. I wish to foreground the workings of the anthropomorphic imagination as a tool *for*, or *as*, political art.[6] *Before* getting close enough – mind the temporal gap! – the viewer only sees beautiful, enticing suggestions of form, but that form is not at all anthropomorphic. It remains "safely" abstract. Abstraction seems a condition for the tranquil enjoyment of beauty as an escape from politics. *After* the approach, in contrast, the viewer is beyond the divide that separates art from life, or word from world.

A worn shoe, with traces of sweat and dirt, of corns and the distortions of bones that come with aging and labor, of the idiosyncrasies of toes and bones of a particular individual whom we have never met and never will because she is dead or otherwise disappeared – is that art? It is, and more than that: *only* that, or something that operates in that way, can be art, says this work – but only thanks to the fact that it is *not* a representation. Like the furniture, these shoes are real, but they are art to the extent that they are traces. As such, they establish a sharply painful indexical connection between the former live body of the wearer and the actually live presence of the viewer, now standing, in shoes, in front of these niches. They also hover between invisibility and over-visibility, between abstraction and overly precise figuration, toppling over from representation into simulacrum. But even though there are no "original" shapes of shoes and every single shoe is as banal as any copy of a copy, they are, at the same time, hyper-real, transcending their reality and particularity by means of their hyper-particularity, which bridges the gap between the former wearer, whose staying power is in the trace, and us, who are in charge of perpetuating that staying power. But *because* we are not allowed to know who that individual is, we "bring her along" into the general. This ongoing dialectic between particular and general cannot accommodate a universalism as its endpoint. Instead, this "bringing along" of the particular into the general, which preserves the traces of the particular that enriches the general, and transfers back to the particular the generality of the political domain where violence must be dealt with, is a form of metaphor, as in a stubbornly literal sense of *translation*.

The Act of Metaphoring

Metaphoring as an engagement and dialogue between particular and general happenings – here, of violence – stands for the possibility for art to act. This possibility is important, because the fast pace of today's world does not allow for procrastination or discouragement, both of which lead to indifference. In the face of disaster, violence, and terror, in the presence of the war that Etienne Balibar has analyzed as enduring, hence as *in the present*, Salcedo's metaphoring beyond the distinctions between referential and semiotic, literal and figurative, or world and word shows that art is a worthy – no, indispensable – contribution to the collective efforts toward making societies livable.

Whenever we use the word "political," as distinct from the affiliated yet opposed notion of "ethics" with which it is often confused in the humanities, we are necessarily framing whatever this word qualifies in a specific time and place. If the domain of the ethical is or aspires to be universal, the political is particular. Hence the question I see Salcedo grappling with is that of political art today: is such art possible? Is it relevant? How can it achieve something? Because of the very nature of the political as always occurring within specific situations, times, and places, not to speak of the nature of art itself, this question cannot be answered in any generalizing sense, at least, no generalizing view of artistic agency will suffice. What particularity is involved, then, and how can metaphoring encompass it? [7]

Central to Salcedo's work is *extreme violence, disturbed (inter)subjectivity*, and *displacement*. I am trying to show the inextricable intertwinement of these issues by establishing connections between them, by means of these seemingly simple, straightforward – "literal" – shoes. But there is a further reason for the relevance of Salcedo's work. Violence, subjective "deviance," and displacement are of all times, yet they have taken on a global status since "the war" in our present began.[8] The current state of the world-at-large is one of *war*. Hence if the qualifier "political" in the phrase "political art" means anything, violence is likely to be within its orbit. In different ways, something similar can be said of the other issues, of subjective deviance and displacement.

In Salcedo's *Atrabiliarios*, the motif of shoes receives yet another meaning. Shoes are for walking, the simplest, most elementary means of travel. But the owners, the inhabitants of these shoes, walked under coercion. Displacement is an inherent facet of violence. In terms of *place*, the current state of the world is paradoxical. It is clear that the present-day manifestations of violence, in particular, are no longer contained, although many try hard to make us believe they are limited to the Middle East. The attacks on New York and Washington, D.C. in 2001 demonstrate the impossibility of containing violence. On the other hand, although violence is of all times and all places, the universalization of violence puts it out of reach and facilitates the kind of intellectual laziness that condones indifference. More importantly for my argument, this violence, pervasive as it is, takes on different particularities in different places. My argument is that, instead of numbing us, insight into the "globalization" of violence can reactivate us to look around at other places where violence is the order of the day, and help us to better understand its "differences within" and to militate against the generalizations that make its victims invisible and forgotten. This is one of the knots that exist between violence, subjectivity, and displacement.

Indeed, the three issues are inherent in each other. Their articulation is a task of translating where no "original" exists. Translation, therefore, is at the heart of this paper, its major critical tool, perhaps even its utopian goal, but it needs acts of metaphoring in order to be meaningfully performed. Instead of universalizing violence, therefore, I argue that the violence of one place can and must be metaphored into that of another. This necessity informs my choice for the art I am alleging here.

In an essay on the predicament, in anthropology, of the compulsion and impossibility of defining "culture," Johannes Fabian offers a convincing plea for a rigorously negative (non)definition of this concept. He contends that it is helpful to invoke confrontation and negotiation as the moments during which "the cultural" emerges. This formulation both avoids positive, reifying definitions that are inherently "othering" and foregrounds process as the domain of culture. Thus it involves temporality, agency, and plurality, without falling into the traps of self-congratulatory celebrations of multiplicity and freedom, of idealizations of the possibility of democracy, and of the insidious imposition of particular values as universal (Fabian).

Along similar lines, I would like to learn, from Salcedo's *Atrabiliarios*, how to grasp the idea of political art – without imprisoning it in positivity and reification. Indeed, the phrase "political art" traditionally possesses a number of meanings that we can now discard or bracket. First, obviously, political art is not overtly and explicitly *about* politics. Such a thematic concentration would dis-empower art, which may be more effective for not being explicit. Second, the phrase cannot mean state-sponsored and/or -censored art. In fact, I tend to try to steer away from the sensitive issue of censorship that this conception entails. This tradition, which, in the West, has its starting point in Plato's *Republic*, limits the notion of political art to art that either resists or supports "official" politics. This perspective unwarrantedly makes invisible the infractions of politics on people's private lives. It would thus defeat the purpose of Salcedo's art, since this work insists on how the breakdown of the distinction between public and private is, in fact, an imposing feature of war. Hence, rethinking reasons to protect that distinction may well be the most poignant area for an inquiry into political art. In an unfortunate misunderstanding of the phrase, the "conceptual overview" article in the recent *Encyclopedia of Aesthetics* bases its conceptualization of the issues of political art on just such a simplistic relationship between art and politics. In such cases, art and politics remain two separate domains that are more or less incidentally connected. The obsoleteness of that binary – of support versus critique – is one of the reasons we need, I think, to rethink political art (Stopford).

Third, we cannot see political art as punctual protest, as a singular political statement presented within the framework of the art world. For such art is not political *qua* art, it just happens to have a political meaning. Its limited range may well hinder, rather than help, our understanding of how art can act politically. Such art may be effective, as effective as protest marches, parliamentary lobbying, or actual warfare, but if so, it is not effective *qua* art.

These three senses in which the phrase "political art" functions have in common that they suggest, as their alternative, a universal, and universally valuable, kind of art that protects itself from political "contagion." This art is pure, ethereal, and aesthetic only; what Adorno disparagingly calls "the work [of art] that wants nothing but to exist." It advocates forgetting that, as the philosopher added, this fetishization of aesthetics is "an apolitical stance that is in fact highly political" ("Commitment" 240).[9]

There are three other meanings of political art, however, that are more difficult to discard, because they are not caught up in this false binary of political versus aesthetic. These meanings emerge from another opposition, that between art and life rather than between aesthetics and politics. They emerged from post-Holocaust philosophy and have in common a delicacy, a modesty, a need to draw limits around the tragedy of "real life" so that victims are not re-victimized. Salcedo's art must be situated in relation to these concerns. They are inevitably bound up with the name of Adorno, who wrote these thoughts not only in the aftermath of the Holocaust but also under the sway of its cultural trauma. To bring this essay as close as possible to the relationship between art and what could be called "the cultural politics of horror," then, I wish to situate Salcedo's deployment of metaphor in relation to the concerns Adorno expressed but was not quite able to resolve.

The first of these meanings is the kind of aestheticizing or, as Adorno would say, stylizing, of real-world politics, including – especially, I would add – violence. It is, in my view, the fourth meaning of political art that needs to be suspended in this little exercise in negativity: art that represents events or effects of violence. Representation is here perceived as turning violence – events, victims, consequences – into something that can be perceived as "art" rather than as documentation, journalism, or critical writing. This is fundamentally the problem of representation, a cultural form of expression whose problems have been examined in great detail by cultural analysts since the 1970s. But Adorno offers alternatives that I also propose to bracket. Political art made under the banner of representation would either refuse art itself, limiting itself to documentary commemorialization, or refuse the representation (of violence).

This does not mean that representation in all its guises must be tabooed, as Adorno's initial statement has often been taken to mean. By definition, representation stylizes. I submit that it does not, however, necessarily stylize violence away. The mode of representation can be such that it works to "undercode" the violence it is addressing. I contend that Salcedo has been exploring artistic languages that enable her to do neither of these two things. Instead, she undercodes the violence so that its presence in the resulting work, which is partly representational and partly anti-representational, is all the more tenacious and acute. Her tool is that of metaphoring between the particular and the general.[10]

In its various formulations, Adorno's objection remains as paradoxical as it is valid. He argued that turning horror into beauty, far from being a civilized thing, is, indeed, barbaric. Allegedly, art would destroy the civilized world, or at least be in collusion with that destruction, because it makes the violence palatable, even risks making it pleasurable. The effect is the total obliteration of the violence. For there is no more radical way of erasing violence or, to anticipate a later concept, of "translating" it, than to make something appealing out of it, thus mitigating it, giving it beauty, and, unwittingly, redeeming it.

Adorno's indictment of art "after Auschwitz" – to cite the title of one of the later essays in which he discussed this – has been extensively alleged in Holocaust studies, often to advocate documentation as the only "proper" way of representing the Holocaust (1973).[11] Its influence has been such that it is worth revisiting today. The original statement appears in the context of a rather savagely critical examination of what was to become cultural studies: the progressive, critical study of culture. One of the typical, enigmatic, dialectical paradoxes he refers to in the essay "Cultural Criticism and Society" where the indictment first appeared, is something that cultural studies has taken to heart insufficiently: "such [cultural] criticism is ideology as long as it remains mere criticism of ideology" ("Cultural Criticism and Society" 153). The reason for this severe judgment becomes clear in a later formulation, which states that the problem appears to lie with the definition of culture underlying this critique of ideology. Hence, Adorno prefigures Fabian's negative and dynamic concept of emerging culture: "Such critical consciousness remains subservient to culture insofar as its concern with culture distracts from the true horrors" ("Cultural Criticism and Society" 155). This "distraction" is what Salcedo's acts of metaphoring attempt to overcome. In line with these attempts, which I have characterized above as attempts at translation between the particular and the general, Adorno writes:

the task of criticism must be not so much to search for the particular interest groups to which cultural phenomena are to be assigned, as to decipher the general social tendencies that are expressed in these phenomena and through which the most powerful interests realize themselves. ("Cultural Criticism and Society" 158)

This task has been ill understood and snowed under by a US-style identity politics of which we have only recently become weary. And although some of Adorno's statements in "Cultural Criticism and Society" suggest that self-reflection is urgently necessary, he equally relentlessly points out the limitations of that activity: "Even the most radical reflection of the mind on its own failure is limited by the fact that it is only reflection, without altering the existence to which *its failure bears witness*" ("Cultural Criticism and Society" 160; emphasis added). It is within this last phrase that resides the continuing relevance of Adorno's thoughts on post-Holocaust art for cultural reflection. Is it possible, Salcedo's shoes appear to ask, to deploy art not only as reflection, but also as a form of witnessing that does alter the existence of what it witnesses?

It is at the end of this in-depth commentary on radical cultural critique that Adorno's famous indictment of poetry after Auschwitz first appears. In protest against the frequent isolation of this sentence, I quote the preceding and the following one as well, so as to foreground the fact that Adorno's addressee is the cultural critic, whether an academic or not:

Cultural criticism finds itself faced with the final stage of the dialectic of culture and barbarism. To write poetry after Auschwitz is barbaric. And this corrodes even the knowledge of why it has become impossible to write poetry today. ("Cultural Criticism and Society" 162)

Adorno wrote this in 1949. I don't think we are finished addressing this statement yet. Especially if we see it in light of an even earlier, remarkable piece, "Out of the Firing Line," written in the Fall of 1944.

In that short text Adorno describes, in one devastating sweep, the permanent state of war that the world is in and which we are only now beginning to notice; the role of the media in obliterating this state; and the financial interests of global proportions that sustain that war and even make it indispensable. *Atrabiliarios* deploys different ways of engaging these same issues. It is no more able to come up with a non-contradictory answer than Adorno is. But it does, at least, attempt to address the situation on its own, real terms, by profiting from the fact that art, too, is a medium.

Conclusion: Metaphor as Skin

In later writings, Adorno alleges three slightly different reasons for his aversion, each entailing an implicit or explicit alternative. In one of his most famous formulations, from *Negative Dialectics*, his negative judgment concerns his fear that art may suggest some sense where the horror did not and cannot make sense:

After Auschwitz, our feelings resist any claim of the positivity of existence as sanctimonious, as wronging the victims; they balk at squeezing any kind of sense, however bleached, out of the victims' fate. ("After Auschwitz" 361)

It is worth noting that in terms of Adorno's conception of negative dialectics, the word "positivity" already points to a near-total ban on representation, at least representation with a claim to "matching" its object. Stylized representation makes matters worse because it diminishes the suffering while rendering its representation enjoyable. "Sense," as Adorno uses the word here, would emerge from stylizing representation. Stylizing, then, entails cutting off affect from meaning.

In a later essay, devoted to what he calls "committed art," and in which he again primarily discusses literature, the issue is not *sense*, as in entry into acceptance or even redemption, but, plainly and disturbingly, *pleasure*:

The so-called artistic rendering of the naked physical pain of those who were beaten down with rifle butts contains, however distantly, the possibility that pleasure can be squeezed out from it. ("Commitment" 252)

That same verb, "squeezed," betokens the violent relationship between art and horror, whether sense or beauty is the blood squeezed out of the victims. The danger, here, to put it bluntly, is akin to the effect of pornography. Needless to say, any art that risks exposing its viewers to this effect would not even begin to qualify for the status of political art as I am trying to articulate the concept here.

On the other hand, though, in both "After Auschwitz" and "Commitment," Adorno qualified his indictment almost immediately. The result is the fifth meaning of political art that I wish to bracket. This meaning is related to expressionism, to making the voice of the victims audible so that they can speak out and be heard. This possibility made Adorno nuance his forbidding original formulation, albeit only to displace the burden from the poet onto the survivor, and from the ethical domain onto the psychological. This shift not only gave his essay the status of a politico-aesthetic guideline, but also showed his deep understanding of trauma.

The following excerpt, from which the title of the recent Adorno volume was derived, contains a formulation that suggests an intimate bond between the two domains of ethics and psychology:

Perennial suffering has as much right to expression as a tortured man has to scream; hence it may have been wrong to say that after Auschwitz you could no longer write poems. But it is not wrong to raise the less cultured question whether after Auschwitz you can go on living – especially whether one who escaped by accident, one who by rights should have been killed, may go on living. His mere survival calls for the coldness, the basic principle of bourgeois subjectivity, without which there could have been no Auschwitz; this is the drastic guilt of him who was spared. By way of atonement he will be plagued by dreams such as that he is no longer living at all, that he was sent to the ovens in 1944 and his whole existence since has been imaginary, an emanation of the insane wish of a man killed twenty years earlier. ("After Auschwitz" 362–63)

In view of the painful state of the survivor described in the major part of this excerpt, the first part almost passes unnoticed in its particular aesthetic. To summarize the issue rather succinctly: art as "scream," as expression, is both legitimate and, Adorno says, necessary. In light of my discussion on political art in this essay, let me say that this expressionist aesthetic serves a political purpose (which may be utterly necessary), but not, by definition, an artistic one. The two can go together, but that again, to put it strongly polemically, is a more or less fortuitous coincidence. The reason for this is that the expressionist view leaves open what art can *do* that documentation, journalism, and critical writing cannot. More importantly, it also remains caught up in a primary particularity that is confining and in tension with the need for art to mobilize translation. This second reason is related to the first, so that it makes the question of "high" art versus (?) other domains of culture a moot one, even though this question appears to be embedded within the first reason.

Finally, the kind of art from which *Atrabiliarios* seems most at pains to distinguish itself as political art is the utterly particularizing, "sympathizing," sentimentalizing art that induces commiseration. Compassion, without an identification that is both specific *and* heteropathic, leads us to an emotional realm where the fear of violence can be made object-less and where it can be turned into a vague thrill of feel-good sentimentality about violence. Hence, between our gaze and the trace of life wrenched out of the victims, yet visible in the shoes that remain, a layer of translucent skin distorts and discolors the hyper-visible particularity. It is that layer, and the stitches that bind it to the negative space of the niches, that embodies the severance as well as the connection between the particular and the general, through our own particular experience of violence witnessed or undergone; different, but capable of being mobilized, without merciful sentiment. That sheet of skin allows for the connection, up to a point. Like the two sides of a sheet of paper – Saussure's metaphor for the connection and severance between signifier and signified – the sheet of skin is a metaphor of metaphor: translucent, impermeable, imprisoning the eye caught in distortion, in a negative space where indifference is not possible. "People do not have skeletons in their cupboards" said the narrator of Haddon's novel. But they do have skins that hurt, and eyes that see.

Notes

1. Van Alphen, *Art in Mind*. I have written on this issue in *Quoting Caravaggio*.

2. For a lucid survey of theories of metaphor, see Culler.

3. The quotation is from Deleuze and Parnet (*Dialogues* 3), quoted by Paul Patton in "Mobile Concepts" in the present volume.

4. The need to bind metaphor to truth claims is the hornet's nest in Donald Davidson's theory of metaphor, from 1978 to 2001.

5. Culler wrote this before either Derrida or Deleuze and Guattari had achieved their influence on thinking about metaphor.

6. With the term "anthropomorphic imagination" I refer to a range of strategies in literature and the visual arts where "thinking through the body" (Gallop) is the primary rhetoric. The most obvious instances are the human figure in art and the character in literature, but also, in humanistic scholarship, the "hand" of the artists, the "voice" of the narrator, and any interpretation of texts in terms of the unconscious or the psyche.

7. In the 1980s and '90s, when "politically correct" was still a positive term (as reflected in the attempts to implement identity politics, and, most importantly perhaps, a specific kind of reading), large contingents of the humanities were involved in political thought. In the mid-1990s, the key term suddenly became "ethical."

This alternative came from those who most opposed the political turn, yet it was endorsed by formerly politically-inclined scholars, probably in an attempt at reconciliation following the "culture wars." I wish to argue that this replacement is problematic and, at the present time, no longer tenable.

8. To give the current war against various Arabic and Asian countries a somewhat arbitrary start, I follow Etienne Balibar, who proposes the date of 1992 (the Gulf War) as the beginning and assigns no end date at all. The name of the war has changed from Gulf War to "War on Terrorism," and it encompasses the war against Afghanistan that began in 2002 and is still continuing, as well as the war against Iraq, begun in March-April 2003.

9. All further quotes from Adorno are taken from the recent collection of his writings related to his initial indictment of "poetry after Auschwitz" (*Can One Live After Auschwitz?*), on which more below. This publication will hopefully make an end to the indirect and decontextualized, often untraceable, citations of Adorno's position that have savaged critical theory for the last decade.

10. For the notion of undercoding, see Eco.

11. Strangely, this essay, "After Auschwitz," is not included in the 2003 volume. For a lucid discussion of the two implications of Adorno's initial position (the ethical and the semiotic inadequacy of art after the Holocaust), see Van Alphen *Caught by History*.

Works Cited

Adorno, Theodor W. "After Auschwitz." *Negative Dialectics*. Trans. E.B. Ashton. London: Routledge and Kegan Paul, 1973. 361-65.

—. *Can One Live After Auschwitz? A Philosophical Reader*. Trans. Rodney Livingstone et al. Ed. Rolf Tiedemann. Stanford: Stanford UP, 2003.

—. "Commitment." *Can One Live After Auschwitz? A Philosophical Reader*. Trans.

Rodney Livingstone et al. Ed. Rolf Tiedemann. Stanford: Stanford UP, 2003. 240-58.

—. "Cultural Criticism and Society." *Can One Live After Auschwitz? A Philosophical Reader*. Trans. Rodney Livingstone et al. Ed. Rolf Tiedemann. Stanford: Stanford UP, 2003. 146-62.

—. "Out of the Firing Line." *Can One Live After Auschwitz? A Philosophical Reader*. Trans. Rodney

Livingstone et al. Ed. Rolf Tiedemann. Stanford: Stanford UP, 2003. 44-47.

Alphen, Ernst van. *Caught by History: Holocaust Effects in Contemporary Art, Literature, and Theory*. Stanford: Stanford UP, 1997.

—. *Art in Mind: How Images Shape Contemporary Thought*. Chicago: U of Chicago P, 2005.

Bal, Mieke. *Quoting Caravaggio: Contemporary Art, Preposterous History*. Chicago: U of Chicago P, 1999.

—. *Travelling Concepts in the Humanities: A Rough Guide*. Toronto: U of Toronto P, 2002.

Balibar, Etienne. "What is a War?" Lecture. School of Criticism and Theory. Cornell University. 23 June 2003.

Barthes, Roland. *Camera Lucida: Reflections on Photography*. Trans. Richard Howard. London: Vintage, 1993.

Burke, Kenneth. *Language as Symbol*. Berkeley: U of California P, 1968.

Culler, Jonathan. "The Turns of Metaphor." 1981. *The Pursuit of Signs: Semiotics, Literature Deconstruction*. New York: Routledge, 2001. 209-33.

Davidson, Donald. "What Metaphors Mean." *Critical Inquiry* 5.1 (1978): 31-47.

—. *Inquiries into Truth and Interpretation*. Oxford: Oxford UP, 2001.

Deleuze, Gilles, and Felix Guattari. *A Thousand Plateaus: Capitalism and Schizophrenia*. Vol. 2. Trans. Brian Massumi. London: Athlone Press, 1988.

Deleuze, Gilles, and Catherine Parnet. *Dialogues*. Trans. Hugh Tomlinson and Barbara Habberjam. London: Athlone Press, 1987.

De Man, Paul. *Allegories of Reading*. New Haven: Yale UP, 1979.

Derrida, Jacques. "White Mythology." *New Literary History* 6 (1974): 5-74.

Eco, Umberto. *A Theory of Semiotics*. Bloomington: Indiana UP, 1976.

Fabian, Johannes. *Anthropology with an Attitude: Critical Essays*. Stanford: Stanford UP, 2001.

Gallop, Jane. *Thinking Through the Body*. New York: Columbia UP, 1988.

Genette, Gérard. "Métonymie chez Proust." *Figures III*. Paris: Editions du Seuil, 1972. 41-66.

(English: *Figures*. Vols. 1-3. English Selections. Trans. Alan Sheridan. New York: Columbia UP, 1982).

Gombrich, E.M. "Review of Charles Morris, Signs, Language and Behavior." *Art Bulletin* 31 (1949): 68-73.

Haddon, Mark. *The Curious Incident of the Dog in the Night-Time*. New York: Doubleday, 2002.

Nietzsche, Friedrich. "On Truth and Lie in a Nonmoral Sense." 1873. *Philosophy and Truth: Selections from Nietzsche's Notebooks of the Early 1870's*. Ed. and Trans. Daniel Breazeale. Atlantic Highlands, NJ: Humanities Press, 1979. 77-97.

Patton, Paul. "Mobile Concepts, Metaphor and the Problem of Referentiality in Deleuze and Guattari." *Metaphoricity and the Politics of Mobility*. Ed. Maria Margaroni and Effie Yiannopoulou. Amsterdam and New York: Rodopi Press, 2006. 31-56.

Richards, Ivor A. *The Philosophy of Rhetoric*. Oxford: Oxford UP, 1936.

Stopford, John. "Culture and Political Theory." *Encyclopedia of Aesthetics, Vol. 4*. Editor-in-chief Michael Kelly. 4 vols. New York/Oxford: Oxford UP, 1998. 16-19.

List of Figures

Contributors

Mieke Bal, a well-known cultural critic and theorist, is Professor of the Theory of Literature in the Faculty of Humanities at the University of Amsterdam. Her most recent book is *Travelling Concepts in the Humanities: A Rough Guide* (University of Toronto Press, 2002). *A Mieke Bal Reader* is forthcoming from the University of Chicago Press. She is also a video artist.

Tim Cresswell is Professor of Social and Cultural Geography at the University of Wales, Aberystwyth. He is the author of *The Tramp in America* (Reaktion, 2001) and *Place: A Short Introduction* (Blackwell, 2004). He is also co-editor of *Engaging Film: Geographies of Mobility and Identity* (Rowman and Littlefield, 2002) and *Mobilizing Place, Placing Mobility* (Rodopi, 2002). He is currently finishing a book on the politics of mobility.

Stuart Elden is a reader in political geography and the Academic Director of the International Boundary Research Unit at the University of Durham. He is the author of *Mapping the Present: Heidegger, Foucault and the Project of a Spatial History* (Continuum, 2001), *Understanding Henri Lefebvre: Theory and the Possible* (Continuum, 2004), and *Speaking Against Number: Heidegger, Language and the Politics of Calculation* (Edinburgh University Press, 2006). He is currently working on a history of the concept of territory.

Gareth Hoskins graduated in Geography at the University of Wales, Aberystwyth in 2000. After a year as a visiting research graduate based at the University of California, Berkeley, he returned to complete a Ph.D. on the ways in which the exclusion of Chinese immigrants from America is being remembered at Angel Island Immigration Station, San Francisco. Gareth is currently a lecturer in human geography and teaches in the sub-fields of cultural, historical and urban geography.

Marcia Landy is Distinguished Service Professor in English/Film Studies with Secondary Appointment in the French and Italian Department at the University of Pittsburgh. Her recent books include *Italian Film* (Cambridge, 2000), *The Historical Film: History and Memory in Media* (Rutgers, 2000) and *Monty Python's Flying Circus* (Wayne State, 2005). Her essays have appeared in *Screen*, *Cinema Journal*, *boundary 2*, and *Critical Quarterly*.

Maria Margaroni is Associate Professor in Literary and Cultural Theory at the University of Cyprus. She is co-author (with John Lechte) of *Julia Kristeva: Live Theory* (Continuum, 2004). Her essays have appeared in *Modern Drama*, *European Journal of English Studies (EJES)*, *Camera Obscura*, *Hypatia*, *Parallax* and *Philosophy Today*.

Nikos Papastergiadis is Associate Professor and Reader at the Australian Center, University of Melbourne. His major publications include, *Modernity as Exile* (1992), *Dialogues in the Diaspora* (1998), *The Turbulence of Migration* (2000), *Complex Entanglements* (2003), *Metaphor and Tension* (2004). In 2005 he was the Willy Brandt Guest Professor at the University of Sweden.

Paul Patton is Professor of Philosophy at the University of New South Wales, Sydney, Australia. He translated Deleuze's *Difference and Repetition* (Athlone/Columbia, 1994), and edited *Deleuze: A Critical Reader* (Blackwell, 1996) and (with John Protevi) *Between Deleuze and Derrida* (Continuum, 2003). He is the author of *Deleuze and the Political* (Routledge, 2000).

Ginette Verstraete is Professor at the De Vrije Universiteit Amsterdam. She is also the Director of the M.A. Program in Cultural Analysis and member of the Amsterdam School for Cultural Analysis. She is the author of, among others, *Fragments of the Feminine*

Sublime in Friedrich Schlegel and James Joyce (State University of New York Press, 1998). She has co-edited books and issues on mobility, globalization and cultural studies. She is currently finishing a book-length manuscript on various cultural practices of travel, migration, and globalization in Europe.

Rinaldo Walcott is Associate Professor in the Department of Sociology and Equity Studies at the OISE/University of Toronto. He is Canada Research Chair of Social Justice and Cultural Studies and the author of *Black Like Who?: Writing Black Canada* (second revised edition, 2003).

Effie Yiannopoulou is lecturer in English and Cultural Theory at the School of English, Aristotle University of Thessaloniki, Greece. She has received an M.A. from Lancaster University (UK) and a Ph.D. from the Centre for Critical and Cultural Theory, Cardiff University (UK). Her publications are in the field of twentieth-century women's writings and have appeared in book collections and international journals.

Index

Age Rage and Going Gently

Stories of the Senescent Subject in Twentieth-Century French Writing

Oliver Davis

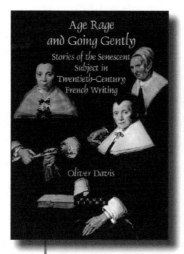

This wide-ranging study looks at how the ageing process has alternately been figured in and excluded from twentieth-century French literature, philosophy and psychoanalysis. It espouses a critical interdisciplinarity and calls into question the assumptions underlying much research into ageing in the social sciences, work in which the negative aspects of growing older are almost invariably suppressed. It offers a major reappraisal of Simone de Beauvoir's great but neglected late treatise, *La Vieillesse*, and presents the first substantial discussion of a lost documentary film about old age in which Beauvoir appears and which she helped to write, *PROMENADE AU PAYS DE LA VIEILLESSE*. Questioning Beauvoir's own rather reductive reading of Gide's work on old age, this study analyses the way in which his *Journal* and *Ainsi soit-il* experiment with a range of representational models for the senescent subject. The encounter between psychoanalysis and ageing is framed by a reading of Violette Leduc's autobiographical trilogy, in which she suggests that psychoanalysis, to its detriment, simply cannot allow ageing to signify. This claim is tested in a critical survey of recent theoretical and clinical work by psychoanalysts interested in ageing in France, the UK and the US. Lastly, Hervé Guibert's recently republished photo-novel about his elderly great-aunts, *Suzanne et Louise*, is examined as a work of intergenerational empathy and is found, in addition, to be an important statement of his photographic aesthetic. Navigating between the extremes of fury ('age rage') and serene acceptance ('going gently'), this study aims throughout to examine the role which ageing plays in formal, as well as thematic, terms in writing the life of the subject.

Amsterdam/New York, NY,
2006 225 pp.
(Faux Titre 283)
Paper € 45 / US$ 59
ISBN-10: 9042020261
ISBN-13: 9789042020269

USA/Canada:
295 North Michigan Avenue - Suite 1B, Kenilworth, NJ 07033,
USA. Call Toll-free (US only): 1-800-225-3998
All other countries:
Tijnmuiden 7, 1046 AK Amsterdam, The Netherlands
Tel. +31-20-611 48 21 Fax +31-20-447 29 79
Please note that the exchange rate is subject to fluctuations

rodopi

Orders@rodopi.nl—www.rodopi.nl

Understanding Problems of Social Pathology

Edited by
Przemysław Piotrowski

A social reality (including social pathology) is constantly being constructed anew in the process of confrontation of perspectives and definitions of individuals, institutions and social groups. Therefore what interests the authors of the book more than the disputes on the right definition, is the *understanding* of social pathology phenomena — their causes, mechanisms, and social costs. Complex and multidimensional as it is, social reality is best described from various perspectives. For that reason, a potentially interesting and fruitful interdisciplinary approach characterises the book. It contains mainly texts of psychologists who work at the Jagiellonian University in Cracow. The articles of sociologists, lawyers, and one theoretician of education broaden the horizon and thus contribute new insights to the entirety of the book. The body of articles predominantly relates to Polish reality, as well as stems from the experience of the Polish society in the period of political transformation. No less interesting are the articles on the pathology of political discourse, community-policing problems in France, and issues of social concern (victims of violence, problems of the elderly, and collective behaviour).

The volume is of interest for social scientists and professionals as well as for students.

Amsterdam/New York, NY,
2006 XIX-246 pp.
(At the Interface/Probing
the Boundaries 33)
Paper € 53 / US$ 69
ISBN-10: 9042020253
ISBN-13: 9789042020252

USA/Canada:
295 North Michigan Avenue - Suite 1B Kenilworth, NJ 07033,
USA. Call Toll-free (US only): 1-800-225-3998
All other countries:
Tijnmuiden 7, 1046 AK Amsterdam, The Netherlands
Tel. +31-20-611 48 21 Fax +31-20-447 29 79
Please note that the exchange rate is subject to fluctuations